Culture and Customs of Gambia

Culture and Customs of Gambia

ABDOULAYE SAINE

Culture and Customs of Africa
Toyin Falola, Series Editor

GREENWOOD

AN IMPRINT OF ABC-CLIO, LLC
Santa Barbara, California • Denver, Colorado • Oxford, England

Library of Congress Cataloging-in-Publication Data

Saine, Abdoulaye S.,
   Culture and customs of Gambia / Abdoulaye Saine.
      p. cm. — (Culture and customs of Africa)
   Includes bibliographical references and index.
   ISBN 978-0-313-35910-1 (hardcopy : alk. paper) — ISBN 978-0-313-35911-8 (ebook)
1. Gambia—Civilization.   2. Gambia—Social life and customs.   I. Title.   II. Series:
Culture and customs of Africa.
   DT509.4.S25   2012
   966.51—dc23   2011052170

ISBN: 978-0-313-35910-1
EISBN: 978-0-313-35911-8

16 15 14 13 12   2 3 4 5

This book is also available on the World Wide Web as an eBook.
Visit www.abc-clio.com for details.

Greenwood
An Imprint of ABC-CLIO, LLC

ABC-CLIO, LLC
130 Cremona Drive, P.O. Box 1911
Santa Barbara, California 93116-1911

This book is printed on acid-free paper ∞

Manufactured in the United States of America

The publisher has done its best to make sure the instructions and/or recipes in this book are correct. However, users should apply judgment and experience when preparing recipes, especially parents and teachers working with young people. The publisher accepts no responsibility for the outcome of any recipe included in this volume and assumes no liability for, and is released by readers from, any injury or damage resulting from the strict adherence to, or deviation from, the directions and/or recipes herein. The publisher is not responsible for any reader's specific health or allergy needs that may require medical super-vision, nor for any adverse reactions to the recipes contained in this book. All yields are approximations.

To Abdoulaye Isaac Marget-Nakopa Saine, and Sajo Maimuna Sowe
who left us much too soon.

Contents

Series Foreword

AFRICA IS A vast continent, the second largest, after Asia. It is four times the size of the United States, excluding Alaska. It is the cradle of human civilization. A diverse continent, Africa has more than fifty countries with a population of over 700 million people who speak over 1,000 languages. Ecological and cultural differences vary from one region to another. As an old continent, Africa is one of the richest in culture and customs, and its contributions to world civilization are impressive indeed.

Africans regard culture as essential to their lives and future development. Culture embodies their philosophy, worldview, behavior patterns, arts, and institutions. The books in this series intend to capture the comprehensiveness of African culture and customs, dwelling on such important aspects as religion, worldview, literature, media, art, housing, architecture, cuisine, traditional dress, gender, marriage, family, lifestyles, social customs, music, and dance.

The uses and definitions of "culture" vary, reflecting its prestigious association with civilization and social status, its restriction to attitude and behavior, its globalization, and the debates surrounding issues of tradition, modernity, and postmodernity. The participating authors have chosen a comprehensive meaning of culture while not ignoring the alternative uses of the term.

Each volume in the series focuses on a single country, and the format is uniform. The first chapter presents a historical overview, in addition to information on geography, economy, and politics. Each volume then proceeds to examine the various aspects of culture and customs. The series highlights the mechanisms for the transmission of tradition and culture across generations: the significance of orality, traditions, kinship rites, and family property distribution; the rise of print culture; and the impact of educational institutions. The series also explores the intersections between local, regional, national, and global bases for identity and social relations. While the volumes are organized nationally, they pay attention to ethnicity and language groups and the links between Africa and the wider world.

The books in the series capture the elements of continuity and change in culture and customs. Custom is represented not as static or as a museum artifact but as a dynamic phenomenon. Furthermore, the authors recognize the current challenges to traditional wisdom, which include gender relations, the negotiation of local identities in relation to the state, the significance of struggles for power at national and local levels and their impact on cultural traditions and community-based forms of authority, and the tensions between agrarian and industrial/manufacturing/oil-based economic modes of production.

Africa is a continent of great changes, instigated mainly by Africans but also through influences from other continents. The rise of youth culture, the penetration of the global media, and the challenges to generational stability are some of the components of modern changes explored in the series. The ways in which traditional (non-Western and nonimitative) African cultural forms continue to survive and thrive—that is, how they have taken advantage of the market system to enhance their influence and reproductions—also receive attention.

Through the books in this series, readers can see their own cultures in a different perspective, understand the habits of Africans, and educate themselves about the customs and cultures of other countries and people. The hope is that the readers will come to respect the cultures of others and see them not as inferior or superior to theirs but merely as different. Africa has always been important to Europe and the United States, essentially as a source of labor, raw materials, and markets. Blacks are in Europe and the Americas as part of the African diaspora, a migration that took place primarily because of the slave trade. Recent African migrants increasingly swell their number and visibility. It is important to understand the history of the diaspora and the newer migrants as well as the roots of the culture and customs of the places from where they come. It is equally important to understand others in order to be able to interact successfully in a world that keeps shrinking. The accessible nature of the books in this series will contribute to this understanding and enhance the quality of human interaction in a new millennium.

Toyin Falola
Frances Higginbothom Nalle Centennial Professor in History
The University of Texas at Austin

Preface

THE GAMBIA IS the smallest noninsular country in Africa, with a population of 1.7 million. It has a rich history, and just as dynamic a people and culture. What The Gambia lacks in geographic size it more than makes up for by interethnic harmony and religious tolerance, especially in a world riveted by sectarian violence. Each ethnic group, while retaining its own cultural traditions and practices, shares much in common with other groups. Islam and Christianity rather than forces for disharmony are the glue that has given this country, sometimes called the "Smiling Coast," and its people a distinctively open and tolerant character. With slavery and colonialism, many traditional institutions and economies as well as social relations changed. This book captures both the diversity and complexity wrought by these forces by focusing on overarching themes and institutions that permeate The Gambia's many subcultures. This has not made writing the book easy, but certainly easier than if I were to discuss each group exhaustively, which could easily have run into hundreds of pages, if not more. Therefore, limited space and efforts to keep the book at a reasonable length while making it readable for the nonspecialist served as the motivation and guiding principle. In the end, all ethnic groups and emergent social classes in The Gambia will, in varying degrees, see themselves reflected in these pages.

Western media and academic discourse on Africa and Africans typically frame Africa as the problematic "other," different, inferior, and needing to be tamed, changed, and normalized. This frame of Africans is the construction of outsiders rather that of Africans themselves. Europeans did not enslave and later colonize a people waiting to be saved and civilized—Kipling's "white man's burden." Rather, Senegambians built and administered complex medieval empires, kingdoms, and state systems that were comparable to or sometimes more sophisticated than those of Europeans. Framing Africans as "noble savages" along with Hegel's characterization of Africans as not having a history served as ideology for the enslavement and colonial subjugation of Africans. Similarly, "tribe" is yet another frame. This term was used by European colonizers and anthropologists to reorganize, control, and normalize once fluid social organizations for the primary purpose of economic exploitation through taxation. Lying at the confluence of three major civilizations—African, Arab, and European—Gambians were a part of an international commercial system that predated European contact well before the 1400s. In this era of economic and cultural globalization, Gambian society is reshaping and being shaped by forces of change, order, and fragmentation.

This book seeks to offer the general reader a nuanced understanding of The Gambia. It attempts to destabilize or problematize the dominant or conventional framing of Africa and Africans, which this series also seeks to do. In doing so, it is hoped that it will show complex sociocultural, political-economic, and literary histories of a people as agents, resisters, and survivors of an insidious imperial system that put in motion a process of dependency and underdevelopment, which must be critically analyzed and resolved.

Finally, there is considerable variation in the spelling of words and proper names in the literature; Umar or Omar, Taal or Tal, as well as the title, Al Hajj and Alhaji. Both are used depending on whether the person is Gambian or Senegalese. American spelling is used for non-English words, which for the most part are in italics, for example, *mansa* (king), with the French spelling of some words sometimes placed in parentheses, for instance, Jola (Diola). Suggested readings are provided in each chapter, and the selected bibliography is also a good source for additional reading material.

Acknowledgments

Writing a book of this sort, as with any other, is seldom an individual endeavor. I have benefited greatly from discussions with colleagues, friends, and relatives about some aspects of Gambian culture, and the book is clearly better because of them. I am particularly grateful to OB Silla, Baba Galleh Jallow, Abou Jeng, Ebrima Ceesay, Ebrima Sankareh, David Perfect, and Assan Sarr for their careful reading and suggestions on the manuscript, and to Kairaba Fatty, Njie Mbye, Banna Touray, Yama Fatty, Tumani Kanteh, Essap Saine, Alhaji Pa Cheboh Saine, and Haddijatou Cham, for providing me useful cross-ethnic comparisons and information. This work also stands on the shoulders of numerous Africanist scholars, including Gambianists, and Gambians to whom I am deeply indebted for helping me clarify my thoughts and arguments and for making the book more readable. Is to my family and wife, Professor Paula Saine, in particular that I am most indebted for her unfailing support and encouragement. I am also grateful to Miami University and my home department, political science, for an eight-month sabbatical that allowed me to focus on this and other scholarly pursuits, giving me time to write, think, travel, and regenerate. To students in my spring 2008 University Honors Program course, *Politics and Global Issues* (Alison Blackmore, Andrew Bosarge, Abbey Brinkman, Michael Bucci, Ian Callon, Veronica Chasser, Michael Davis, Ida Doutt, Brandon Gay, William Heimach, Steven Heston, Kate Jacob, Daniel Lakis, Elaine Martini, Andrew Ohl, Melanie Reynolds, Jessica Shvarts, Michael Silverstein, Sarah Wagner,

Kristen Wedzikowski, and Chad Workman), I am grateful for your research assistance and interest. I wish to express my heartfelt gratitude to Kaitlin Ciarmiello, my editor, for her patience for having several times extended the deadline to complete the manuscript, and for her careful editing. I am especially grateful to her and Professor Toyin Falola, the series editor, for the opportunity to showcase the country of my birth to a larger global audience. I am also indebted to Barbara Walsh for the meticulous copy-editing work she did on the manuscript. My heartfelt gratitude is also extended to Rajalakshmi at Apex Covantage for her support in seeing the manuscript to publication. I am grateful to Buharry Gassama of Stockholm, Sweden, for permission to use his pictures; these have added so much to the book. It is to The Gambia that I owe the biggest debt of gratitude. Needless to say, I alone take responsibility for the views expressed, as well as the errors therein.

This book is dedicated to diaspora Gambians, Gambians at home, and all who wish to learn more about this once improbable nation and its peoples; but more so for young Gambians in the diaspora to understand better the customs, history, religion, literature, politics, and land from which their parents and grandparents came. If in the process of reading this book you accomplish this, my goal will have been realized. To my children, grandchildren, nephews, nieces, and namesakes, may you also benefit from reading this book and understand a part of yourselves.

To the people of Kaur, Ballanghar, and Saloum for their support and kindness and their salt-of-the-earth values, and to the ancestors who rest there and in Senegal, particularly my late grandmother, Haddy Faal Gajega.

To Momodou Sambou, Musa Fatty, Ebrima Sanyang, (Alhaji) Sheikh Joof, Ousman A. Ndow, and all my former teachers at Kaur School and Armitage High for serving as role models to me and countless others with exacting standards and expectations that still serve as signposts several decades later. To (Alhaji) Hon. Omar B. Sey, George Thomas, and the late Jane Garlick for inspiring me to write and appreciate literature.

To Professor Sulayman Nyang for his important scholarly contribution to African and Gambian studies and his friendship and service as mentor to countless number of Gambians and Africans. To non-Gambian Gambianists, past and present, we value your dedicated and immense contributions of many years to Gambian Studies; and especially to Professor Arnold Hughes and the Center of West African Studies (CWAC) for their continuing support of Gambian studies.

To the memory of Essa T. Jeng; James J. Ndow; Sainey L. Bojang; Anthony L. R. Blain, Imam; (Alhaji) Pa Makumba Jaye; Pa Serign Ceesay; Pa Njanko B. O. Njie; Kekoto Manneh; M.B.H. Njie; Saim Kinteh; Bamba T.

Njie; Sedia Sanyang; Dawda Faal; Prince G. Baker; Dr. Mam Biram Joof; Marie Jeng; and Belinda Faal-Bidwell for their dedication and contributions to educating thousands of Gambians.

This book is also dedicated to the memory of Dr. Lenrie Peters, Pan-Africanist, novelist, poet-surgeon, and doyen of Gambian literature for his unflinching service and love of The Gambia and its people.

To the memory of Professor David Gamble for his pioneering scholarship on The Gambia; he will be remembered for having cleared the intellectual brush to create disciplinary paths on which Gambianists today travel. And to his many Gambian informants who along with Professor Gamble bequeathed to us and the world knowledge of The Gambia and its people. Last, but certainly not least, to Professor John Wiseman for his great contributions to African studies, generally, and Gambian studies, specifically; he departed this life much too soon.

Abbreviations

AFPRC	Armed Forces Provisional Ruling Council
APRC	Alliance for Patriotic Reorientation and Construction
AU	African Union
BBC	British Broadcasting Company
CDC	Colonial Development Corporation
CRR	Central River Region
DFI	Direct foreign investments
ERP	Economic Recovery Program
EU	European Union
GAMCOTRAP	Gambia Committee on Traditional Practices Affecting the Health of Women and Children
GNA	Gambia National Army
GPMB	Gambia Produce Marketing Board
GPP	Gambia People's Party
GPU	Gambia Press Union
GRTS	Gambia Radio and Television Services
GSRP	Gambia Socialist Revolutionary Party
IEC	Independent Electoral Commission
IMF	International Monetary Fund

LGAs	Local government areas
LRR	Lower River Region
MOJA-G	Movement for Justice in Africa—Gambia
NA	National Assembly
NADD	National Alliance for Democracy and Development
NAM	National Assembly Member
NBR	North Bank Region
NCAC	National Council for Arts and Culture
NCC	National Consultative Committee
NGO	Nongovernmental organization
NIA	National Intelligence Agency
NPC	National Convention Party
NRP	National Reconciliation Party
OIC	Organization of Islamic Conference
PDOIS	People's Democratic Organization for Independence and Socialism
PIEC	Provisional Independent Electoral Commission
PPP	People's Progressive Party
R&B	Rhythm and blues
RFI	Radio France International
RTS	Senegal Radio and Television
SoS	Secretary of State
UDP	United Democratic Party
UK	United Kingdom
UNDP	United Nations Development Program
UP	United Party
URR	Upper River Region
VOA	Voice of America
WID	Women in Development
WR	Western Region

Chronology

A.D. 1200s	Fula migrate southward into Senegambia region.
	Abd al Qadir Jilani found the *Qadiriyaa* Brotherhood in Baghdad, Iraq.
1400–1600s	Region is part of the Mali Empire.
1455	Portuguese explorers arrive in The Gambia. Groundnuts and Christianity are introduced.
1765	May 25: Colony of Senegambia is established and headquartered in St. Louis.
1772	Phyllis Wheatley's book, *Poems of Various Subjects, Religious and Moral*, is published in the United States. Wheatley was enslaved as a child and is believed to have been born in Niumi, a state in precolonial Gambia.
1794	Al Hajj Sheikh Umar Tal is born in Futa Toro.
1807	Trade in enslaved Africans is abolished and James Island is used to stop the illicit traffic in enslaved Africans. Groundnut production for export replaces the trade in enslaved Africans.
1816	The King of Kombo signs treaty with Captain Alexander Grant to build the city of Bathurst.
1821	October 17: The Gambia is administered as a crown colony from Sierra Leone.

1852	"Strange farmers" begin to arrive in The Gambia from neighboring Guinea and Mali to help with groundnut cultivation.
1854	The Royal Victoria Hospital is built in Bathurst.
1861	Maba Jahou (Dahou) Bah conquers the king of Baddibu and established it as a theocracy.
1864	Al Hajj Umar Tal is killed in battle at Massina.
1865	Maba Jahou (Dahou) defeats French troops at the battle of *Pathebadiane*, Senegal.
1867	Maba is killed at the battle of *Somp* in Sine, Senegal.
1869	A cholera outbreak in Mocam town (later renamed Half-Die) in Bathurst kills 1,162 people out of a population of 4,000.
1871	*Bathurst Times* newspaper is founded by Thomas Brown, an English merchant opposed to ceding The Gambia to France.
1890	Edward Francis Small is born in Bathurst.
1894	Slave trading in the Protectorate (Gambia) is abolished.
	Foday Silla Touray is exiled by the British.
1899	*Ahmadiyya* Movement is founded in India.
1900	Traveling Commissioners F. C. Sitwell and F. E. Silva are killed along with six of their assistants in Sankandi.
1901	Foday Kabba is killed effectively ending the Soninke-Marabout Wars.
1903	Mohammedan School is established in Banjul.
1917	Edward Francis Small serves at the Methodist Church in Ballanghar.
1919	Musa Molloh, the King of Fulladu, is deposed and exiled by the British to Sierra Leone.
1924	May 16: Dawda K. Jawara is born in Barajally Suuba.
1925	William Conton, author of *The African,* is born in Bathurst.
1927	Sheikh Amadou Bamba, founder of the *Moride* Brotherhood, is exiled.
	Armitage School is founded for the sons of Chiefs in Georgetown (Janjangbureh).
1929	Under Francis E. Small's leadership, the Bathurst Trade Union, which he founded, organizes one of the most successful strikes in colonial Africa before World War II.
1931	Musa Molloh dies in Kaserikunda.

1932	Lenrie Peters Jr., Pan-Africanist, poet, novelist, and surgeon, is born in Bathurst.
1939–45	Gambians fight in World War II. The Gambia contributes £45,000 to the war effort.
1940	An Anglican boarding school for boys is founded at Kristikunda.
1943	President Franklin D. Roosevelt makes an overnight stop in The Gambia on his way to Casablanca and is appalled by the living conditions of Gambians.
1947	Edward Francis Small is elected to the Legislative Council.
1958	Kebba Foon and M. B. Jones establish *The Vanguard* newspaper.
1963	Gambia gains internal self-government.
1964	700 workers at the Marines and Public Works Departments are laid off.
	July: Independence talks begin in London.
1965	February 18: Gambia gains independence from Britain.
	May: Yahya Jammeh is born (celebrates birthday on May 25, the same day as Africa Liberation Day [ALD]).
1970	April: The Gambia attains republican status.
1981	July 30: Senegalese troops intervene to abort a civilian-led coup (Kukoi Samba Sanyang) to overthrow Sir Dawda Jawara's government.
1982	Senegambia Confederation is established between The Gambia and Senegal.
1985	An Economic Recovery Program (ERP) is launched and several hundred employees are laid off.
1987	Halifa Sallah, Sedia Jatta, and Sam Sarr establish *Foroyaa* newspaper.
1990	Deyda Hydara and Pap Saine establish *The Point* newspaper.
1994	July 22: Yahya Jammeh along with three junior officers topple President Jawara's government.
1996	The United Democratic Party (UDP) is formed and lawyer Ousainou Darboe is elected Secretary General.
	August 9: A new constitution is ratified.
	September 27: Yahya Jammeh "defeats" Ousainou Darboe, Halifa Sallah, and Hamat Bah in elections not deemed free and fair.
2000	April 10 and 11: A peaceful demonstration turns deadly when security forces fire on students in Banjul and up-country; at least 14 students and a journalist, Omar Barrow, lose their lives.
2001	President Jammeh wins another five-year term in a presidential election.

2002   April: Sir Dawda Jawara and his immediate family are granted amnesty by President Jammeh.

2004   February 17: President Jammeh announces the discovery of oil in "large quantities," saying the offshore find would eliminate poverty and hunger in The Gambia.

               December 16: Deyda Hydara, editor and co-owner of *The Point* newspaper, is shot and killed by unidentified gunmen. The slaying has yet to be solved.

2005   May: National Alliance for Democracy and Development (NADD) is launched by five opposition political parties.

               December: Journalists petition government to investigate and bring to trail Deyda Hydara's killer(s).

               December 16: Lawyer Ousman Sillah survives an attempt on his life.

2006   February 1: NADD disintegrates after Ousainou Darboe's (UDP) resignation from the coalition.

               March: *The Independent* newspaper is closed following a report that a former minister was involved in a recently "discovered" coup attempt.

               March 21: Daba Marenah, director general of Gambia's National Intelligence Agency, is allegedly executed along with other prisoners en route to prison in Janjangbureh.

               July 1–2: African Union (AU) Summit is held in The Gambia to which presidents Hugo Chavez of Venezuela and Mahmoud Ahmadinejad of Iran are invited.

               September 23: Yahya Jammeh is reelected to a third five-year term.

               December 13: National Assembly passes a law that awarded ex-presidents a lucrative pension.

2007   February 22: President Jammeh expels UNDP Representative Fadzai Gwaradzimba after she criticized Jammeh's claims of having found a cure for AIDS.

2009   March 18: About 1,000 people are forced to drink potions by Guinean witch doctors to determine whether they were witches.

               November 22: President Ahmadinejad pays a 24-hour working visit to The Gambia.

2010   April: Femi Peters, propaganda secretary of the United Democratic Party, is sentenced to a one-year prison term.

               June: Two tons of cocaine worth about US$1 billion bound for Europe and the United States and believed to be from South America are seized in The Gambia along with a large sum of money and firearms.

November 22: Iranian Government officials are given 48 hours to leave the country, following a seizure of arms from Iran allegedly destined for The Gambia to support Casamance rebels.

2011 June 7: Former minister Amadou Janneh is arrested along with others for allegedly trying to destabilize the country.

October 20: Moammar Gadhafi, financial supporter and mentor of President Jammeh, is killed in Libya.

October: Gambian opposition leaders fail in their efforts to form a coalition against President Jammeh in the 2011 presidential election.

November 25: President Jammeh wins a fourth, five-year term as president.

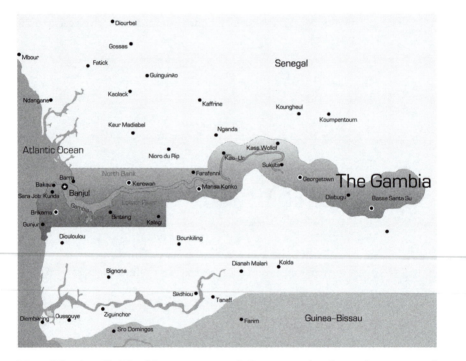

Map of Gambia. (© Olira | Dreamstime.com) Georgetown(on the map) was renamed Janjangbureh.

1

Introduction

A Brief History

The Republic of The Gambia is the official name of Africa's smallest non-insular state of approximately 4,000 square miles, roughly the size of the U.S. state of Delaware. It has a population of about 1.7 million but is one of Africa's most densely populated countries, with a birthrate of about 3.09 percent annual growth. At independence in 1965 life expectancy for men stood at 32 years and was considerably less for women of childbearing age. Today, life expectancy hovers around 56 years for women and 52 for men. While infant mortality rates have improved since the mid-1970s, thanks in part to a health care delivery system that has emphasized primary care and prevention, mortality rates for infants still remain high at 76.3 per 1,000 live births. Banjul, the capital, formerly known as Bathurst, sits at the intersection of the Atlantic Ocean and the Gambia River. Banjul is a leading port in West Africa from which imported goods are re-exported to neighboring Senegal, Guinea, Guinea Bissau, and Mali.

Humans have for centuries inhabited the region that present-day Gambia occupies, and the Jola (Floops) are believed to have been some of the earliest inhabitants of the area, with the Fula arriving from Futa Jallon around the 1200s. The region was also a part of the medieval empires of the western Sudan region, which included Ghana, Mali, and Songhai, and from 1400 to 1600 Gambia was a province of Mali. With Mali's collapse in the late 1600s, however, groups of Mande-speaking people that included the Mandinka settled in what today are Mauritania, Senegal, Gambia, and Guinea Bissau. By the late 1600s Mali was superseded by Songhai, and in later years Songhai, too, would collapse, predominantly from internal weaknesses and attacks from the Almoravids.

In the early 19th century, there were 10 mostly Mandinka kingdoms on the south bank of the Gambia River: Kombo, Foni, Kiang, Jarra, Niamina, Eropina, Jimira, Tomanna, Kantora, and Fulladu (Fula). Along the north bank were five kingdoms: Niumi, Baddibu, Niani, Saloum (Wolof), and Wuli. While these kingdoms differed in size and leadership style, they nonetheless shared many key features that included social and political organization based on caste: freeborn citizens, artisans, and slaves. Each kingdom had a king (*Mansa*) chosen from a royal lineage, a council of elders and advisors, and a standing army. Each kingdom was also subdivided into territorial units of village, ward, and family compound, and each village in turn was governed by a member of the founding lineage and a council of elders and advisors. Agriculture, and to some degree slavery, served as the material foundations of these kingdoms. Trade in kola nuts by the *Dyula* (*Djula*), a Mandinka trading group, also was an important source of wealth. The *Dyula* too were important agents in the spread of Islam; as they traveled from one place to another to sell their wares, so did they spread Islam. Education in Arabic was also introduced in schools, mostly by foreign clerics throughout these kingdoms.

While Islam, the dominant religion in The Gambia, was introduced as early as the 11th century by Berber clerics, it didn't take root until the late 19th and early 20th centuries, as a result of the Soninke-Marabout Wars. These wars, which took place from roughly the mid-1850s to 1901, sought to impose a stricter adherence to the *Sunni* teachings of Islam. According to Sulayman Nyang, the spread of Islam and resulting distribution of Muslim communities in Senegambia Major (Senegal, Gambia, Mauritania, Mali, Guinea, and Guinea Bissau) were due to two key historical waves of advance. The first wave saw the slow spread of Islam by the Almoravids from the 11th to the 17th centuries through the agency of traders and clerics. This wave was typified by the adoption of Islam by the ruling classes; it was the religion of the kings and the religious-commercial class. The second wave came in the 19th century with the Fulbe, Fulani, and Tukulor movements that led to the formation of Islamic theocratic states, followed by a period of consolidation under European occupation.

European conquest and occupation led to accommodation and the flourishing of Sufi brotherhoods that included the *Qadiriyya tariqa*, which was founded by Abd al Qadir Jilani in Baghdad in the 12th century. *Tijaniyya*, another Sufi order, was founded in Morocco by Sheikh Ahmad Tijan in the 18th century. These Sufi orders—*Qadiriyya* and *Tijaniyya*—spread throughout the Sahel and Senegambia, and the peoples there adopted and modified them to suit their spiritual needs and sensibilities. *Muridyaa*, also a Sufi sect, originated in Senegal at the turn of the 20th century and was established by a Wolofized-Tukulor marabout (Muslim clergy), Sheikh Amadou Bamba M'backe, in central Senegal. In time, the religious leadership built symbiotic relationships with various colonial powers.

European contact occurred in the mid-1400s with the arrival of Vasco da Gama, who engaged in trade and the enslavement of Africans. Though Christianity was introduced at this time, it did not take root until the mid-1900s. In 1816, Bathurst was established as a settlement by the British to resettle liberated Africans, known as recaptives, and later created a colony in the western Kombo region and a protectorate covering the rest of the country.

Competition over the region among Portuguese, British, and French colonialists was intense because of the lucrative trade in enslaved Africans as well as territorial expansion. In the end, Britain gained control over the strips of land lying on both sides of the Gambia River. During the 17th and 18th centuries the region was also a major source of enslaved Senegambians. When Britain and some Africans finally helped stem this trade in humans in 1807, it met with resistance from both European slave traders and their African middlemen, resulting in the establishment of a military post on James Island to aid antislavery campaigns. Slavery was finally abolished in The Gambia around 1894.

Political and economic development in The Gambia lagged considerably compared to the bigger and more populated British colonies of Nigeria, Gold Coast, and Sierra Leone. It was not until 1947 before the Aku, descendants of liberated African slaves, and Gambians of other ethnic groups became elected members of the Legislative Council. And, unlike other colonies that went through protracted bouts of violence and conflict with the British, as was the case in Kenya and to some degree the Gold Coast, Gambia's transition to independence was relatively peaceful, going through various phases that began with internal self-government in 1963 and culminating in independence on February 18, 1965.

Under Prime Minister Dawda Jawara's watch, The Gambia became a republic in 1970, ending British oversight and Sir Farimang Singhateh's tenure as Governor General. Despite this political change, The Gambia remained a member of the Commonwealth of Nations, an association of former British colonies with strong links to and dependency on Britain. With modest development goals influenced mostly by the reality of The Gambia's weak economic base, President Jawara went on to establish a functioning democracy and an economy that operated roughly on market principles with a heavy dose of state controls and concentration of political power in the executive.

LAND

The Gambia is about 300 miles long and not more than 15 miles wide. It follows the meandering outline of the Gambia River, one of Africa's most navigable rivers. Flowing east to west, its water is sourced from the Futa Jallon highlands and empties into the Atlantic Ocean. During most of the year, the river is navigable by large ocean liners for approximately 150 miles, as far as Kaur; smaller ships can go even farther. The Gambia River is an important waterway that connects the country and its peoples. Dotted by mangrove swamps, it supports rice farming along its banks but remains generally underutilized for larger agricultural schemes. One exception was the Jahali Pacharr Rice Project in the late 1970 and early 1980s, which failed largely as a consequence of poor government management (specifically, the People's Progressive Party [PPP]).

Lying in the tropics, The Gambia has two distinct seasons—the rainy season and the dry season. The rainy season begins generally in mid-May or early June and ends in late October to early November. It is also The Gambia's planting season for groundnuts, the main export crop, and subsistence crops that include rice as well as a variety of cereal crops like millet and coos.[1] The dry season begins around December, ushering in the trade season during which groundnuts are sold to local groundnut traders or representatives of foreign firms and subsidiaries. Following the end of the trade in enslaved Africans, Britain adopted groundnuts as an alternative commodity, which in subsequent years shaped both the colony's and the postcolonial state's political economy.

Kenneth Swindell and Alieu Jeng have analyzed the intricate symbiotic economic nexus between foreign firms, their representatives, and the colonial state on one hand, as well as the consequent marginalization and exploitation of Gambian farmers and seasonal migratory "strange farmers" from neighboring Guinea and Mali on the other.[2] While the colonial state accumulated considerable revenues from trade in groundnuts, Britain never invested much in improving the lives of colonial subjects or the colony. Rather, The Gambia's revenues, especially during times of surplus, helped to shore up dwindling resources in Britain and support expensive war efforts. On one occasion, U.S. president Franklin D. Roosevelt was visibly shaken by colonial Bathurst's misery and squalor following an overnight stop on his way to a conference in Casablanca in 1943. Upon meeting Sir Winston Churchill at the conference, President Roosevelt did not mince his words regarding the deplorable state of Gambians under British colonial rule and the need to improve health facilities and education.

Colonialism, whether imposed by the British in Kenya and South Africa or the French in Algeria, was a brutal imposition conducted with brute force to subjugate a people for profit and empire. Gambians, as other Africans, suffered and continue to suffer from the direct violence and the structural violence colonialism engendered. British benign neglect of The Gambia and insistence on carving out the country along the river to serve its own interests laid the foundation for The Gambia's deplorable state and the general misery of its citizens. It disrupted viable trade in the subregion and replaced it with cash crops and economies that would forever reduce The Gambia, once a constellation of viable states, into an unviable strip of a microstate.

The oldest British colony in Africa, The Gambia and Gambians had little to celebrate at independence. In the 1950s, the Colonial Development Corporation (CDC) squandered millions of pounds on failed poultry, groundnut, and fishery projects rather than investing in health services and good roads. Most Gambians remained poor, unhealthy, and uneducated, and not until the Jawara administration came into power after flag independence did conditions improve. Jawara's tenure saw many improvements in health, education, infrastructure, and social services, changes that Gambians aged 50 years or older would readily accept and appreciate. In contrast, travel during the colonial era was almost impossible, as there were few roads and outbreaks of disease were common. For instance, in 1869 a cholera epidemic in Mocam Town, a section of Bathurst later renamed Half-Die, claimed the lives of 1,162 people out of Bathurst's population of 4,000 people.

By the mid-1970s and early 1980s, The Gambia and neighboring countries were suffering from prolonged drought, and collective vegetable gardening was introduced, with women taking the lead to improve family and personal incomes. Richard Schroeder's study on women's gardens in Kerewan, the regional headquarters of the North Bank Region, showed how this moneymaking venture improved and empowered women and their families.[3] Drought conditions in the 1970s and 1980s increased poverty and resulted in poor soils, which have lost valuable nutrients partly because of overuse and erosion. This has resulted in the red coloration of once fertile farming soils. This state of affairs has contributed to frequent floods throughout The Gambia. Clearly, climate change as well as groundnut cultivation are major contributing factors. Land pressures resulting from a growing population and desertification remain creeping challenges. These are being countered by the planting of trees and stringent laws to curb the cutting of trees for charcoal and other uses.

Gambia is home to many animal and bird species that attract numerous tourists, as do spectacular sunsets over a palm-tree-lined coast and beaches. (© Piscari | Dreamstime.com)

Administrative Divisions

The Gambia has six administrative regions, including Banjul and its environs, which constitute the Greater Banjul Area. The remaining administrative regions are Lower River (LR), with Mansakonko as its capital; Central River (CR), with Janjangbureh as its capital; the North Bank Region (NB), with Kerewan as its capital; the Upper River (UR), with Basse as its capital; and the Western Region (WR), with Brikama as its capital. The Gambia is further subdivided into 37 districts; see Table 1.1.

The Greater Banjul Area and the Western Region are the most populous and in general have relatively better infrastructure. Banjul's population has, however, declined drastically, from around 60,000 in the 1970s to 35,000 in 2003 and possibly less than 30,000 in 2010. The Greater Banjul Area also enjoys better services—water, electricity, schools, and roads—and is home to the major tourist attractions, such as beaches, ecotourism sites, and markets. Postindependence development patterns more or less followed colonial ones, which neglected infrastructure and services in the regions (formerly called provinces). While some modest infrastructure development and services were once evident in the major towns of Mansakonko, Basse, Janjangbureh, Kun-

Table 1.1 Administrative Division of The Gambia: 6 Regions, 8 LGAs, and 37 Districts

Regional Local Government Area (LGA) Districts

Greater Banjul Region

Kanifing LGA Kombo St. Mary/Kanifing Municipality (Greater Banjul Area)

Western Region

Brikama LGA

Kombo North, Kombo South, Kombo Central,

Kombo East, Foni Berefet, Foni Bintang, Foni

Kansala, Foni Bondali, Foni Jarrol

Lower River Region

Mansakonko LGA

Kiang West, Kiang Central, Kiang East, Jarra

West, Jarra Central, Jarra East

North Bank Region

Kerewan LGA

Lower Niumi, Upper Niumi, Jokadu, Lower

Baddibu, Central Baddibu, Upper Baddibu

Central River Region

Kuntaur LGA

Lower Saloum, Upper Saloum, Nianija,

Niani, Sami

Georgetown LGA

Niamina Dankunku, Niamina West, Niamina

East, Fulladu West

Upper River Region

Basse LGA Fulladu East, Sandu, Wuli West, Wuli East,

Kantora

Each region is headed by a governor who is appointed and answerable to the president of the republic. Each region, in turn, has an Area Council consisting of elected and nominated members and presided over by an executive officer and his staff who all are under the supervision of the governor. The regions are also subdivided into districts, which are headed by district chiefs, and at the village levels, by an Alkalo (village head).

Source: Kasper Juffermans and Caroline McGlynn, "A Sociolinguistic Profile of The Gambia," *Sociolinguistics* 3, no. 3 (2009): 329–55.

taur, Kaur, and later Farafenni, much of The Gambia still remains rural and depopulated, and commercial towns that were vibrant 30 years ago are virtual ghost towns today. Many citizens in these areas, particularly the younger ones, have moved to the urban centers on the coast or nearby areas in hopes of accessing opportunities. This was not the case in the major towns of Kaur and Kuntaur, which as late as the 1970s were homes to groundnut processing mills. Soma, located in Jarra Central in the Lower River Region, and Farafenni, in the North Bank Region, are both strategically located on the Trans-Gambia Highway, which links Dakar to the Southern Region of Casamance. Both towns witnessed significant population growth as early as the mid-1970s, to the extent that Farafenni overtook both Kaur and Kuntaur following the closure of mills operated by The Gambia Produce Marketing Board.

Today, not only is Soma a bustling town, it also serves as an important refueling and refreshment hub for vehicles and passengers traveling to Basse and beyond Basse, though slightly depopulated, continues to serve as a major commercial town for businessmen, predominantly, and some women from Guinea, Mali, and Senegal. Lying at the Senegalese border next to Kolda, Basse remains a major trading center. Janjangbureh, on the other hand, has lost its once dynamic commercial life and in the last two decades has been overtaken by Bansang, a bustling commercial center. And while Kerewan has seen some infrastructure development in the last 30 years, it, too, has lost its population to the Greater Banjul Area and Kombos. Ease of transportation following the construction of the North Bank Highway and a bridge at the river's juncture between Dasilami and Kerewan may help reverse the pull to the urban centers. Better access to water and electricity and improved opportunities in the rural areas may in the long term reverse the drift from rural to urban. The coastal as well as the North Bank highways have significantly reduced travel time, and with the completion of the South Bank Highway, travel time to most points of this small country will be drastically reduced.

The Gambia, however, remains an underdeveloped country, though it has considerable potential. The Gambia River and the Atlantic Ocean into which it empties remain underutilized. Diversified export products, including fruit, fruit juices, fish, and other industries, remain opportunities that have yet to be fully exploited. The Gambia River also holds out the promise of producing enough electricity to meet domestic as well as export consumption needs. With a sunny climate all year round, solar energy is a potentially lucrative resource for domestic use and export. And tourism, which today is by far the largest earner of foreign exchange, has yet to live up to its full potential. Close proximity to Europe and the United States, beautiful beaches, a friendly and hospitable people, and favorable exchange rates between the dalasi and major international currencies augur well for the future development of this sector.

PEOPLES AND LANGUAGES OF THE GAMBIA

About ten major languages are spoken in The Gambia, including Mandinka, Fula, Wolof, Serer, Jola, and Serahule; minor languages spoken include Manjago, Bambara, Jahanka, and Balanta as well as Karoninka and Aku. However, none of these are spoken exclusively in The Gambia; all of them can also be found in Senegal, Guinea Bissau, Guinea, Mauritania, and Mali. Languages in The Gambia fall into the Niger-Congo family group of languages, which can be divided further into two main branches: Mande languages and Atlantic languages. Mande languages include Mandinka, Bambara, and Jahanke. According to Juffermans and McGlynn, these Mande languages are to a certain degree mutually intelligible, and the people share a common history and culture. Serahule (Soninke) is related to the Mande languages but is not close enough to be included in the group. Gambian languages in the Atlantic group can be subdivided into Senegambian (Wolof, Fulani/Fula, Serer) and Bak (Jola, Manjago, Balanta) languages, plus Bainunka. The internal differences within the Senegambian and Bak groups are more substantial than those between languages of the Mande family. Aku is an English-based Creole language. While not strictly an indigenous language, it has been included in this section as a local language.[4] The Gambia is a multiethnic, multireligious country with traditions that have coexisted peaceably, in general, following the demise of the Mali empire and the subsequent dispersion of various groups throughout the Senegambia subregion.

Mandinka

While the Mandinka constitute the majority group in The Gambia, the Fulani or Fula, as they are called in The Gambia, run a close second, followed by the Wolof, who migrated from the north of Senegal to populate both states. The Mandinka, both men and women, have historically been tied to the land as farmers, even though a branch of this diverse group called the *Dyula* was associated with long-distance trade for centuries. Also, the Baddibu-based Mandinka in the North Bank of The Gambia have also been known to be skilled traders. Today, along with the Serahule, they dominate the retail sector trade in Banjul's Albert Market. As the largest ethnic group, they also fared well in the civil service under President Jawara, who is Mandinka. They continue to do so in other sectors, even though their influence as a group has been eclipsed with the coming to power of Yahya Jammeh, who is Jola. As noted earlier, the Mandinka are a diverse group, which may also include Jola (Floop), and Bainuka elements with strong links to ancient Mali and societies that are highly stratified, with the Mannehs and Sannehs known to have been *nyancho* (warrior class). Patience Sonko-Godwin and

Dawda Faal provide good information on all the major ethnic groups in The Gambia. Charolotte Quinn's (1972) *Mandingo Kingdoms of the Senegambia: Traditionalism, Islam, and European Expansion* provides a detailed historical analysis of these kingdoms specifically, and Gambian history generally.[5]

Fula (Fulani)

The Fulani or Fula, as they are commonly called, are made up of a variety of ethnic groups and are generally grouped as Hallpullar (those who speak Fula, including the Peul, Tukulor, Laube, Torodo, Firdu, and several other subgroups). Originating from Futa Jallon, they can be found throughout West Africa and as far as Chad and Cameroon in Central Africa. The Fula, in general, speak the same language, with slight variations in pronunciation. Many Fula in The Gambia and elsewhere have traditionally been associated with cattle herding, traveling the entire subregion of West Africa in search of pasture and water for their herds. Fulani Bororojie (herders) settle in a place just long enough to meet the needs of their herds before moving on to greener pastures. In the meantime, however, they build symbiotic relationships with their sedentary hosts, mostly agriculturalists, providing them with milk, butter, and ghee from their herds in exchange for millet and other cereals. Yet not all Fula are nomadic; many, in fact, live sedentary urban lifestyles (Fulanai Gidda), and some have taken well to farming in villages that sometimes number less than five households. The Laube, a subgroup of the Fula, speak a dialect of Fulani and can be divided further into two sub-subgroups: Laube-ette (wood-carvers), and Laube-*Dyula*, those who engage in long-distance trade.

Finally, some Fulani can also be distinguished by skin color. Most have Negroid features while some are light-skinned with distinct Caucasian characteristics. It is theorized that the light-skinned subgroup of the Fulani is the by-product of mixing between black Africans and Berbers around the 11th century and after. As clerics, judges, and advisors to African rulers, many Berbers married African women, and their offspring often reflected this mixture. This branch of the Fulani, the Tukulor, were also responsible, albeit not exclusively, for the spread of Islam in West Africa. These include Othman Dan Fodio and Sheikh Umar Tal of Futa Toro, who in the 18th and 19th centuries waged jihads against so-called infidel rulers. Yet there was once a relatively large pocket of non-Muslim Fula in the Upper River Region of the country who held onto their spiritualist traditions. By the early 1930s, however, many traditionalist Fulani had converted to Christianity, as the Bandeh and Jawo families of Mansajang Kunda.

Wolof

The Wolof in The Gambia are predominantly located in Saloum, Banjul, Bakau, and Serrekunda; there are also various communities in Niamina and several pockets of Wolof in Baddibu. The Banjul Wolof consist of descendants of Wolof from St. Louis, Goree, and other towns and villages in Senegal, where they constitute the majority. Urban Wolof once enjoyed high social status, especially those tied to commerce and the civil service during the colonial and postcolonial eras. Their influence, however, goes beyond these areas to impact both the social and cultural milieu of The Gambia and Senegal. The Wolof who live up-country in The Gambia, commonly known by the Mandinka as *jambakatang Surwa* (green-leaf Wolof), or, as they call themselves, *fana-fana, kaw kaw* (up-country), are an industrious and down-to-earth folk whose men cultivate groundnuts and various cereal crops while the women engage in rice farming and vegetable gardening. Spoken urban Wolof differs from up-country Wolof in pronunciation and intonation. Like other ethnic languages, urban Wolof in both Gambia and Senegal borrowed heavily from Portuguese, English, and French and as a result may have lost some authenticity. This, however, is compensated for by the wide use of Wolof as a lingua franca in both countries, providing, as it does, a convenient tool for cross-ethnic communication. In fact, before the 1730s, Wolof was also the lingua franca in the Southern states of colonial America because of that region's heavy concentration of enslaved Senegambians. Like the Fula, the Wolof are also made up of several ethnic groups that have assimilated Wolof culture.

Closely related to the Wolof are the Serer and Lebou, who inhabit villages dotted along the Senegal River where the men are primarily engaged in fishing. Linguistically, Wolof is also close to Serer, Lebou, and Fulani. In fact, the Wolof are believed to be an offshoot of the Serer, given the similarities in their kinship systems and language. Cooperation and exchange rather than conflict typify social relations between and among these ethnic groups through the institutionalization of joking relationships, *kall* (Wolof), *senowya* (Mandinka), and *dendiragall* (Fula). These joking relationships also occur between the Jola and Serer and several ethnic groups as well as between cousins, grandchildren, and grandparents. Their social function is to diffuse potential tension and conflict and serve as a strong basis for economic and other forms of social interaction.

Jola (Diola)

The Jola, who call themselves *Ajamatau* or Floops, as they were once called, are generally recognized as the original inhabitants of the area where modern-day Gambia is now located and are found in the Casamance region of modern Senegal and Guinea Bissau. As the fourth largest group in The Gambia, the Jola (a Mandinka-derived term that means one who pays debts) have long been associated with agriculture. Fiercely independent and adherents of their traditional belief system or religion, the Jola, which are made up of several subgroups, including the Bainuka, have historically refused to embrace Islam or Christianity; the bulk of them having converted to either religion only in the mid-1950s, and perhaps later.[6] Unlike the other Senegambian ethnic groups, the Jola do not have a caste system and do not have a strong centrally organized authority structure. Thus, the village system remained central to social life under a nonhierarchal structure. This changed, however, around the 1900s, at which time British colonial authorities appointed Mandinka chiefs to collect taxes and maintain order. Mandinka chiefs were later replaced by Jola chiefs. Also, the Jola, like many Senegambian ethnic groups, were deeply implicated in the trade in enslaved Africans, and today, the Jola are just as likely as other ethnic groups to have chiefs and a hierarchal social structure. Under President Jammeh, many have fared well beyond what their numbers would suggest. They maintain key positions in both the army and security forces as well as in the civil service.

Serahule (Soninke)

The Serahule (Sarakole) or Soninke are the fifth largest group and live mostly in the Upper River Region of The Gambia, especially in the urban centers of Basse, Alungkhare, Kantora, and their environs. They are believed to be of mixed heritage that includes Mandinka, Tuareg, and Fula. Known as the Jews of The Gambia, they are enterprising risk takers and in general manage their resources well. They are not ostentatious and generally live modestly—some say, frugally. Serahule men, especially those who remain in the Basse and Fatotto area, also engage in groundnut farming, and some accumulate enough capital from this to establish small businesses. Serahule families are often corporations unto themselves, with each successful relative helping other relatives by providing start-up funds. The women generally make and trade household pottery utensils and beautiful, high-quality dyed cloth. The Serahule or Soninke (some Serahule may take offense to this name), like other ethnic groups in The Gambia, are immigrants, having arrived in The Gambia after the collapse of the Ghana empire, which they ruled from the 8th to the 11th centuries. They too have a proud tradition and until recently have been resistant to Western culture. Some Serahule families have, however, taken to urban ways, sending their children to school and engaging in large-scale export trade in kola nuts or diamonds, which has taken them as far as Congo Democratic Republic, Angola, Europe, and the United States.

Serer

Like the Fula, the Serer (also known as the Serere) are made up of different subgroups, including the Serer-Sine, the Serer-Niuminka, and several others. In general, they have lived in The Gambia for several centuries. The men

A fisherman ventures out into the Atlantic Ocean with a motorized dugout, competing for a dwindling fish catch that is dominated by large commercial fishing boats. (© Trevkitt | Dreamstime.com)

typically engage in fishing and some farming, while Serer women engage in agriculture and trade in fish and *cherreh*, a couscous-like grain made from coos or millet. Pockets of them live in Saloum, once a Serer/Wolof kingdom, and to a great degree Niumi, which accounts for the Niuminka designation. Serer in Saloum and Banjul have by and large assimilated Wolof ways and traditions, and today many consider themselves Wolof. Like the Jola, they too resisted Western influences and Islam and remained traditional worshipers of their *kharem* (idols) until the 1900s, and perhaps later. A few Serer in The Gambia, however, embraced Christianity, as have the Serer in Senegal. In Senegal, the Serer are a much larger group than they are in The Gambia, where they constitute about 5 percent of the population. In fact, Senegal's founding president, Leopold Sedat Senghor, was a Serer from Joal, a fishing village in Senegal. The Serer are linguistically and culturally close to the Wolof, Lebou, Mandinka, and Fula and were once matrilineal. Yet Serer kings of Sine are thought to be of Malinke/Kabu origin, just like the Touray dynasty of Lower Saloum in The Gambia. The Serer are *kalls* to the Fula and Jola.

Manjago (Njago)

The Manjago, also known as the Manjak or Njago, may have arrived in The Gambia in the late 1800s to the early 1900s from Guinea Bissau, which

Wetland fisherman subsistence fishing for protein to complement a typical Gambian diet that is based on grains and vegetables. (© Susan Robinson | Dreamstime.com)

was, along with several Gambian states, part of the kingdom of Kabu. Manjago men have typically served as sailors on ships and barges that ply the Gambia River transporting groundnuts from the trading posts and towns upriver to Kuntaur, Kaur, or Sarro, where the crops would be processed for export. The women typically engage in agriculture. The Manjago are mostly Christian today, and following independence many acquired an education and today hold important positions in the civil service and education sectors. Like the Jola, some have only recently converted to Islam.

Bambara (Bamana)

The Bambara population in The Gambia, unlike in Mali, where they constitute the majority, is relatively small. They come from as proud and rich a tradition as that of the Mandinka, having arrived in The Gambia as early as the 1800s and established a significant presence in the Banjul area by the 1900s. Like the Serahule, they first arrived as seasonal "strange" farmers and gradually settled predominantly in Mandinka and Wolof communities, where they practiced agriculture. The Bambara, like other numerically small ethnic groups, have assimilated, some becoming Mandinka or Wolof with few maintaining the Bambara traditions.

Aku (Krio/Creole)

The Aku, sometimes called Creole or Krio, are descendants of liberated enslaved Africans (or recaptives) of mostly Yoruba and some Ibo stock whose ancestors arrived in The Gambia at the end of the slave trade in 1807 or shortly thereafter. By the 1830s an established Aku community was already in Bathurst, with a smaller Aku settlement as early as 1818. While not constituting an ethnic group in the traditional anthropological sense of the term, they share fundamental characteristics of language, tradition, and religion to make them one. As with other ethnic groups in The Gambia, Aku identity is also constructed or imagined and united by Christianity and their de-ethnicized status, for the most part.

The Muslim element among the Aku are generally referred to as the Oku-marabout and are of Yoruba and Hausa descent. Some Christian Serer, Jola, Mandinka, and Wolof have adopted the Aku culture and generally are considered Aku, even if their last names (e.g., Sonko, Senghor, Mboge, Joof, Bahoum, Ndow) tell their ethnic origin. They played prominent roles as educators, merchants, and administrators in both the colonial and postcolonial civil service and in the professions. They, along with Wolof Methodists, specifically, were among the first to receive Western educations and served as leaders in the struggle for independence. Edward Francis Small, an Aku whose mother was Jola, is considered the father of Gambian nationalism.

Following the second decade of independence, the Christian Aku influence began to wane as other ethnic groups gained more access to education, jobs, and professions once dominated by the Aku. Marriages between the Aku and other urban-based ethnic groups has increased, with younger Aku men and women typically converting to Islam and sometimes assuming Islamized or traditional Senegambian names while maintaining their European last names. Only a few have dropped their European last names. Many young Aku, as well as some older ones, have in fact integrated well into the larger Gambian cultural mosaic, speaking several ethnic languages and over the years building friendships with Gambians across the ethnic spectrum. In doing so, many Aku, both young and old, who live in the greater Banjul area (few, if any, live in rural areas) have at one time or another in their youth lived the *ndongo* experience—a street lifestyle characterized by adventure, light truancy, and time spent playing beach (*tati-perreh*) soccer and other games while building bonds of friendship that last a lifetime. There is also a large Aku diaspora in the United Kingdom who maintain ties with their Gambian cousins and churches.

Lebanese/Syrian

The Gambia is also home to a small Lebanese community of Christian and Muslim ancestry that engages predominantly in business—more specifically, the purchase of groundnuts. Many arrived in The Gambia in the early 1900s and live in the major trading towns of Kaur, Farafenni, Kuntaur, Georgetown, Basse, and Banjul. Some intermarried with their Mandinka, Wolof, and Jola hosts, and their offspring, generations later, are more Wolof or Jola than their parents, who were born in The Gambia. Following the collapse of the groundnut trade in the 1970s and thereafter, many relocated to Banjul and Greater Banjul. There once was a distinct Syrian community that over time assumed a Lebanese identity, and now the two have generally been lumped together. Together, they have assimilated further to assume an Aku identity. Several, including Henry Madi, rose prominently not only in business but in politics as well.

Other ethnic groups include the Narr Gannar, whose ancestry is traceable to Mauritania and who are of mixed heritage—Bambara, Wolof, and Soninke—but they speak a language close to Arabic and can communicate with the Lebanese, with whom they often intermarry. There once was a distinct, albeit small, group of Gambian mulattos, the offspring of liaisons and marriages between African women and European men that occurred in the 18th and 19th centuries. Their descendants, mostly of Christian stock, have for all intents and purposes assimilated into Gambian society and did so as early as the 20th century.

In the 1760s this mostly Portuguese-mulatto community was active in business, particularly the trade in enslaved Africans as well as the establishment of factories along the river, especially in ports including Kaur. Fenda (Penda) Lawrence was one such businessperson. As the widow of a wealthy English trader, Fenda is believed to have inherited part of her fortune from her former husband but also gained great profits as a slave trader and slave owner in Kaur. In the late 1760s she moved to the state of Georgia in the United States with some of her children and slaves and lived as a free black woman, having been granted this status by the governor of the state. Dr. Florence Mahoney has written about these Gambians and their very colorful, interesting history in her book *The Signare*.[7] In an edited volume by Paul Lovejoy, *Identity in the Shadow of Slavery*, Lillian Ashcraft-Eason's chapter, "She Voluntarily Hath Come: A Gambian Woman Trader in Colonial Georgia in the Eighteenth Century," tells the fascinating story of Fenda Lawerence as a free black (mulatto) woman who traveled with her children and several slaves to colonial Georgia to provide them all the opportunity for a good education.[8]

The 1980s and 1990s saw a new wave of immigrants to The Gambia who arrived as refugees from the war-torn countries of Liberia and Sierra Leone. At the turn of the twenty-first century many more immigrants arrived, this time from Nigeria, Ghana, and Sierra Leone as teachers, bankers, judges, and pastors—this last group catering to the spiritual needs of the newly arrived. Intermarriages between the newly arrived and Gambian women are introducing another dynamic to the ethnic composition of the country. The offspring of these unions have Ibo, Yoruba, and other last names but may not speak the corresponding languages. The new immigrant influx has resulted in the dramatic growth of the Christian population as well. In the absence of national census data, it is difficult to say how much the Christian population has grown. Anecdotal data, however, suggests an increase in their numbers, sometimes measured by the number of new churches.

THE FLUIDITY OF ETHNIC COMPOSITION

Ethnic group and individual identities in The Gambia and Senegal, Senegambia Minor, generally are extremely fluid, and as a result many Gambians have multiple ethnic identities owing to the high rate of interethnic marriages. Similarities in traditions, such as caste, Islam, joking relationships, and so-called Wolofization, that cross social divisions have tended to make Senegambian society seamless, which in turn helps assuage or dampen potential social tensions. For instance, many offspring of mixed-ethnic marriages are today more likely to claim both identities rather than one over the other. And because Wolof and Aku serve as a lingua franca, many have easily adopted these languages. Surnames likewise reflect the fluidity of ethnic identities in Senegambia in that they no longer are markers of a specific ethnic group. Jallow or Jeng could be Wolof, as much as Dibba, Manneh, or Jammeh could be Mandinka or Jola, and Taal (Tal), Ndure, Jeng, or Faal could be Wolof, Narr, Serer, or Fula. The Wolof saying *santa amut kerr* (last names have no homes) succinctly captures this sentiment of shifting ethnic identities.

This is especially true in the urban areas, where generations of Fula, Jola, Serer, and Mandinka youth speak Wolof or Aku better than their own languages, or speak their ancestral tongues haltingly or not at all. Islam and Christianity have also been unifying forces for most Gambians. As noted earlier, interethnic harmony is further enhanced by the institutionalized joking relationships. These joking relationships are a source of fun, no matter one's social class or standing in society. It involves teasing and sometimes cajoling one's *kall*. Food is a frequent topic, and *kall*s tease one another or exchange jokes over their love of food or money. The Baddibunka Mandinka are teased routinely, even by other Mandinka, for their alleged love of money. If done well, joking relationships reinforce bonds of friendship and community. In-stitutionalized joking relationships engender a community spirit, and the institution has survived wars and dates back to medieval Mali.

LANGUAGES

While English is the official language for business and government and is taught in schools, pidgin Aku or Krio is widely used as a lingua franca. In fact, Krio also serves the role of a lingua franca even between those who ordinarily speak standard English but prefer the former, especially among the Aku. Many ethnic languages, as outlined earlier, also thrive, and neither the English language nor Arabic has been able to overshadow them, even though during the colonial period students in schools were prohibited from speaking their languages and ridiculed and often punished for doing so. Today, these languages are spoken widely in government as well as on television and radio broadcasts. Thus, the fear often associated with globalization and its threats to ethnic languages has not been borne out by evidence from The Gambia. More research on this is needed.

EDUCATION

The Gambia and Gambians, generally, have had a long history and tradition of education in Arabic and Islamic studies, dating back centuries but taking firm root only in the late 18th and early 19th centuries. Western-style education was brought to The Gambia by various Wesleyan, Methodist, Anglican, and Catholic missionaries, who established schools, in Bathurst mostly, and a few in the Protectorate (territory outside the established British Crown Colony and administered by chiefs and British traveling commissioners). The Wesleyans as well as the Methodists had an early presence in MacCarthy Island (Georgetown), renamed Janjangbureh following the relocation of liberated Africans on the island in 1823. And between 1833 and 1866, Wesleyan missionary activity on the island was intense but failed to convert many of the island's inhabitants. Despite being predominantly Muslim, urban Gambian youth attended missionary schools. The Methodist Boys High School, founded in 1875 and later renamed The Gambia High School, educated a significant number of Aku and future leaders of postindependent Gambia, including Dawda Jawara, Gambia's founding president. His biography, *Kairaba* (big peace), provides excellent narratives of life in colonial Bathurst during the 1940s and 1950s.

The fact that there were no Islamic schools until the founding of Moham-medan School in Bathurst in 1903 attests to the contribution that Christian missionaries made to educating young Muslim Gambians. St Augustine's

High School, also located in Bathurst, educated and sometimes converted many students to Christianity, many of whom went on to become prominent in the professions and politics. Founded in 1927 in Georgetown, Armitage School was first a preserve for the education of the sons of chiefs. In later years, however, it had an open-admission policy that allowed many rural Gambians to gain an education, with room and board for a modest fee. A government-run school to this day, Armitage also went on to educate not only the sons of chiefs but many prominent Gambians at the time as well, combining as it still does Western-style education and Qur'anic and religious instruction. In fact, Armitage was the school of choice for most Gambian Muslim parents because of its dual emphasis on Western and Qur'anic education and the inculcation in students of important moral values and life principles.

Predictably, entrance into these high schools was very competitive, requiring students age 11 or older to perform well on the Common Entrance Exam to gain admission. Only The Gambia High and later St. Augustine's had the Sixth Form, a preparatory grade for university education abroad. Selection to the Sixth Form was very competitive, as only a few seats were available, leaving many worthy students to take up jobs or train as teachers at the only post-secondary teacher's college at Yundum. Following independence, the Jawara government made a concerted effort to increase access to education, which resulted in the construction of numerous primary schools. Saudi Arabia, Kuwait, Libya, and other countries in the Middle East saw that it was in their interest to promote Islamic/Qur'anic education, which led to the establishment of Muslim and Nusrat High Schools in the 1970s. Without a national university, a select number of Gambian students who completed their studies at the Sixth Form received government scholarships to study abroad.

After the 1994 bloodless coup by young army officers who overthrew the 30-year government of Sir Dwada Jawra, many more high schools were built by the new Armed Forces Provisional Ruling Council (AFPRC) regime, which significantly expanded student access to education, especially for girls. Even in the provinces (formerly the-Protectorate), where access to education remained relatively limited, many more children began to attend school. Today, under President Yahya Jammeh, except for in a few remote villages, access to primary and secondary education has improved. Access to education was enhanced further with the establishment of a new university in 1999, which enabled many more Gambians to receive a university education. Despite these changes, however, literacy rates in The Gambia remain low.

And while education for girls has also improved, it lags behind that of boys. This is due partly to the once common practice of privileging male education over that of females and the general tendency then to marry off young school-aged girls or keep them at home to help out with household chores.

Under President Jammeh a lot has changed, and today government continues to support education for girls with many incentives, such as subsidized school fees and feeding programs to keep them in school. Access to Qur'anic and Islamic education for both boys and girls has also improved because of the increase in scholarships now available for study in the Middle East. In fact, as early as the late 1950s and 1960s many young Gambians ventured to the United Kingdom and the United States to seek university educations. This eventually increased the number of Gambians who today hold various undergraduate, postgraduate, and professional degrees.

CITIES

Bathurst, renamed Banjul in 1973, is located on an island, and its population in 2009 stood roughly at 30,000 inhabitants. Congestion in the early 1970s led many inhabitants to relocate to nearby Serrekunda and the Kombo region, making Serrekunda the largest city in the country with a population estimated at 336,000 in 2009. Serrekunda was a relatively small town prior to the large wave of Banjulians, internal migration from the provinces, and an influx of new immigrants from neighboring countries. It grew subsequently to incorporate the adjoining towns of Churchill's Town and Dippakunda. It has a bustling business center that in the past has suffered numerous fires sometimes started by faulty electrical wiring.

Brikama, in the western region of the country and less than 25 miles from Serrekunda, has also seen rapid growth in its population because like Serrekunda, it has come to incorporate newer settlements in recent years. Its population now stands close to 100,000 or more. The remaining towns of Bakau, Farafenni, Mansakonko, and Basse have populations that range from 40,000 to 60,000 inhabitants or more each. Basse in particular has now incorporated the once distant village of Mansajang Kunda. These towns or major population centers, including Kanifing, are ethnically diverse and attract people from far and wide because of the opportunity and amenities they provide. This has resulted once more in congestion, leading to new settlements such as Brusubi and Woollingkahnma on the coast and the growth in population of once small villages like Sabiji and Sanyang. Population pressure from the subregion and Europe has resulted in higher land prices and land grabbing by the well-to-do for later sale to Europeans.

RESOURCES, ECONOMY, AND OCCUPATIONS

The Gambia is predominantly an agricultural country even though tourism has in recent years become the major source of foreign exchange. The country is endowed with abundant rich farmland, marine resources, fruits, and vegetables. Groundnuts, still cultivated by peasants on relatively small parcels of land, have lost their importance as the primary engine for the economy. There is a small light-manufacturing industrial base, but the absence of heavy minerals (ilmenite was discovered in the early 1950s but was found not to be commercially viable) has kept industrialization low. Today, there is talk of commercially viable oil deposits; however, oil has yet to flow.

The Gambia's economy, therefore, remains small and undiversified, relying heavily on imports to meet domestic consumption needs and for reexport to neighboring countries. Reexports, which follow the old trade routes of centuries past, are a major source of foreign exchange, providing stimulus to the economy and some employment, but not enough to make a dent in the high unemployment and underemployment rates. Outside of agriculture, government remains the largest employer, with service workers in the tourist industry in the pre-coup period totaling about ten thousand. In the private sector, employment remains low. Given these economic challenges,

GT Bank on Kairaba Avenue in Serekunda. This commercial strip is by far the priciest piece of real estate in the country. It is home to malls, supermarkets, and numerous other businesses. (Courtesy of Buharry Gassama)

The Gambia relies heavily on external economic assistance, which accounts for about 70 percent of its annual budget. Corruption and low economic productivity have combined to increase poverty rates, which stand at about 65 percent of the population, leaving about 65 percent of Gambians living on less than $2 a day.

Gambians work in professions that include law, medicine, education, banking, and business. Lower down the scale, Gambians work as tailors, bus and taxi drivers, individual entrepreneurs, police officers, and carpenters; some are self-employed and others work for the state or businesses. A strong work ethic thrives, and for the most part, Gambians rely on their own efforts rather than on government. Thus, family provides the needed safety nets for young children and aged parents; in turn, aged parents help with child rearing. In these economic hard times, however, family obligations, solidarity, and strength are slowly eroding to make life difficult for many. This makes remittances from The Gambia's relatively large diaspora in the United States, Europe, and elsewhere all the more important for Gambians. Total remittances are estimated at $75 million annually.

GOVERNMENT

In 1970, The Gambia became a republic, thus doing away with the titular post of the governor general. Under President Jawara, The Gambia remained a functioning democracy until his ouster in a coup of 1994. Since then, a military-turned-civilian government has run the country. In addition to the executive branch of government that dominates, there is the National Assembly, whose members are elected from several individual constituencies, with seven voting members appointed by the president. Since the 1994 coup presidential and National Assembly elections have been held in 1996/1997, 2001/2002, and 2006/2007, with presidential elections last held in November 2011.

There are no presidential term limits in The Gambia's constitution. Limits were expunged from the draft constitution before it was ratified. Jammeh also lowered the age requirement from 40 to 30 to enable him to run for the presidency. The constitution provides for the protection of civil liberties and guarantees basic rights to assembly. It also guarantees a fair trial and forbids detention without charges for more than 72 hours. Except for religion, these protections and guarantees are routinely abridged. Constitutionally, the president is also head of the armed forces. President Jammeh also serves as secretary of defense and at one time or the other has served as secretary of agriculture and energy.

Now more than ever, government office has become the instrument through which government leaders misappropriate national resources for personal gain. President Jammeh has used the state to amass considerable wealth and influence, making him not only the richest Gambian but also one of the wealthiest heads of state in Africa. Jammeh has used the state not only to amass considerable wealth for himself and his immediate family, but also to dole out favors to his supporters, friends, and relatives in order to garner votes from key constituencies during national elections. The consequences are political and economic instability as well as widespread deprivation.

EARLY HISTORY

The state of Niumi serves as a metaphor for the economic incorporation that was to occur in the surrounding region. Related to the period of industrialization in Europe, Niumi's incorporation in the global-capitalist economy resulted in far-reaching political and economic changes. In place of political autonomy, power, self-reliance, and social cohesion began the process of colonization, dependence, and underdevelopment in the region, generally, and Niumi, specifically. In time, The Gambia's prospects for autonomous indigenous development were sidetracked and distorted to serve European interests and needs. Taxation, in particular, forced Gambian farmers into groundnut cultivation from the mid-1850s; it also allowed for the purchase of a whole range of commodities imported by the trading firms. The pervasiveness of small-commodity production effectively locked the Gambian farmer into the global-capitalist economy of unequal exchange. The Gambia's incorporation into this evolving world-capitalist system intensified further between the 1750s and 1900, driven by the need for capital accumulation. In fact, Donald Wright argues that Niumi's reliance on European imports in exchange for foodstuffs in the last third of the eighteenth century forced Niumi residents to transition into a new relationship of dependency on the growing world market.[9]

Clearly, these circumstances have had far-reaching economic consequences on rice production for domestic consumption. Because of the cash incentives provided to groundnut farmers, food production declined drastically, leading to increased rice imports as early as the 1900s. In fact, rice imports to The Gambia in the 1890s, according to Swindell and Jeng, were meant to feed not a growing urban population, as in other countries in the region at the time, but rather Gambian rice farmers, ironically.[10] Here lies one of the root causes of The Gambia's historic food insecurity.

BRITISH RULE

The Gambia owes its separate existence from Senegal to British slave-trading activity, which by 1816 led to the establishment of Bathurst as a settlement for liberated Africans. With its location at the mouth of the Gambia River, Bathurst also served as a military base from which the British sought to stem the trade in enslaved Africans. While both France and Britain recognized the country's odd and precarious location in the heart of Senegal, negotiations to incorporate both colonies into a single French colonial entity broke down. This breakdown resulted in part from conflicting and limited British economic interests focused on the Gambia River, and from Britain's failure to invest in both the people and infrastructure of the colony. For a while in the 1800s, both Sierra Leone and The Gambia were jointly administered by a resident governor in Freetown and a lieutenant governor or administrator in Bathurst; the administrator answered to the governor.

This arrangement turned out to be less than optimal, which led the Colonial Office to propose exchanging The Gambia for French territory. This proposal was later abandoned owing to forceful protests against it from a small yet influential group of liberated Africans, or Aku. Continued concern over The Gambia's viability as a nation saw yet another proposal, this time from the United Nations (UN) in the 1960s following Britain's request for a feasibility study to explore The Gambia's incorporation into Senegal. Once more, this proposal met with strong opposition from an emerging class of Gambian nationalists who were determined to see a free and independent Gambia.

Britain's colonial policy of indirect rule saw the division of The Gambia into a colony and a protectorate in 1894, the former administered by a British governor and a coterie of civil servants and in the latter by British traveling commissioners, Gambian chiefs, and village heads (*alkali*). Together, they saw to the stability and maintenance of British colonial policy. As the term implies, indirect rule saw British officials at the apex of the administrative pyramid with Africans in the middle and lower rungs. In the lower rungs, traditional cultural mores would coexist with those of the British, except where they conflicted with Britain's operational and cultural values. British colonial policy, like that of the French, had a so-called civilizing ethos, as Africans and Gambians were deemed racially inferior. British and all European colonizers had conveniently forgotten that Africans had or were part of sophisticated kingdoms and empires that were just as rich and complex as their own during the 14th and 15th centuries and even later.

It took European firepower and decades of pacification wars to conquer Africans, and thus began the takeover of their lands and authority through colonization.

British colonial rule, which began in 1821, was limited to the new settlement of Bathurst, named after the Secretary of the Colonies, Earl Bathurst. The Colony consisted of Bathurst and a few other scattered settlements along the Gambia River and did not include the rural interior, in part because of ongoing jihads in the area and efforts by the British to keep administrative costs low—a cardinal principle of British colonial policy in Africa and elsewhere. The Legislative Council was the main administrative body, which was tasked with lawmaking and administration. It was headed by a governor, who was assisted by some British administrators and merchants, with limited African representation from 1883. In time, however, Aku and Gambian Muslims and chiefs represented both colony and protectorate interests.

Following negotiations between the British colonial office and Gambian nationalist leaders in London, internal self-government was granted, which culminated in independence on February 18, 1965. The Gambia gained independence eight years after Ghana, five years after Nigeria, and four years after Sierra Leone.

COLONIALISM AND CULTURE

Gambians generally consider their enslavement and colonization by the British as two of the country's most formative and destructive experiences, reshaping not only their political economies but their psychological state as well. In fact, many Africans believe that in order to understand Africa's past, current, and future status and prospects, and The Gambia's in particular, it is important to comprehend the impact that slavery and colonialism had on the continent and its peoples. While formal colonialism may have lasted some seventy years, on average, it nonetheless reshaped or modified African traditional institutions, usurped African authority, and subordinated Africans to serve European colonial interests. Colonization was an affront to African cultural values. Christian missionaries introduced Christianity and were driven by the belief that Africans needed to be saved through the Gospel. Islam had a similar mission and coexisted with some African traditions and institutions until the Soninke-Marabout Wars that were fought to cleanse Islam of these so-called Africanisms. Africans, especially those located in coastal areas, were converted in small numbers to Christianity. The Jola in particular resisted Christianity, but in time missionaries

The entrance to Banjul International Airport was refurbished and remains one of President Jammeh's triumphs of infrastructure development following the 1994 coup. (Courtesy of Buharry Gassama)

built schools and educated a growing number of young Jolas, Serers, and other Gambians. The Jola likewise resisted Islam and began to embrace it only in the 1900s. Paradoxically, Christian missionary and colonial education, rudimentary as it was, became the catalyst for African and Gambian independence.

Like other colonies, The Gambia had a share of both forms of education that complemented Qur'anic education, which tended not to be formalized until much later. Through colonial and missionary education the English language spread, and new consumption patterns were introduced and old ones reinforced. Ultimately, women were further relegated to producing food crops while men focused on cash crops for export. Where relative gender equality or matrilineal relations existed, patrilineality ensued. And where relative food self-sufficiency existed, food dependence, especially on rice, took root.

INDEPENDENT MOVEMENTS

Edward Francis Small, an Aku nationalist journalist and trade unionist, is considered the father of Gambian nationalism. A persistent thorn in the side of the colonial administration, Small became the first African to be elected to the Legislative Council in 1947, with Chief Tamba Jammeh of Illiasa and Reverend J.C. Faye of Bathurst appointed to that body in the same year. The road to The Gambia's independence was characterized by political subterfuge among party leaders and between the leaders and the colonial administration, and on July 22, 1964, under the chairmanship of the Honorable Duncan Sandys, Secretary of State for the Colonies, independence talks began. Forty-one officials attended these talks: six from the Colonial Office; three from the Foreign Office; two from the Home Office; and 14 from the Gambian government, including Sir John Paul, the governor. Among the Gambian delegation on the government side were Prime Minister Dawda Jawara, Sheriff Sisay, S.M. Dibba, J.C. Faye, and others. The Gambian opposition delegation included P.S. Njie, M.C. Cham, I.M. Garba Jahumpa, I.A.S. Burang-John, and Kebba Foon.

In the 1950s, some opposition party leaders, including Jahumpa, advocated a political arrangement similar to the Malta Plan, in which representatives from The Gambia would sit in the British Parliament. Others, including P.S. Njie, argued in favor of delaying independence, whereas Jawara, along with other members of the newly formed the People's Progressive Party (PPP), a party of mostly educated provincial young men, demanded independence. By the time the talks began, however, they were united in their demand for political independence. In fact, the PPP had an independence manifesto that emphasized, among other things, internal self-government by May 1961, raising living standards, and a guaranteed producer price for groundnuts. Printed in Nigeria while Jawara was attending Nigeria's independence celebrations in 1960, the PPP manifesto established the party as the leading advocate for independence in The Gambia. However, Sanjally Bojang, an influential founding member of the PPP, advocated the formation of a single-umbrella party and, together with J.C. Faye and Garba Jahumpa, denounced Jawara for refusing to go along with the idea. At a party congress in Brikama, Bojang was expelled from the PPP. Following the distribution of the party manifesto, according to Sir Dawda, Governor Windley threatened him with detention, but he never followed through with his threat.

The 1962 elections, which saw Jawara's rise to the position of prime minister, prompted a gradual British withdrawal, which led to internal self-government in 1963 and independence on February 18, 1965. Yet along with flag independence came myriad social, political, and economic challenges that had their origin in British colonial indifference. This meant that the newly independent state had only two government-owned hospitals and high schools and very poor infrastructure. Like other ex-colonies, The Gambia gained independence while relying predominantly on a single export crop, groundnuts, as a source of revenue to improve poor social services, education, and health. Although the British government provided modest financial assistance initially, The Gambia was nonetheless trapped in a cycle of dependence and vulnerability, attributes that would define its postindependence existence. Limited natural resources, an odd geographic location, and a generalized state of underdevelopment led the American journalist Berkley Rice to question the viability of the country, which he termed an "improbable nation."[11]

Prime Minister Jawara's work, along with that of his cabinet and a small civil service, was clearly daunting. Without saying so, they worked to prove Berkley Rice wrong by putting in place an open market system and, even more important, a functioning democracy. While many newly independent African countries and their leadership engaged in constructing massive prestige-driven development projects, Jawara and his government instead moved modestly and worked to build health care and communication systems that once were considered some of Africa's best. In time, access to education improved, as did life expectancy, and before long this relatively well-governed "improbable nation" began to enjoy worldwide respect and support.

It is worth reiterating that life in postindependent Gambia was nothing short of hellish. Life expectancy was around 30 years; infant mortality and adult deaths from disease were extraordinarily high; and roads, if you wished

Car park at Bakoteh on the Kotu Highway, with street vendors displaying their wares as pedestrians and vehicles go by. (Courtesy of Buharry Gassama)

to call them that, were impassible. It took days to travel from Bathurst (Banjul) to Basse, and roads were impassible in August and September because of heavy rains. Access to education was severely limited and employment went to a few Gambians who worked for the state and for foreign firms. Life in the rural areas was at best difficult, especially during the rainy season when food supplies were low or unavailable, forcing many rural dwellers to subsist on small rations of food before their cereal crops ripened. Unscrupulous businessmen seized this dismal situation, termed the "hungry season," to lend farmers cash and goods in return for exorbitant profits. Thus, rural farmers were caught in a perpetual cycle of debt and seldom made enough to improve their lives or the lives of those who depended on them.

PPP HEGEMONY AND THE FURTHER ASCENDANCE OF JAWARA

Nine months after political independence in 1965, Jawara faced a major challenge when he sought republican status for the country, and in so doing to establish the post of executive president. This initiative failed due to opposition spearheaded by the main opposition, the United Party (UP), whose fortunes and influence in Gambian politics began to decline soon thereafter. In the 1966 elections, the UP was dealt a blow that ultimately would spell its death. Representation by the UP fell further when its leader, P. S. Njie, was expelled from Parliament for failing to attend meetings. Indeed, this paved the way for Sir Dawda Jawara's dominance (he was knighted in 1966). In 1970, The Gambia became a republic, an event that saw the ascendance of Sir Dawda to the presidency. Subsequent elections in 1972 and thereafter consolidated PPP rule.[12]

Jawara's rise to political prominence would continue to be challenged nonetheless. Characteristic of his generation of African presidents and heads of government, his rule became increasingly personalist, characterized by patron–client relationships and the co-optation of opposition party members. Jawara's political breakup with his former vice president, Sheriff Dibba, over the butut affair in early 1972 was to begin a series of political breakups. As a unit of The Gambia's currency, the butut was deemed valuable in neighboring Senegal, where it was melted for its copper and made into jewelry. In 1972 Dibba's brother was caught transporting this merchandise illegally.

Vice President Dibba resigned his position over the butut affair but was then appointed ambassador to the European Union. He subsequently formed the National Convention Party (NCP) in 1975, while the 1980s saw the mushrooming of several other opposition political parties. Assan Musa Camara, another former vice president under Jawara, formed The Gambia People's Party (GPP) in 1987, a splinter party of the PPP. The People's Democratic Organization for Independence and Socialism (PDOIS) was founded by

Halifa Sallah, Sedia Jatta, and Sam Sarr in 1986; it advocated a new vision while raising issues critical of the PPP government. Two Marxist-oriented parties were banned—the Gambia Socialist Revolutionary Party (GSRP) and the Movement for Justice in Africa—The Gambia branch (MOJA-G), headed by Tijan "Korro" Sallah. Sheriff Sisay, a founding member of the PPP, also broke ranks with Jawara and the PPP after he resigned as finance minister. Sisay would, however, return to the party and later serve as governor of the Central Bank and minister of finance. Under Sisay's watch in 1985 the Economic Recovery Program (ERP) was introduced by the World Bank to reform The Gambia's economy.

THE 1981 ABORTIVE COUP

For the most part, The Gambia remained an oasis in a continent of instability and coups d'état, but not for long. In 1981, while away in Europe, Jawara faced the greatest challenge to his rule and the legitimacy of his government when an ex-politician turned Marxist, Kukoi Samba Sanyang, and some members of the Field Force (an unarmed quasi-military security establishment) sought to overthrow him. Though the coup was foiled by Senegalese troops and Jawara was restored to power, it nonetheless brought to the fore the regime's growing weakness and vulnerability. Social inequality and a deepening division between an emergent political and economic class against a backdrop of grinding poverty among the mass of the population, coupled with infighting and factionalism within the PPP, exposed Jawara and his government to adverse criticism. Additionally, the erosion of competitive party politics within the larger political arena and the repression of dissent and dissidents within the PPP, of which the splinter parties headed by Dibba and Camara were examples, left the PPP and Jawara vulnerable to further attack. The loss of life, estimated at 500 but possibly more, and property following the abortive coup shattered the political innocence of Gambians and the long-held beliefs in The Gambia's peaceful and stable character. Senegal's intervention to quell the coup once more raised Gambian fears of a Senegalese takeover of the country. Therefore, the attempted coup and Senegal's intervention to restore Jawara back to power became an important card in President Abdou Diouf's hand to pressure Jawara for some sort of political union.

THE SENEGAMBIA CONFEDERATION

Fears of a Senegalese takeover were not farfetched because three weeks after the attempted coup, plans were under way to establish the Senegambia Confederation. Critics opined that President Jawara had mortgaged The Gambia's future to regain power. President Diouf got just what he wanted and served as the confederation's first president while Sir Dawda became his vice president. A new Gambian army, a confederal parliament, and a cabinet were set up. Yet the establishment of a new Gambian army raised serious security concerns for The Gambia and for Jawara himself. In accepting the creation of a new Gambian army, his critics maintained, Jawara exposed himself to a future coup. In hindsight, Jawara was caught in a catch-22 situation. By signing the Senegambian accords to save himself and his government, The Gambia had in effect become, in principle if not in fact, an equal member of the confederation. And with this came the expectation that it would contribute equally to the newly created institutions of the confederation. However, owing to a variety of political and economic factors that included disagreement over the rotation of the post of president between Presidents Diouf and Jawara, coupled with economic challenges, the ill-fated Senegambia Confederation ultimately collapsed in 1989 amid much acrimony. Jeggan Senghor's book *The Politics of Senegambia Integration, 1958–1994* documents these events well.[13]

THE ECONOMIC RECOVERY PROGRAM

Following the abortive coup, political reconciliation and economic reconstruction became key objectives of Sir Dawda's government. In response to the charges of corruption leveled against his regime, he undertook several political and economic reforms, including the passage of several anticorruption laws as remedy. This was partly precipitated by embarrassing scandals in several government offices in which many key civil servants were implicated. President Jawara also initiated much-needed economic reforms under the supervision of the World Bank. Supported by generous international financial support, Jawara was able to restore domestic and international confidence in large measure because of prudent domestic and foreign economic policy choices. Under the World Bank–directed economic reforms, in which Sheriff Sisay played an important role, the economy grew at a modest pace of about 3–5 percent for the period between 1986 and 1993, with inflation remaining at reasonable limits, bolstered by a stable dalasi.[14] In time, The Gambia's macroeconomic framework began to improve as foreign reserves also began to strengthen to support imports months into the future.

Despite these macroeconomic policies, or perhaps because of them, unemployment and underemployment, which remained problems for the Jawara administration, increased. Hundreds of civil servants were retrenched or laid off in an effort to reduce government spending. Government-owned firms or firms in which the government controlled major shares were privatized, including the Gambia Producing Marketing Board (GPMB), a government-owned parastatal that controlled the sale and purchase of groundnuts. While resentment against these economic reforms was apparent, it never resulted in political protests against the regime, as it had in other countries in West Africa. Nonetheless, economic reforms sharpened further the preexisting social and economic divide between the haves and the have-nots, especially between urban and rural dwellers. Political reforms, which were never as far-reaching as the economic ones, deepened political factionalism within the ruling PPP and severely eroded government legitimacy. The resulting toxic and equally acrimonious political environment added to the country's perceived precipitous decline.

Meanwhile, political instability and volatility in the subregion during the 1990s, especially in Nigeria, Liberia, and Sierra Leone by way of coups d'état, and civil war in Liberia, specifically, spilled over to generate expectations of an army takeover in The Gambia. To an increasingly vocal minority, this was seen as the only solution to The Gambia's economic and political crises. And despite Sir Dawda's gallant efforts to bring to a peaceful resolution Liberia's deepening civil war, he was overrun by regional and domestic events. At the domestic level, elements within the Gambian national army grew increasingly restive. Already divided, the army suffered from internal factionalism as well, which also generated grievances based on rank and nationality, as the bulk of senior officers were Nigerian. Poor salaries and inadequate living quarters and conditions heightened tensions within the army, which led to the bloodless ouster of President Jawara by four young officers, led by Yahya Jammeh, in July 1994. The literature on the causes and consequences of the coup is large. Ebrima Ceesay's book, *The Military and "Democratisation" in The Gambia: 1994–2003,* and Abdoulaye Saine's, *The Paradox of Third-Wave Democratization in Africa: The Gambia Under AFPRC-APRC Rule, 1994–2008,* provide excellent background and analysis of this period in Gambia's political development and history. The personal accounts of the coup by retired colonel Samsudeen Sarr and deputy inspector general of police Ebrima Chongan, *Coup d'état by the Gambia National Army* and *The Price of Duty, Balangba,* respectively, provide fascinating narratives of this event.[15]

Transition to Civilian Rule by the Military Government, 1994–1996/7

Following the coup, the constitution was suspended and political activity was banned.[16] The Armed Forces Provisional Ruling Council (AFPRC) was established and headed by its new chairman, Yahya Jammeh. The new junta promised to root out corruption and introduce democracy and the rule of law. The AFPRC promised accountability, transparency, and probity in government and proceeded to replace many civil servants in the previous Jawara administration with their own supporters. The regime thereafter began a program to build and resurface roads and construct schools, hospitals, and a new airport. The AFPRC became increasingly populist in its rhetoric and appealed to the population to join them in their "revolution."

In time, however, it became apparent that the regime was more interested in the welfare of their own members and before long, they adopted the same flamboyant lifestyles for which they had criticized Jawara and the PPP. They seized properties belonging to citizens they thought guilty of corruption and distributed these properties to senior military officers and their supporters. Increasingly, the regime became very repressive, with some council members engaging in widespread brutality against civilians.

An alleged coup in November 1994 was brutally repressed by the regime, resulting in the deaths of many officers. Meanwhile, economic sanctions and advisories by Britain and Scandinavian governments to their citizens to suspend travel to The Gambia began to have a negative economic impact and before long stemmed the flow of tourists from Europe. The United States and the European Union suspended all aid except humanitarian aid and insisted on a speedy return to civilian rule. To counter the negative economic effects arising from these sanctions, the AFPRC undertook an aggressive foreign policy strategy to cultivate new friends internationally as it desperately sought to shore up its dwindling economic resource base. Taiwan, partly because of its own political isolation—its lack of international recognition and conflict with the People's Republic of China—became a major economic benefactor, along with Libya.

Pressures continued to mount, however, both nationally and internationally for a return to civilian rule. The regime responded defiantly, promising not to hold elections or that it would do so only when they were ready. Chairman Jammeh threatened that whoever opposed them "would "go six feet deep." In the end, the AFPRC was forced to cut back its timetable to civilian rule from four years to two. The National Consultative Committee (NCC), chaired by Dr. Lenrie Peters, was formed to sound Gambians' opinions as to the length of the transition period. The regime held a referendum over a hastily drafted national constitution, which was ratified but not before Jammeh doctored it to expunge a two-term limit for the president and to lower the presidential age limit from 40 to 30 in order to enable him to contest the presidential elections slated for September 1996.

Jammeh imposed another ban of up to 25 years on all politicians and political parties of the first republic except for a few small parties that did not pose much of a threat to his continued rule. To bolster his chances of winning, Jammeh also passed Decrees 70 and 71, essentially to muzzle the press and make it extremely difficult for all aspiring presidential candidates to run against him.[17] He imposed what many believed to be unreasonable financial requirements for presidential candidates. He proceeded to single-handedly establish and appoint members to the Provisional Independent Electoral Commission (PIEC) to conduct the forthcoming presidential and National Assembly elections. In the months leading to the presidential vote, Jammeh ratcheted up his repressive machinery, which he used to violate, detain, or arrest leaders of the opposition parties and their supporters.

Chairman Jammeh then proceeded to resign his commission; form his own political party, the Alliance for Patriotic Reorientation and Construction (APRC); and in effect take control of the national television station, which he had just built to relay his message of change to the population. In the end, Jammeh was declared the winner against Ousainou Darboe and his newly formed United Democratic Party (UDP) and other opponents. The results, however, were widely condemned by the Commonwealth because of numerous electoral irregularities that included vote buying; voting by Jammeh's coethnic Jola from Senegal, who crossed over from Casamance to cast votes for him; and widespread violence and intimidation of voters. Jammeh prevailed in the election and was then sworn in as The Gambia's second president, but not before the results were widely criticized internationally.

Under President Jammeh the economy continued to deteriorate along with human rights, as extrajudicial killings and disappearances ensued. Ex-President Jawara, who now lived in exile outside London, England, with his immediate family and a crop of former officials and supporters, lobbied the United States and several African and European governments to help him bring to an end the APRC's stranglehold on the country. This was not to be, as subsequent elections in 2001 and 2006 saw Jammeh reelected to power. With the armed forces along with the National Intelligence Agency (NIA) under his control, The Gambia was a democracy only in name, as horrendous individual and press freedoms were systematically abridged to insulate Jammeh from adverse criticism.

Jammeh began to engage in bizarre medical practices and made incredible claims, much to the dismay of both the domestic and international communities. He claimed to have found the cure for AIDS, cancer, diabetes, high blood pressure, and infertility, among many other ailments. Throngs lined up to receive his herbal concoctions and potions under the glare of domestic and international media. Several people were said to have died or suffered serious medical harm after ingesting these potions. Many AIDS patients claimed to have been cured after Jammeh's medical intervention, and many more became negligent and stopped taking antiretroviral cocktail drugs, which Jammeh had demanded of participants who wished to remain in his program. Critics maintain that Jammeh's so-called cures were the product of a failed health delivery system that despite the hype did not deliver to the majority of Gambians. While infant immunization improved, thanks in part to international donors, health care for the average Gambian has not improved by much, so thousands have died and many still die needlessly from easily curable diseases.

Jammeh also oversaw a nationwide hunt to rid the country of witches, who in his estimation harbor ill will against him and his family. His witch-hunters forcibly administered potions to individuals to prove their innocence or guilt. Many were reported to have died from taking these concoctions while many others suffered from hallucinations or severe bouts of diarrhea. Many believe that Jammeh's witch hunts targeted people he suspected of being sympathetic to the opposition. In a country where these beliefs still hold much sway, it was viewed as a legitimate means to protect himself, the country, and its people from these sinister individuals.

In October 2010 a group of Jammeh supporters consisting of district chiefs and some elders traveled the country advocating that Jammeh be crowned king of The Gambia, because of his "tremendous economic development achievements" since coming to power in 1994. This was widely seen for what it was—Jammeh's veiled efforts to test the waters regarding his wish to become king. This effort was widely criticized and ridiculed by supporters and detractors alike and was in the end abandoned, at least for now. Yet this was not the first time Jammeh tested the waters for something he wanted to do. Shortly before the 1996 presidential elections, a group of provincial women supporters held political rallies in support of a "no elections" option. This too died from lack of support.

In December 2010, Senegal and its president, Abdoulaye Wade, were insulted by secretary-general and head of the civil service, Njogu Bah, following the interdiction of an arms shipment from Iran in Nigeria bound for Kaninlai Farms—Jammeh's hometown. Nigerian officers inspected the containers, labeled as building materials, only to find a cache of arms that many believe were bound for the rebels in Casamance. Senegal immediately reported the matter to the United Nations, as the arms shipment was in violation of an arms embargo against Iran. Bah's orchestrated attack criticized President Abdoulaye Wade and his government and characterized President Wade as a disingenuous Pan-Africanist. Bah threatened that The Gambia was ready to defend itself against friend and foe alike. This was an unprecedentedly undiplomatic speech against Senegal, Wade, and Wade's government.

The immediate fallout from the arms bust was the rupture in relations between The Gambia and Iran, a move believed to have been forced on Jammeh by the U.S. government. Earlier in 2010 a $1 billion drug bust was made by British agents in collaboration with their Gambian counterparts. Hidden in a warehouse outside the capital, Banjul, agents found cocaine and other drugs neatly concealed by a façade of a wall. Several Nigerians and other foreign nationals were arrested or implicated. Many believe that Jammeh himself could be involved in the sale and transshipment of drugs from South America via The Gambia to Europe and is handsomely paid for his services. There is no evidence of this, however, and now that little has been heard of this bust and those individuals linked to the drugs, some see this as evidence of complicity among lower-security personnel.

What the arms and drug busts reveal is the growing trade in small arms in the subregion, which are allegedly destined for secessionist groups who use it to foment instability in countries like Senegal. Also, the growing presence of South American drug cartels in the subregion, Guinea Bissau and The Gambia, specifically, has not only increased the level of government criminal activity, as government officials in both countries have been implicated, but it has also heightened the level of drug use, with devastating negative social and economic effects.

Finally, since the coup, Jammeh has sought to transform his image from that of a soldier to that of a generous, religious statesman or *mansa* (king). He possesses various honorific titles to bolster this image. Among these are Professor, Dr., and Sheikh, none of which he earned; he would, however, severely punish anyone not addressing him without them. Jammeh has over the years been awarded or claims to have been awarded numerous medals in honor of his contribution to The Gambia's development. One was a medal of admiralty, a tongue-and cheek award that was allegedly given to him by the governor of Nebraska, arranged by an Iranian-American; this was quickly withdrawn. Jammeh also claimed to have received from President Barak Obama a title and award, but upon further investigation by the press, this was found to be false. The White House came out to categorically deny that it had awarded President Jammeh a medal.

Jammeh's image adorns offices, and he is engaged in all sorts of economic ventures and has a hand in almost every economic enterprise in The Gambia. He prides himself as a successful farmer; coerces senior civil servants, including secretaries of state, to labor on farms without pay; and admonishes Gambian men for being lazy. In 2002, following protracted negotiations, Jammeh amnestied and welcomed back ex-president Jawara to The Gambia but not his exiled supporters; Jammeh gave him back his home and other properties, provided him with a security outfit and put him on a pension. The amnesty was widely criticized, however, by supporters as well as critics of Jawara since it was limited to him and his immediate family.

In the presidential elections held in November 2011, Jammeh defeated his key opponents. He secured 72 percent of the vote to Ousainou Darboe's 16 percent and Hamat Bah's 11percent, rendering the divided opposition its most severe thrashing. Not because Jammeh is hugely popular—though he enjoys some measure of popularity among his coethnic Jola, women, and youth—but because the electorate may have lost confidence in the current crop of opposition politicians, especially since the collapse of the National Alliance for Development and Democracy (NADD) in 2006. A coalition of several political parties, NADD was formed shortly before the 2006 presidential election to run against Jammeh. Internal divisions along with differences in ideology, however, led to its demise, which was precipitated by the UDP's Darboe following his resignation from the coalition.

CULTURAL ISSUES

As the chapters that follow show, Gambian culture is rich, diverse, and ever changing, shaped by African traditions, Islam, and Christianity. It is necessary to emphasize that Gambian culture is part of a larger tapestry that includes the much larger cultural region, Senegambia Major, a cultural expanse that includes modern-day Mali, Guinea, Senegal, The Gambia, Guinea Bissau, and Mauritania. And, for a period spanning over five centuries, Senegambia Minor played both important and minor roles in the larger Senegambian configuration, especially during the times in which the empires of the western Sudan were in existence. Therefore, centuries of coexistence, intermarriage, and cooperation as well as conflict between various ethnic groups has had both integrative and disintegrative consequences. Centuries of coexistence also led to social and ethic differentiation and homogenization with Islam and Christianity, which in the end served simultaneously as unifying forces. Today, as in the past, ethnic relations are fluid—as some would say, constructed over time, what Benedict Anderson called "imagined communities."[18] This makes the term *tribe* all the more problematic as an explanatory tool for social and political association in Africa generally and The Gambia specifically. As an anthropological term, it is deeply implicated in Britain's colonial policy of organizing Africans for the primary purposes of taxation, domination, and control. It also constructs Africans in the ethnographic present, that is, Africans as lacking social dynamism and forever trapped in the past. Nothing could be more removed from Senegambian history and reality, as noted earlier in the preface.[19] In the preindependence period, Africans used ethnicity (*tribe*) as a tool around which to organize for political and economic change. And in the postcolonial era, Africa's emergent political class has also used it to drum up support for their policies and as a means to maintain order through ethnic balancing in the distribution of jobs, goods, and services in society.

Individual social and ethnic identities constructed over several centuries therefore provide a sense of belonging informed by mutual social obligations to family, ethnic group, and self. Consequently, even today, many primordial customs persist alongside contemporary ones, often mediated by changed and changing global circumstances. Technological globalization has to a large degree not only preserved many languages but strengthened them as well, though some may be threatened elsewhere. This attests to the fact that cultures in both Senegambia Major and Senegambia Minor have not been static and have consequently experienced and continue to experience appreciable degrees of change and dynamism.[20]

Television, the camcorder, instant messaging, and the ubiquitous mobile phone have reshaped people's lives, cultural traditions, and practices the world over and especially in Senegambia. Add to this the phenomenon of The Gambia's growing diaspora who remit millions of dollars to the country and in doing so have begun to reshape the population's values and global outlook. And there is no doubt that political Islam, as well as other forcers of globalization, simultaneously reshape and are reshaped by The Gambia's own cultural values. It is against this backdrop that we must understand contemporary Gambian culture and worldview.

NOTES

1. *Coos* is a cereal crop from which cherreh, rui, and laah are made.

2. Kenneth Swindell and Alieu Jeng, *Migrants, Credit and Climate: The Gambia Groundnut Trade, 1834–1934* (Leiden: Brill, 2006).

3. Richard A. Schroeder, *Shady Practices, Agroforestry and Gender Politics in The Gambia* (Berkley, CA: Berkley University Press, 1999).

4. Kasper Juffermans and Caroline McGlynn, "A Sociolinguistic Profile of The Gambia," *Sociolinguistics* 3, no. 3 (2009): 323.

5. Patience Sonko-Godwin, *Ethnic Groups of the Senegambia Region* (Banjul: Sunrise Publishers, 2003); Dawda Faal, *A History of The Gambia, AD 1000–1965* (Banjul: Edward Francis Small Printing Press, 1999); Charolotte Quinn, *Mandingo Kingdoms of the Senegambia: Traditionalism, Islam, and European Expansion* (Evanston, IL: Northwestern University Press, 1972). Sonko-Godwin's book is used widely in high schools in The Gambia and it provides a detailed discussion of the various ethnic groups in The Gambia.

6. For a detailed discussion of the Jola, see Godfrey Nwakikagile, *Ethnic Diversity and Integration in The Gambia: The Land, the People and Culture* (Dar-es-Salaam, Tanzania: Continental Press, 2010).

7. Florence Mahoney, *A Signare: Mulatto Woman,* Gambian Studies (Banjul, 2008).

8. Lillian Ashcraft-Eason, "'She Voluntarily Hath Come': A Gambian Woman Trader in Colonial Georgia in the Eighteenth Century," in *Identity in the Shadows of Slavery,* ed. Paul Lovejoy, 202–22 (London: Continuum, 2000).

9. Donald R. Wright, *The World and a Very Small Place in Africa: A History of Globalization in Niumi, The Gambia,* 2nd ed. (Armonk: M. E. Sharpe, 2004)

10. Swindell and Jeng, *Migrants, Credit and Climate.*

11. Berkley Rice, *Enter Gambia: Birth of an Improbable Nation* (New York: Houghton Mifflin, 1967).

12. Arnold Hughes and David Perfect, *A Political History of The Gambia: 1816–1994* (Rochester, NY: University of Rochester Press, 2006), 189.

13. Jeggan C. Senghor, *The Politics of Senegambian Integration, 1958–1994* (Oxford: Peter Lang, 2006).

14. For a good article on this, see Tijan M. Sallah, "Politics and Economic in The Gambia," *The Journal of Modern African Studies* 28, no. 4 (1990): 621–48.

15. Ebrima Ceesay, *The Military and "Democratisation" in The Gambia: 1994–2003* (UK: London, Trafford Publishing, 2006); Abdoulaye Saine, *The Paradox of Third-Wave Democratization in Africa: The Gambia Under AFPRC-APRC Rule, 1994–2008* (Lanham, MD: Lexington Books, 2009); Samsudeen Sarr, *Coup d'etat by the Gambia National Army, July 1994* (Philadelphia: Xlibris, 2007); Ebrima Chongan, *The Price of Duty, Balangba* (London: Lulu, 2010).

16. Abdoulaye Saine, *The Paradox of Third-Wave Democratization in Africa: The Gambia Under AFPRC-APRC Rule* (Lanham, MD: Lexington Books, 2009), 39.

17. Both decrees were passed by the Armed Forces Provisional Council (AFPRC), requiring new and existing newspapers to deposit the sum of US$10,000 before they could operate.

18. Benedict Anderson, *Imagined Communities: Reflections on the Origin and Spread of Nationalism* (London: Verso, 2006).

19. For a fascinating study of The Gambia's and Bathurst's early beginnings, see Florence Mahoney's Ph.D. dissertation, *Government and Opinion in The Gambia, 1816–1901* (London University, 1963), and Charlotte Quinn's *Mandingo Kingdoms of Senegambia: Traditionalism, Islam and European Expansion* (Evanston, IL: Northwestern University Press, 1972).

20. For a good discussion of this and similar positions, see Paul Nugent, "Putting the History Back into Ethnicity: Enslavement, Religion and Cultural Brokerage in the Construction of Mandinka/Jola and Ewe/Agotime Identities in West Africa, c. 1650–1930," *Comparative Studies in Society and History* 50, no. 4 (2008): 920–48.

2

Religion and Worldview

RELIGION IS A pillar underpinning Gambian culture and society. The worldview is more expansive, as it includes a mélange of African traditional beliefs derived from different ethnic groups as well as Islam and Christian beliefs. Together, but not always coherently, these multiple beliefs inform worldview, which in turn defines a person's relationship to self, creator, society, and the world, both temporal and spiritual. The coexistence of Muslim and Christian values alongside African belief systems has engendered high levels of blending, sometimes indistinguishably. Yet in other instances they have become strange bedfellows. Part of Islam's appeal to the peoples of Senegambia Major and Senegambia Minor lay, in part, in the common institutions that Arabs and Berbers shared with Africans. Both are or were at one time agrarian and heavily male-dominated, with traditions and kinship systems based mostly along patrilineal lines of descent, even if some groups are or once were matrilineal. In other words, the privileging of male heirs over female ones also served as a unifying force. Colonialism and Christianity reinforced these institutions and their worldviews as well.

Clearly, while about 5 percent of Gambians are Christian, Christian beliefs through conversion and missionary education also left an important imprint on the worldview of Gambians. Colonialism imposed its worldview on Gambians and also provided an alternative viewpoint to those views they held. Traditional or spiritual beliefs were perhaps the most emphatic rejection of both Islam and Christianity. The Jola, Serer, Manjago, and Fula ethnicities

Banjul Pharmacy, located not in Banjul but in Bambo, London Corner, is one of the oldest pharmacies in this teeming city, with a population of approximately 300,000. (Courtesy of Buharry Gassama)

once held strongly to their beliefs in the occult and magic and offered libations to facilitate intercession by ancestors and spirits in personal and family affairs. Even among the devoted practitioners of both Islam and Christianity, libations and charity, including the sacrifice of chickens, goats, or sheep, are often carried out to appease spirits and avert doom. From marabouts, whose authority is assumed to be based on the Qur'an, to fortune-tellers, whose authority is said to be derived from magic and other supernatural entities, being either Muslim or Christian does not bar one from seeking these services. The Soninke-Marabout wars that ended in 1901 sought to bring to a decisive end the spiritualist traditions among new converts to Islam. Today, only about 1 percent of Gambia's population practice traditional religions.

INDIGENOUS RELIGIONS

The continued presence of marabouts in Senegambian and specifically in Gambian culture may very well represent change from an earlier spiritual tradition of the pre-Islamic era. During the pre-Islamic era, soothsayers, traditional healers, midwives, woodcarvers, leatherworkers, blacksmiths, and goldsmiths and *jali* (pl. *jeli*; means bard or *griot*) were considered to be endowed with magical and mystical powers to intervene on behalf of the sick or those whose luck had run out. Individuals so endowed were asked for miracle healing, for fetishes to ward off evil spirits, or to place a curse on a rival. In the contemporary era, the marabout uses verses from the Qur'an—encased in leather, known as amulets or *juju*, just as in the past—to perform the same or similar services as diviners of the pre-Islamic era—a double consciousness. Though Islam and Christianity are the dominant religions today, traditional practices continue to thrive. Therefore, the introduction of Islam and Christianity did not lead to the disappearance or destruction of these old belief systems. In fact, African traditional belief systems absorbed and modified the new religions, engendering new practices and innovations.

Dream interpretation was and still is an important tool in the hands of diviners and fortune-tellers, as dreams are considered a mirror into the other world and things yet to come. For instance, a pregnant woman in a dream is a sign of impending trouble. A monkey in a dream signifies future failure or downfall, and a piece of white cloth means that the death of a friend or close relative is imminent. Yet not all dreams spell doom. Dreaming of raw fish means the birth of a child. Nighttime, that is, from sunset to dawn, is an especially dangerous period for mere mortals. This is when evil spirits, witches, and devils roam the streets to prey on humans. Consequently, no one visits the sick at night or sits under trees, because this is where spirits reside. Witches are believed to possess powers to kill and consume humans, whereas whirlwinds are believed to be the domain of evil spirits because of the force that accompanies them. By dawn all witches have returned home and become humans once more, following a night of being owls. In fact, in much of Senegambian culture, owls, monkeys, hyenas, and bats are feared by many to this day because of the belief in the power of witches to disguise themselves in those forms. Superstition also has it that witches are particularly dangerous during periods such as circumcision, when they can prey on circumcised boys or girls.

Individuals are not without recourse, however. The diviner, medicine man, or his or her equivalent must provide certain potions, charms, or antidotes or perform certain rites to ward off devils, witches, and persons suspected of casting spells against others. Certain tests can be performed on individuals by way of potions to determine if someone is a witch or wizard. This is what witch doctors or medicine men did under President Jammeh's watch. If a witch or wizard drinks these potions, it makes them be truthful about their supernatural activities. Bitter tomatoes or pignut when eaten by a witch or wizard is expected to elicit admissions of guilt, prompting witches to confess and recount the humans she has consumed. Rain on a sunny day can mystically prompt witches to confess as well. Yet the skills as well as the evil that witches are assumed to possess, according to traditionalist folklore, are passed from mother to child, and to girls in particular. Wizards (*knhorr* in Wolof) are generally deemed harmless and do not possess the repertoire of tricks and evil that witches are assumed to have.

As a form of social control diviners could cast spells on any person or persons guilty of antisocial behavior. A cheating husband could be rendered impotent by either his mistress's husband or his own wife. Stealing a neighbor's belongings could lead to blindness. *Mangkaneh* (potions or decorated horns) could be used to punish or deter thieves from stealing from a mango orchard or other people's belongings. Many kids, even to this day, avoid orchards out of fear of being negatively impacted by the *mangkaneh*—a good potion has the ability to keep you standing at the crime scene until the owner arrives to release the culprit, but not before administering the cane.

Senegambian culture, like most cultures, cherishes bravery. Young men are taught not to fear death or adversity. Particular amulets are believed to withstand bullets from guns; blunt knives used in a stabbing or a potent amulet could lead to a girl or woman falling in love with a suitor she despises. Even in competitive sports like soccer and wrestling, the team or wrestler with the strongest *juju* is believed to have his chances of winning enhanced. Yet, just as there are many ways to do harm, equally, several other means exist to perform good deeds. Similarly, it would not be unheard of for a senior civil servant convicted of corruption to spend considerable sums of money on a marabout to "save" him from serving a long prison term or dismissal. Individuals seeking travel visas to Europe or the United States will often retain the services of a fortune-teller or marabout to ease the interview process so as to ensure a successful outcome.

Many of the examples detailed in this section have been discredited through either experience, education, or adoption of Islam or Christianity. Yet many remain just below the surface of these religious beliefs and can be evoked during light moments or in times of stress when every other remedy seems to have failed. Some Christians may also resort to diviners, fortune-tellers, and marabouts when all else has failed or sometimes as a first line of action to ward off an impending problem. However, the strong influence that these beliefs have had for centuries has reduced significantly, due mostly to growing social awareness, education, and travel. Thus, when President Jammeh initiated witch hunt to weed out witches, he was evoking a latent belief and fear was once pervasive and some still believed to be true. It should also be noted that superstitions are present in all societies and while science and technology may have disproved their validity for the most part, some remain.

Dream reading or interpretation, for instance, is not unique to The Gambia but can be found in all major religions, including Judaism, Christianity, and Islam. It should also be noted that traditional religious beliefs in The Gambia, especially among the Jola and Serer, include a concept of God, gods, and diviners who are the mediators between the living and the dead. Also, traditional Gambian beliefs, similar to others on the continent, maintain that there are strong bonds with ancestors, who are believed to be alive in the spiritual world. Pouring drops of palm wine or putting a mound of rice on the ground before partaking of either commodity is done in reverence to the ancestors, who can also intercede directly to change one's earthly circumstances. These practices are seldom seen today in The Gambia, except among the few *cheddo* (traditionalist worshipers).

The extent to which ancestors are revered in Gambian society is amply demonstrated by the griot or *jeli*, whose mastery of the spoken word and recollection of genealogies of patron(s) are generally seen as a gift of supernatural proportions. Patrons take great pride in their ancestry and a *jali*'s skills of recounting intricate genealogies that span generations, which also includes retelling acts of gallantry, is often handsomely rewarded. Funerals also are an occasion to honor a dead relative on the day of death (departure) and then 3, 7, and 40 days later. This is often a time for mourners to indulge in delicious food and drink as a sign of respect and reverence. The underlying belief is that the departed only transition to the other world, where they will continue to live. It once was common in pre-Islamic cultures for the dead to be buried with some personal belongings, items they would surely need in the next world. This is not the case today.

Festivities that surround the enforced seclusion of the circumcised, whether male or female, are occasions for merriment and also for the payment of respects to the ancestors who watch over people to shoo away witches. Among the Mandinka, a masquerade known as *kankurang* is often deployed to ward off evil as well as to entertain onlookers. Dressed in reddened tree bark from head to waist and a skirtlike outfit made of leaves covering the waist down and chewing a piece of bark, the *kankurang* dances into a frenzy while striking onlookers, especially women, with a whip. With pulsating drums, the *kankurang* is believed to be in a trance—perhaps in another world or possessed by spirits. *Fambondi* (the one who takes himself out), a more sophisticated version of the *kankurang*, is endowed with fabulous spiritual powers to protect vast territory, including the circumcised, and is believed to enter into a rage as he flies to protect his domain, brandishing machetes and swords, and killing everything in his way. Unlike the *kankurang*, whose red-bark garment and skirt of green leaves is mounted by humans, *Fambondi* needs no one to mount his gear; he comes out dressed by no one.

There is a Wolof equivalent of *Fambondi* called *Mam*, whose feats are just as legendary. He too comes to protect the new initiates by warding off witches and evildoers. The Jola and Manjago, as well as the Aku-marabout, cousins to the Christian Aku, also have elaborate masquerades for different occasions—the *Kumpa, Egugu, Pakin,* and *huntin,* respectively. All exemplify the strong links between the living and ancestors. Among the Serer and Wolof, the *Simbe* or *Simba*, a masquerade of fierce lionlike characteristics, also serve the primary purpose of warding off evil. The *N'dape* ceremony among the Lebou of Senegal also has a similar function, as does the *njam* (the tattooing of young women's gums, lower lip, and chin into a blue-black color), which is practiced by most ethnic groups, especially the Hallpullar. During such occasions diviners are typically present to dissuade witches from consuming the blood of the initiated during the tattooing process. Senegambian traditional beliefs and practices are indeed very rich, and one could easily devote a book to the beliefs of each of the ethnic groups without doing justice to them. This discussion, however, should provide a glimpse into this largely unexplored terrain and inspire Gambianists and younger Gambian scholars, especially anthropologists and sociologists, to shed more light on each group.

Many of these traditions are dying out in The Gambia owing to lack of interest, absence of a cultural preservation policy, and hard economic times. These factors have combined to dampen somewhat the enthusiasm that once accompanied ceremonies, especially homecoming celebrations. Some traditional practices, while not completely abandoned, have been modified by changing circumstances; worldviews, however, are more enduring.

ISLAM

The spread of Islam and the resulting distribution of Muslim communities in West Africa came in two waves, broadly speaking. The first wave, during the 11th to the 17th centuries, saw Islam spread slowly, with the process led by clerics; Islam was then spread by traders, among others, in the 18th and 19th centuries. Thus, for many years Muslims lived under the protection and patronage of so-called infidel kings, whose conversion to Islam was far from complete owing to their continued reliance on fetishes and alcohol. The subsequent establishment of great centers of learning in Senegambia Major—the town of Pirr in Senegal, specifically—and the Sahel aided in the spread of Islam as well, but not enough to have made the kings abandon their traditional practices. Even Mansa Musa of Mali, who had earlier performed a pilgrimage to the holy city of Mecca in 1324–1325, and Askia Muhammed of Songhay were unable, or perhaps unwilling, to rid their monarchies of pre-Islamic beliefs. The famous North African Berber scholar and traveler Ibn

Battuta attested to the existence of these beliefs and practices at the court of Askia Dawud in the 1400s.

As we shall see in Senegambia Major, as was the case in northern Nigeria in the 19th century, Muslim jihadists, a Tukulor warrior class or theocracy, who could no longer coexist with their so-called infidel kings and patrons undertook wars of purification to bring to an end pre-Islamic rituals and practices. This constituted the second wave of Islamization, followed by a period of accommodation and consolidation under European occupation. In the area now occupied by modern-day Mauritania other jihads erupted as well.

It was Al Hajj Sheikh Umar (Futiu) Tal, a Fula cleric and caliph of the *Tijaniyya* sect, who began a quest to establish a theocratic state in the subregion following his return from Mecca. Born in Futa Toro in the Senegal River valley in 1794, Al Hajj Umar would wage jihads between 1852 and 1864 in the Western Sudan from his native Futa. He succeeded in establishing a theocratic state from Futa Jallon to Timbuktu, occupying both sides of the Niger River and converting the Bambara to Islam. Sheikh Umar was killed in a campaign trying to convert his coethnic Fula in Massina in 1864, but not before he appointed his son as successor. Sheikh Umar was a major influence in the spread of *Tijaniyya* and its subsequent adoption by his coethnic Fula disciples Maba Jahou (Diahou) Bah and, to a limited degree, Alpha and Musa Molloh on the Gambia River's north and south banks, respectively. In time, the Mollohs were driven less by a desire to spread Islam than by a desire to build, expand, and consolidate their territorial gains.[1]

The Soninke-Marabout Wars, 1850s–1901: An Overview

In the mid-1850s to 1901, The Gambia went through jihadist waves led by Tijaniyya disciples of Al Hajj Umar. Maba Jahou Bah, a Tukulor cleric, had in the earlier part of the 19th century helped defeat the key Wolof state of Cayor and converted its populations to Islam, winning the allegiance of its king, Lat Dior Diop (Jobe) and gaining him as an ally. Maba sought to replicate Al Hajj Umar's feat by trying to establish a theocratic state, first by seizing Baddibu in 1861 and driving out the traditional rulers. His advance on Niumi was repulsed by British forces; it took several decades of action by his deputy, Amar Fall, before Niumi was finally subdued in the 1880s. Maba's ambitious and expansive outreach attracted French interests, which allied with him initially to weaken the power and appeal of traditional kings in Cayor and Jollof but later turned against him. At the battle of Pathebadiane in 1865, Maba narrowly defeated the French, but subsequent efforts to come to the aid of Amar Faal in Niumi and Lat Dior Diop (Jobe) in Cayor severely weakened him and his forces. The last threat to Maba's territorial ambitions was the Serer kingdom of Sine. In his 1867 campaign to subdue the Serer, Maba was slain at the battle of Somp, one of the most crucial battles of the Soninke-Marabout Wars.[2]

Following Maba's death his brother Marmur (N'erri) Nderri Bah maintained his control over Baddibu but never succeeded in defeating Sine, due mostly to the French presence in the area and beyond. The kingdom was lost to the French in the late 1800s, when Maba's son, Sait Mati Bah, was routed by the French. His uncle Mamur (Mamut) then became leader of a much-reduced Baddibu state. Maba Jahou had an important ally and supporter in Biram Ceesay Sise of Kaur, Saloum. Following Maba's death, Sise's alliance with the Bah dynasty also ended. Ceesay Sise's political struggle with and against Mamur, in particular, was aided by Musa Molloh, a Fula ruler of the kingdom of Fulladu, but he could never defeat Sait Mati, and in the end he agreed to a British-brokered settlement.

The second phase of the Soninke-Marabout Wars affected all states on both sides of the Gambia River and was pursued with much violence into the 20th century. While Maba waged his wars of purification in the North Bank states of Baddibu and Niumi, states including Kombo enjoyed relative peace and in fact welcomed refugees from these regions, according to Florence Mahoney.[3] The western region of Kombo and Foni suffered the heaviest loss of human life and the most population dislocation. In Kombo, Foday Silla Touray, Almamy of Gunjur from 1853–1855, along with Omar of Sabiji, a Moor, ransacked the region, converting the Mandinka kings to Islam. Foday Silla was uncompromising in his conversion strategy, and when he attacked a British garrison in the area and inflicted defeat on the British, it required British reinforcements and considerable effort to defeat him. This area was, in the 1850s, already a boiling cauldron of British resistance and Muslim militancy.

In the 1860s, Foday Kabba Dumbuya led campaigns against Kiang and Foni and was relatively successful in converting the Kiangkas, but not the Jola of Foni, to Islam. The Jola continued to resist conversion and were protected in part by the British because of Foni's lucrative trade and British efforts to stem the resurgence of the Atlantic slave trade. On the whole, British colonial authorities, though anti-marabout for the most part, mostly stayed out of the Soninke-Marabout Wars until their interests were threatened. In 1900, when two British traveling commissioners, C. F. Sitwell and F. E. Silva, along with the chief of Battelling and six assistants, were killed in Sankandi, a French force pursued Foday Kaba Dumbuya into Medina, a town then under French control, and they killed him in 1901. Chief Dari Darbo, along with two of his assistants, were tried by the Supreme Court and executed. During Silla's last campaign in the Kombo in 1875, *Mansa* Tumani Bojang surrendered and was converted to Islam. Foday Silla continued his slave raids and later fell out with the British, who in February 1894 attacked him. Rejected by Foni, Silla retreated to the Casamance but was later captured and exiled to Cayor, where he died in April 1894.[4]

Musa Molloh's father, Alpha, was an elephant hunter who became a *talibe* (student) of Sheikh Umar Tal, whom he met before Umar's death in 1864. Alpha subsequently rose against the Mandinka king of Jimara in the mid-1800s and gradually gained the support of his coethnic Fula in the theocratic states of Futa Jallon and Futa Toro. Musa, his son, would later lead these forces to conquer Tomanna and smaller chieftaincies and extended his domination further to include Foday Kabba, whose family Musa had killed in 1862. Following the death of his father in 1881, a power struggle between Musa and his uncle, Bakary Dembel, ensued. In the end, Musa ousted his uncle and proclaimed himself king in 1892.

The division of Senegambia after 1889 saw Musa Molloh in French territory, and when the French established a military post in Hamdallai, Musa burnt the town and retreated to British territory in 1903. He was later deposed and exiled to Sierra Leone by the British in 1919, following reports of brutality against his subjects. Yet he succeeded in building in Fulladu a centralized state system that was second to none in organization, sophistication, and efficiency. He subsequently returned to Fulladu in 1923 to a much-reduced state, stipend, and status and died at Kaserikunda in 1931. He was succeeded by his son, Cherno Baldeh.

These jihads were waged partly for religious reasons but more for political and economic gain. Having amassed wealth through trade, teaching, and agriculture, the marabouts grew increasingly resentful of the ruling Soninke kings, whose political power and control were complete and exclusive. Additionally, the marabouts had little political influence, or at least their influence was not commensurate with their rising economic wealth and ambitions. This was not the case for Maba Jahou, who came closest to living up to Al Hajj Umar's jihadist tradition and ethic and almost succeeded in establishing a theocratic state that would have encompassed Baddibu, Niumi, Saloum, Jolof, and Cayor before his death in Sine.

For Foday Kabba Dumbuya, Foday Silla, and especially Musa Molloh, all allies of Maba and Al Hajj Umar, political and economic power and their consolidation, particularly in Fulladu, were paramount. Musa Molloh was more interested in preserving the territorial boundaries of Fulladu than he was driven by religious doctrine to convert so-called pagans. And while one could argue that initially, both Foday Silla and Foday Kabba were armed with religious rhetoric, their subsequent campaigns were motivated by the drive not so much to convert the Jola but to participate in the lucrative slave trade, which the British tried to quash to preserve their own commercial interests. The

A neighborhood mosque on Kombo Coastal Highway where neighborhood and business people worship; the Central Mosque is located in Banjul. (Courtesy of Buharry Gassama)

poor in these regions of The Gambia who also flocked to the jihadist armies were motivated primarily by economic gain rather than religious fervor.

Conquest and Accommodation to Colonial Rule

Conquest and European occupation constituted an ugly saga, and even though Gambian leaders resisted British control and registered significant victories in battle over the British, they were ultimately subdued. It is true that Musa Molloh was cruel to his subjects, but his atrocities compared to British violence and the wars of pacification against Gambians and their leaders pale in comparison. In the end, accommodation rather than conflict won the day in Senegal and The Gambia. Foday Kabba Dumbuya, Foday Silla, and Musa Molloh were reduced to fugitives and broken. Sufi leaders such as Sheikh Amadou Bamba, who founded the *Muride* sect in Senegal at the turn of the 20th century, was also exiled several times by the French to Gabon (1895–1903) and Mauritania (1903–1907) and in the end accommodated to French colonial authorities. David Robinson has argued in his book *Paths of Accommodation* that during the period between 1880 and 1920, northern Mauritania and central Senegal witnessed the accommodation of religious leadership to French political interests in exchange for relative autonomy and control over the religious and economic spheres of society. In time, various Islamic sects and their leaders in Senegal were co-opted and became important agents and pillars of the colonial economy.[5]

Today, about 90 percent of Gambians are professed Sunni Muslims, belonging to different sects but united by the five basic tenets of Islam: Ishada, a declaration of belief in Allah and Muhammad as his messenger; performance of the five daily prayers; Zakat (charity) to the poor; fasting during the month of Ramadan; and the obligatory pilgrimage to Mecca when it is financially affordable. The five daily prayers occur at intervals throughout the day; the time for each prayer depends on the season and when the sun rises or sets. The first prayer is at dawn around 6:30 a.m.; the second is performed around 1:00 p.m.; the third is around 4:00 p.m.; the fourth is at sunset; and the last prayer is around 7:30 p.m. Each prayer is preceded by a cleansing ritual (ablution) in which the hands, mouth, nostrils, head, ears, and feet are washed three times. There also are special prayer rituals for the dead, for travelers, and for almost any occasion, including jihad. Considered a complete way of life, Islam provides its followers with a comprehensive worldview, as it integrates small communities into a larger global community, the Ummah, and provides its followers with political ideas to help shape their relationship with central authority.

Conversion to Islam today, unlike during the 19th century jihads, is done peacefully and often involves the prospective convert and an Imam performing purification rites at a mosque. Conversion to Islam requires a purification bath; recitation of the Ishada; a name change; and in some places the shaving of facial hair, including the head. Jihad, a much-maligned term today, also has a more nuanced and less-talked-about meaning: the pursuit of personal spiritual and moral growth and devotion to Allah. This includes efforts to emulate Prophet Muhammad's lifestyle to the closest extent possible. Prophet Muhammad is not only believed to be the founder of Islam, he is also seen as embodying the best qualities of Islam and to have lived a perfect life, though he is not considered to be God or a son of God. Generally, all Muslims in The Gambia follow the five pillars closely irrespective of the *tariqa* or sect.

There is also a small but influential *Ahmadiyya* community in The Gambia that arrived in the late 1960s. Originally founded in India in 1899, the movement is heavily involved in education and medical services, and since its arrival in The Gambia, a predominantly Sunni country, it has won over only a limited number of followers. Regarded with suspicion, perhaps hostility, by some, it maintains a relationship with the mainstream Sunni sect of Islam, which has not been without tensions. In 2002, The Gambia's Supreme Islamic Council declared the *Ahmadiyya* a non-Muslim organization because its teachings, it alleged, were contrary to those of Islam. Infuriated, leaders of the movement left but later returned to The Gambia. The declaration by the Islamic Council that both the beliefs and teachings of the *Ahmadiyya* ran counter to the teachings of Sunni Islam stood against the norm of religious tolerance in the country.

The 1990s also witnessed the growth of a more orthodox, fundamentalist *Wahhabi* political form of Islam influenced in large measure by the continuing Israeli-Palestinian land dispute and the first and second Gulf Wars against Iraq. Radicalization of some Gambian students at Middle Eastern universities inclines some of them to oppose Western interests—and U.S. interests, specifically—in the region and elsewhere. In general, because of their belief in a more orthodox version of Islam, *Wahhabi* Muslims strongly endorse Shari'a. And like the jihadists of the mid-1800s in The Gambia, they also hold the view that Islam, as currently practiced in Gambia, is incorrect and impure, thus requiring a return to the teachings of Abdul Wahhab, the 17th-century founder who advocated a return to the more purist teachings of Islam.[6]

In addition, religious influences emanating from Senegal cannot be discounted as another source of radical Islamist ideology, as the rise and influence of *Dairras* (religious organizations/clubs) by *Wahhabi* Islamists is widespread. These have proliferated and spilled into The Gambia, fueled in large measure by radio and television broadcasts from Dakar. The traditional *Mawlood'Nabi* or *Gammo*, a night of celebration of Prophet Muhammad's birthday and life, as well as religious conferences have combined to disseminate radical political information and teachings about the new revivalist Islamist movement. This is also occurring at a time of great economic hardship in The Gambia, which is partly alleviated by financial assistance from Muslim countries in the Middle East that also help build schools for the propagation of Islam. Consequently, use of the veil has become more common, especially among young women and schoolgirls.

The appointment of Abdoulie Fatty as Imam of the State House Mosque in 1994, as well as the introduction of a secretary of state portfolio for religious affairs represents an important intrusion of Islam or its politicized form into secular politics of The Gambia. This is not to suggest that Islam under President Jawara did not influence the state, but rather that religion under President Jammeh is more consciously utilized. He has also used it sometimes, in combination with secular politics, to serve his interests. Thus, under Jammeh's watch a symbiotic relationship has matured further between secular politicians and Imams. However, Imam Bakawsu Fofana, who has preached against this growing Islamic fundamentalist wave in The Gambia, was not only expelled from The Gambia's Islamic Council but also silenced and banned from leading prayers at his mosque. The ban was recently lifted, however, following a well-choreographed meeting between members of the

Islamic Council, Bakawsu Fofana, and Jammeh. As in Senegal, Gambian Muslims are not a monolith but belong to Mourid and other Sufi sects mentioned earlier. What's interesting about the Gambian Mourids, though, is that many of them are Mandinka Yet, most people relate the Mouridiyya to the Wolof.

THE ENDURING LEGACY OF ISLAM

The Soninke-Marabout Wars that spanned the period between the 1850s and 1901 deeply reshaped Gambia's cultural, religious, and political worldview. While the wars of purification wrought immense human suffering and property destruction, they nonetheless put in place a basis for a Muslim community—*Ummah*. In time, Islam became a unifying force, in that it imposed a common frame of reference among Gambian Muslims based on the Qu'ran, with Prophet Muhammad serving as an exemplar of the religion. Islam also provided a single god, Allah, with strict rules of social and economic interaction and further delineated gender roles and expectations between the ruled and the ruler. Islam also introduced an alphabet, a standardized lunar calendar, and increased literacy in Arabic by way of *madrassa* or *darra* (Islamic schools) that continue to instruct the young in *fiqh*, Qur'anic knowledge and other subdisciplines. Western colonialism to some degree accomplished similar results.

Young Gambians begin religious instruction as early as age five and by age eight enter the Western education system. Today, Qur'anic and religious instruction has been integrated into the daily curriculum of most schools in The Gambia, including high school, with increasing opportunity for students to study abroad to further their education in Islamic studies in Muslim countries such as Malaysia, Indonesia, and those in the Middle East. It was once the case that young Gambians who specialized in Islamic studies were at a disadvantage as compared to students in Western-oriented schools because of their general lack of facility in the English language. This is rarely the case today, as many young scholars of Islam are just as likely to be literate in English as their Western-schooled compatriots. It is the latter, as mentioned earlier, who are largely responsible for the Islamic revivalist wave of the 1990s and beyond. Like the marabouts of the 19th century, they too tend to be purist or puritanical in their desire to rid Islam of impurities or innovations.

Like many Gambian traditional religions, Islam is also deeply patriarchal, which contributed somewhat to its adoption. For instance, polygamy among Muslim Gambians is in general accepted as a matter of course, and Gambian Muslim men who do not have multiple wives are sometimes singled out for light ridicule. Economic hardship, however, along with crowded urban dwellings and high rents have to some extent dampened the enthusiasm for multiple wives, and many men who marry several wives, especially the well-to-do, do so out of love but also as a demonstration of their prestige. In The Gambia, however, Muslim women are not secluded nor do they generally wear veils, even though headscarves are commonly worn by young women and older married women. And contrary to the widely held view by some Westerners of oppressed African women, Gambian women are generally independent and assertive. Notwithstanding the proliferation of women's and other nongovernmental organizations and the passage of the Women's Bill in 2010, which aims to promote the rights of women and girls, women and girls experience lower status than men. Violence against women occurs much too often in The Gambia (as elsewhere in the world).

Perhaps one of the enduring impacts of Islam on Gambians beyond the obvious religious mindset, values, and attitudes is found in the various local languages that have adopted Arabic words into their respective vocabularies. Words like *cadi* (judge) and *alkali* (political village head), among others, prove Islam's enduring legacy in The Gambia, as does the proliferation of Arabic names, which Muslim Gambians adopted several centuries ago. What many Westerners and individuals not familiar with the history of Islam in Africa and The Gambia often lose sight of is the deep and enduring legacy of Islamic scholarship and literacy that was created by renowned African Muslim scholars whose writings, poetry, books, and essays on astrology, medicine, and philosophy thrive to this day. Timbuktu, in modern-day Mali, was renowned for its splendid university, Sankore, and libraries that attracted students and scholars from far and wide.

Islam also gave coherence to large administrative structures such as the empires of Western Sudan—Ghana, Mali, and Songhay—as well as the theocracies of Sokoto, Baddibu, and lesser-known ones. In doing so, Islam helped put in place sophisticated administrative, military, and legal structures to lend stability to these large political kingdoms. Yet Senegambians were not passive recipients of Islamic knowledge; they were innovators of *tariqa* who adopted Islam to meet local and transnational objectives and used the Arabic alphabet to write in their own languages. Some of the most moving Muslim religious hymns and poems dedicated to Prophet Muhammad can be found in Senegambia Minor, written and sung in Fula, Wolof, Mandinka, and other languages. Thus, the notion of the so-called Dark Continent that was erroneously perpetuated and prejudicially applied to Africa and Africans by Europeans was a colossal historical error that regrettably lingers on, albeit less so in modern times.

CHRISTIANITY

Christianity was introduced in The Gambia in the mid-1400s by Portuguese explorers who were the first European navigators to travel the upper reaches of the Gambia River. Diego Gomez and Alvise da Cadamosto's glowing reports of wealth and trade in gold and other precious metals prompted the arrival of Portuguese missionaries who sought to introduce Christianity to Gambians in the area. Christianity never took root among Gambians, however, until the second half of the 19th century, when liberated African Aku/Creole were settled primarily in Bathurst and MacCarthy Island, limiting the religion primarily to the coast. Before this time, however, there was a small group of Luso-Africans living along the north and south banks of the Gambia River who professed to be Catholics. These Luso-African mulattos were the offspring of marriage or liaisons between Portuguese men and African women. And even decades later when they had integrated into Madinka and Wolof cultures and lost their fair complexions, they still remained Christian and considered themselves white. George E. Brooks's book *Euro-Africans in Western Africa* is a rich historical exposé of the lives of Euro-Africans, among whom Luso-Africans in Senegambia were prominent.[7]

A liberated African outpost in MacCarthy Island, Georgetown (Lemain Island), now renamed Janjangbureh, saw the establishment of a Methodist church and primary school in the 1830s. By the late 1950s and early 1960s, however, only a handful of Christian families lived in the Janjangbureh elementary school, like its counterparts in Bathurst, opened its doors to Muslim pupils as well.

The church similarly served a small Methodist congregation consisting of townspeople and students from Armitage High School. An Anglican boarding school for boys was also later established at Kristikunda in 1940 but with limited success. The mission never made many inroads into the local Muslim population, and the school succeeded only in converting some Muslim pupils to Christianity, and also serving as a feeder school for Christian-based schools in Bathurst. In the end, Kristikunda earned the reputation, perhaps undeserved, for being a school for wayward students. Some Fula in the area, however, did convert to Christianity, but the number of converts never met church expectations. E. F. Small had a short stint in Ballanghar as an agent of the Methodist Church before an argument with the district commissioner led to his recall to Bathurst. The mission never took off, as was the case in most upcountry towns and villages in Saloum.

Today, Christians constitute about 5 percent of the population. The Christian Aku are much less influential than they were in the colonial and the postindependence era, yet they continue to reside in the greater Banjul area. The mid-1990s also witnessed a new wave of Christian churches in Serrekunda and Kanifing that cater to the spiritual needs of newly arrived immigrants. The older and more established churches, however, are located in Banjul; the most notable of these is the Catholic cathedral on what was old Hagan Street, which has been renamed Daniel Goddard Street.

Religious tolerance, harmony, and collaboration rather than conflict characterize Christian-Muslim relations in The Gambia. This remains a major achievement for President Jawara, who once was a Christian convert and married to a Christian before his reconversion to Islam in 1965. From many accounts, President Jammeh was born a Christian, and he may have converted to Islam, perhaps when his family moved to his adopted village of Kaninlai as a youngster. Religious tolerance in The Gambia is to a large measure a result of the mix in many Gambian families of members who are Christian and Muslim. Intermarriage between members of the two faiths has also engendered high levels of tolerance and mutual respect. Religious tolerance and harmony in The Gambia was further underscored by visits to the country by Pope John Paul II in February 1992 and the Archbishop of Canterbury in July 2003.

Therefore, from all indications, The Gambia is a model of religious tolerance, thanks to a government policy that recognizes the major religious holidays of both faiths. In fact, Korriteh/Eid ul-Fitr, the celebration following Ramadan and Christmas, is a time for both faith communities to indulge in one another's religious feasts that mark them. Interfaith dialogues have become a permanent fixture of the religious landscape where matters of mutual concern are discussed. Family ties between Christians and Muslims also make weddings as well as naming/christening/baptismal and funeral ceremonies occasions for family get-togethers and interfaith interaction. In turn, this has enabled the Gambian state to maintain a relatively secular policy, with state functions typically preceded by prayers from both holy books.

Religious leaders, both Christian and Muslim, also exchange messages of goodwill punctuated by statements of mutual respect and recognition of their respective prophets and faiths during all major holidays. Religious leaders of both faiths also stress the need to maintain religious harmony to ensure continued peace and prosperity in The Gambia. For instance, in 2003 the Imam of Banjul expressed the respect and high esteem that Jesus enjoys as a prophet among Muslims, with Christian leaders reciprocating similarly in a subsequent Tobaski message to Muslims. Tobaski, also known as Eid al-Adha, "Festival of Sacrifice," marks Prophet Abraham/Ibrahim's obedience to God's command to sacrifice his only son (Ishmael) before being saved by archangel Gabriel/ Gibril who instead offered him a ram in his son's place.

Christianity's lasting impact on The Gambia remains the introduction of Western culture, ideas, and, more importantly, education. Western education not only provided a distinct worldview that sought to replace that of Africans completely, it also whet the appetite of Gambians for more Western education. With Western education, many Gambians received the opportunity to climb up the social and economic ladders, which made it possible to enjoy lifestyles that for the most part were virtually unattainable without it. Rudimentary as it was, missionary education alienated few Gambians from their traditional cultures. Yet many Muslim families, and rural families in particular, refused to send their sons to Western-oriented schools for fear of losing them to *nassaran* (*nassarano* among the Mandinka) (the white man's ways). This, however, did not mean loss of language or culture, necessarily. Rather, the acquisition by many Gambians of the English language, a language of global business and diplomacy and one of The Gambia's official languages, made it possible for many, including women, to leverage opportunities that economic globalization offers. Today, Gambians, especially those in the diaspora, have acquired professional skills and education levels never thought possible. The presence of Gambians in higher education and the professions throughout the world is testimony to this and has its roots partly in missionary education. In the end, Western education—some might say miseducation—contributed to the training of numerous Gambians who constituted the postindependence leadership. And to this day, mission schools continue to educate many young Gambians.

RELIGION AND POLITICS

Religion has always played an important role in the politics of both Senegambia Major and Senegambia Minor, beginning as early as the introduction of Islam in the region during the 11th century but especially in the 18th and 19th centuries. Islam in this region was first adopted, albeit not totally, by the kings and local elite. As the influence of Muslim clerics grew over the centuries, so did their ambition and their ability to usurp political and economic powers. The Soninke-Marabout Wars of the middle 1800s were not solely motivated by a desire to convert the Jola, Serer, Mandinka, and Wolof for the sake of conversion to Islam alone. Indeed, disaffection with material conditions and quest for political power were also important motivating factors. At one point or another, all the major Gambian jihadists collaborated or conspired with Europeans against one another for political and economic gain. This suggests the continuing relationship between spiritual and secular power, between religion and politics.

Since independence in 1965, both President Jammeh, and President Jawara before him, have sometimes, though not always, used religion for their political ends. While the state is secular and generally free of religious interference from both Christians and Muslims, a symbiotic relationship exists between the two, though not to the extent or degree that it does in neighboring Senegal. And, unlike in many countries in the subregion, religion has not yet entered the political sphere to the extent of destabilizing it. The rise of

Wahhabi Muslims and their advocacy for Shari'a may very well be the closest threat to The Gambia's secular state and politics. While Shari'a courts exist to adjudicate marriage disputes and inheritance and custody issues among Muslims by the *cadi* at the village and district levels, it does not apply to national-level courts. The secular character of the Gambian state, as well as the growth in Gambia's Christian population, will likely keep Shari'a law to lower courts and for Muslims exclusively for some time to come.

NOTES

1. For a good historical narrative, see Florence Mahoney, *A Signare: Mulatto Lady,* Gambian Studies (Banjul, 2008).

2. Arnold Hughes and David Perfect, *Historical Dictionary of The Gambia,* 4th ed. (Lanham, MD: The Scarecrow Press, 2008), 213.

3. Mahoney, *A Signare.*

4. See Lady Southorn's *The Gambia: The Story of the Groundnut Colony* (London: George Allen & Unwin, 1952), 197; see also Hughes and Perfect, *Historical Dictionary,* 52.

5. David Robinson, *Paths of Accommodation: Muslim Societies and French Colonial Authorities in Senegal and Mauritania, 1880–1920* (Athens: Ohio University Press, 2000), 2.

6. Momodou Darboe, "Islam in West Africa: Gambia," *African Studies Review* 47, no. 2 (2004): 76.

7. George E. Brooks, *Euro-Africans in West Africa: Commerce, Social Status, Gender and Social Observance from the Sixteenth to the Eighteenth Century* (Oxford: James Curry, 2003).

3

Literature and Media

THE PEOPLES OF Senegambia Major and Senegambia Minor have for centuries preserved their histories and traditions predominantly through the spoken word and to a lesser degree through writing using the Arabic alphabet. Storytelling, fables, creation myths, proverbs, songs, and poetry—in sum, oral-literature—continue to be important vehicles in the transmission of culture to succeeding generations. For much of Africa, and especially for Gambian society, storytelling is a medium through which communally cherished values—honesty, bravery, and respect—are transmitted. Stories about the cunning hare and the greedy hyena, as well as stories about two girls, both named Kumba—one orphaned at birth and poorly treated by her stepmother, and the other treated as a princess—continue to teach and instill among the young cherished societal values that include forbearance. These values and virtues have provided stability, continuity, and change in the Senegambian societies for many centuries.

The task of preservation of family histories or genealogy is reserved for the *jeli, gewel,* griot, or bard—a stratum in Senegambian society whose function, among many, is to serve as repositories of societal and family histories. The *jeli* and *gewel* are in general less constrained, as are the freeborn, by social norms and taboos; when they occasionally transgress societal norms, it is seen as entertaining. Patrons seek to avoid the anger of their *gewel,* as this could earn a patron derisive commentary and shaming, especially in instances when a patron does not readily part with gifts, articles of clothing, and money.

Thus, the griot plays many important roles in Senegambian societies. In the past, some were, in fact, known to accompany their patron kings to war to inspire them in battle, praising them as they battled the enemy.

Historically endogamous, today these social groups and categories, partly because of the opportunities for upward social mobility and education, have greatly eroded. For instance, while in the past it was taboo for a person of slave origin to marry into nobility or the freeborn category or vice versa, it is not uncommon to see such unions today. In fact, owing to the growing wealth of the *gewel* or *jeli* in the early1990s because of multiple patrons, especially in the urban areas, and education, many may be doing better, financially, than their patrons. A popular Wolof song from the 1970s titled *amut gherr amut gewel mbugail la am* (it matters not if you are a griot or freeborn, what matters is love) was one of the first songs to chip at the rigid social stratification systems of The Gambia. Similarly, the famous Gambian kora palyer, the late Lalo Kebba Drammeh, was also known for his strong yet sweet melodic attacks on social divisions and often sang of *kanno* (love). Modern musicians like The Gambia's premier entertainer, Jaliba (big *jali*) Kuyateh, as well as musicians from neighboring Senegal, have further eroded these social divisions and replaced them with *mbugail* (love). Borrowing strongly from a repertoire of traditional songs, these contemporary musicians, who use a combination of traditional and Western instruments, sing songs of love and pain—themes that transcend social standing, culture, and nationality.

It is against this brief backdrop that one must appreciate and situate the traditional role of the griot, *jeli*, or *gewel*. They are walking history books, poets, diplomats, and entertainers, among many other things. Together, they bring to life, as well as maintain for posterity, the oral literatures of Senegambians. Modernization and globalization have together enhanced their roles. Travel overseas to entertain large audiences and admirers and sale of their CDs have transformed them, in general, into a relatively well-to-do class of entertainers. Musicians such as The Gambia's Jaliba Kuyateh and Tata Dinding Jobarteh and Senegal's Youssou N'dour, Baba Maal, Thione Seck, and Fatou Laube, to name a few, are today earning incomes and international acclaim once only dreamed of. Their messages of love, social commentary, and criticism, especially in these days of economic austerity, have enabled them to eclipse the more traditional *gewel*. In fact, while many of the modern musicians of Senegambia Major and Minor are of *gewel* origin, some, like Salif Keita of Mali, are not. These modern musicians nonetheless continue in the tradition of the *jeli* or griot, singing songs of praise and using poetic expressions such as *tassou*, the forerunner of modern rap music in Senegal and The Gambia.

Tassou, as a poetic expression, is performed by both men and women before an individual dance performance, a tune to which the *tassou-kat* dances. The *tassou* could be social commentary; praise of oneself; or a direct or indirect critique of another person, persons in positions of authority, or a spouse. Its rhythmic inflections are often complicated and mimicked by the drummers, especially the *tammakat* (talking drum) drummer. For instance, a popular Wolof *tassou* that has been around for some time goes like this: *ku jan matte sa (m) k'hell dem che deh, bangai dundak bangai deh yep sa(m) k'hell dem chi deh* (whoever gets bitten by a snake, you think about death; whether you live or die, you still are preoccupied by death).

The result is an explosive intricate dance and drumming that plays out the *tassou-kat's* tonal inflections with drum sounds. *Tassou* must, however, be distinguished from *baku*, another poetic form used by wrestlers for self-praise and to intimidate opponents. Another poetic form is used during circumcision ceremonies for boys followed by song. It too invokes good spirits and transmits socially valued characteristics in men. Girls have similar poems and song in their excision ceremonies as well. The *kankurang* and *simba*, among the Mandingo and Wolof, are often accompanied by praise poetry called *jat* among the Wolof. Senegambian languages are generally rich and poetic and harbor forms of expression that most *jeli* and *gewel* would be versed in. All these poetic expressions have found their way into modern literature and the music scene, yet the one that has had the most impact, especially in the urban scene in Senegal and the Gambia, is *mbalax*, followed by *tassou*—rap in Wolof, Mandinka, and Fula. It is also worth noting, as we shall see later in this chapter, that many stories, myths, and fables have become sources on which modern Gambian writers base their novels and poems.

What is often lost sight of among scholars is the important imprint that Senegambian oral literature—stories, fables, poems, and epics—has had on North and South American and Caribbean folktales. These crossed the Atlantic with enslaved Senegambians who were valued not only as good workers, but as record keepers because many were literate in Arabic and as a result fetched a higher price. They were also skilled rice growers. Their skills earned them relative prestige on arrival in Louisiana, Georgia, and North and South Carolina. Judith Carney has shown through her work the rice-growing skills brought over by Senegambians to the South of the United States. This is especially instructive, as enslaved Africans were always deemed to have brought nothing but their labor.

Carney debunks this myth, and in fact shows convincingly that Senegambians taught their masters a thing or two about growing rice and other things. Senegambian women also enjoyed a reputation for their cleanliness and as a result fetched a good price, with their labor often reserved for their master's house. Equally intriguing is the fact that some Senegambians who arrived in the new world were literate in Arabic, especially the Fula captives, who served as clerks in plantations and kept good records for their masters and consequently were spared the harsher realities of slavery. Enslaved Africans also exhibited their military skills in several of the slave revolts in Bahia, Brazil, many having fought in the jihads of the early 1800s. Sylviane Diouf's *Servants of Allah: African Muslims Enslaved in the Americas* details with eloquence these episodes.[1] In fact, there is an extensive body of literature that includes the works of Allan Austin, Michael Gomez, Paul Lovejoy, and Daniel Littlefield, who have documented the lives and experiences of enslaved Africans and Muslims, specifically in the antebellum South and elsewhere in the New World.[2]

One such enslaved African sold on the banks of the Gambia River was Job Ben Solomon Jallow, who as a prince was captured and sold into slavery around 1730 and shipped to Maryland. His vigorous protests to practice his Muslim faith and his revulsion against slavery, along with the intervention of General Oglethorpe, founder of Georgia, won him his freedom. Literate in Arabic, Jallow wrote letters to his father, the king of Bondu, about his enslavement. One of these letters was later translated, which in the end spared him the harsh treatment that enslaved Africans suffered. He later returned to The Gambia around 1734 and befriended Francis More, an English slave trader on the river. Many other enslaved Africans would later return to The Gambia, Senegal, Guinea, and neighboring countries. Allan Austin's book *Muslim Slaves in Antebellum America A Source Book.* New York: Garland Publishers (1984): is a fascinating narrative on several Muslim Africans. Austin argues that most of the Africans brought to New Orleans, Louisiana, in the 18th century were from The Gambia and Senegal. Gwendolyn Midlo Hall makes this case as well in her fascinating book, *Africans in Colonial Louisiana.* One of the best-known enslaved Africans (from the area where modern Nigeria is now located) who was later freed and led a very interesting life was written about in a book by James Walvin, *An African's Life: The Life and Times of Olaudah Equiano, 1745–1797.*[3]

There is also a rich literature in Atlantic diaspora studies that makes a compelling case for an African presence in the Americas long before the arrival of Christopher Columbus in the New World in 1492. Through archaeological finds, which include rock paintings and words and names of plants, historians were able to provide convincing evidence that there were Africans in Mexico and the New World before Columbus. Historian Ivan Van Sertima argued in his book, *They Came Before Columbus*, that a flourishing trade between medieval Mali and the New World existed in the 1300s, and that Mansa Musa's brother, Abubakar II, made a trans-Atlantic journey in 1311 from the Senegambian region, possibly from The Gambia or Senegal Rivers. In his book *Economic Change in Precolonial Africa: Senegambia in the Era of the Slave Trade*, noted historian Philip Curtin argued that Senegambians traded with China and India as early as 1450, if not before.[4]

Similarly, during the Atlantic slave trade, stories of the hare and the hyena invariably found their way into the Southern states of the United States as well as to Trinidad and the Bahamas, among other countries. Senegambian women who tended to the children of their masters retold stories and sang songs and lullabies they had learned as youngsters in Senegambia. One such enslaved Senegambian was Phyllis Wheatley. Captured from the region of present-day Gambia when she was only seven years old, Wheatley not only mastered the English language at a very young age, but also became the most renowned African American woman poet of her time, and the first black woman to have published a book of poems. In sum, Africa, and Senegambia in particular, have given a lot to America and the New World. John Edward Philips's edited volume, *Writing African History*, details these contributions that include religion, cuisine, and the humble peanut. The chapter by Joseph E. Holloway, "What Africa Has Given America: African Continuities in the North American Diaspora," tells a fascinating story of Africa's contribution to the Americas as well as of continuing African cultural and other elements in the United States.

LITERATURE IN ARABIC AND SENEGAMBIAN LANGUAGES

Arabic was the language used most frequently by literate Africans and clerics who served as scribes and teachers in precolonial Senegambian courts and schools. Though a language used mostly by the elite, it nonetheless offered literate Africans a vehicle for self-expression in their own languages. Uthman Dan Fodio wrote close to 500 poems and about 20 books in his native Fula, Hausa, and Arabic. His daughter, Nana Asma'u, wrote close to 20 poems, while her brother, Abdulahi, wrote close to 10 poems. Sheikh Umar Tal was not only a great warrior and strategist but was a prolific writer and scholar as well. Tal would later encourage his disciples or *talibe* to write about the early and middle stages of his campaigns; one of them wrote *laawol Pullaku* (ways and traditions of the Fula). A later poem written in Futa Toro details Umar's campaigns between 1852 and 1855, and a great part of the poem was in praise of Umar and his gallantry.

Sheikh Amadou Bamba of Senegal and founder of the *Muride* Brotherhood was also a prolific writer, having written numerous poems and books in Wolof and Arabic dedicated to Prophet Muhammad. The grand mosque in Touba houses many of his manuscripts, as well as those written by his disciples. They too used the Arabic script to write in Fula, Mandinka, and

Wolof. In fact, the Qur'an was translated into Wolof as early as the 19th century. Some of Sheikh Umar Tal's disciples in The Gambia, including Maba Jahou, were also renowned Fula scholars, and so were many other clerics and heads of sects who followed in the 20th century and beyond. Shiekh Ibrahim Niasse of Kaolack, Senegal, commonly known as Baye Niasse, was a gifted scholar and poet who also dedicated many of his works in praise of Prophet Muhammad.

In The Gambia, Imam Abdoulie Jobe (1910–2004), the late Imam Rattib of Banjul, was a prolific scholar who wrote in both Arabic and Wolof. Literate in both English and Arabic, Jobe wrote a book in Arabic, *The Garden of My Contemporaries,* that was later translated into English but was never published. Also, while studying in Saudi Arabia, he produced a 56-page booklet on Islamic studies as well as many others on poetry and the Haddith (the sayings of Prophet Muhammad). Earlier, the late Alhaji Alieu Badara Faye (1880–1965) was a prolific scholar with a large following from around Senegambia Major. In 1950, Imam Faye founded the town of Boussra several miles from Brikama. He left numerous manuscripts, the bulk of which have yet to be published. Imam Faye also wrote in both Wolof and Arabic and produced a book of about 2,000 verses on Arab grammar that was published in Egypt. His best-known poem in Arabic is "Mimaah katalil Baitil Laasa," which became a famous Gambian national tune frequently performed during Independence Day parades by the Gambian police band.

The late Imam of Bansang, Alhaji Cherno Bubacar Jallow (1909–1989), wrote several books on *Tijaniyaa* theology and *tawheed* (oneness with Allah). His best-known book is *Miftta Us Saadatil Abadiyyafii MaTalibil Ahmadiyya,* published in Tunis in 1963 by Tijan el Mamdi Publishers. Written in Arabic, the book deals with the philosophical foundations of the *Tijaniyya* order and its major prayers. Imam Bubacar Jallow also wrote a long poem in Peul/Fula titled "Mido Jortinnoh" (I have trust and confidence in Allah), which is a detailed poetic guide to the hajj, as well as shorter poems in both Arabic and Peul praising the noble character and qualities of Prophet Muhammad.

To this list must be added Alhaji Pa Makumba Jaye, who after serving as a police officer resigned his commission to pursue his studies of Islam in Senegal. He taught at Armitage High for several decades and in later life served as imam of the Independence Drive Mosque in Banjul. Imam Mam Mamut Saine was also a noted Islamic scholar and teacher who left his native Passy Ngayen to settle in the village of Kerr Demba Kali near Tabananni in the early 1900s, or mid-1800s where he ran a school that attracted students from all over Senegambia Major. Mam Mamut taught the likes of the great Islamic scholar in Bundu, Sayerr Khouma. The late Hatab Bojang, a cleric of great distinction from Kombo Gunjur, was particularly renowned, in part because of his extensive knowledge of the Qur'an, and so was the late *outass* (teacher) Omar Bun Jeng, also of Gunjur.

The current Imam Rattib of Banjul, Alhaji Cherno Kah, an Islamic scholar in his own right, comes from a family of distinguished Islamic scholars in Medina Serign Mass in Niumi. His grandfather, Serign Mass Kah (1827–1936), who founded the village, built a scholarly reputation that few could rival in the region, but unlike Sheikh Umar, he did not engage in the 1800 jihads. Bala Saho's article, "Appropriations of Islam in a Gambian Village: Life and Times of Shaykh Mass Kah, 1827–1936," is a comprehensive treatment of Serign Mass Kah's life and miracles.[5]

In fact, Sheikh Umar Tal visited Bathurst, possibly in the 1840s. During his visit to Bathurst, he was hosted by the Faye family of Dobson Street. Omar Jah Sr., though writing in English, is a world-renowned scholar of Islamic studies, and Sheikh Umar in particular. He writes and speaks fluent Arabic and wrote one of the most definitive dissertations on Sheikh Umar Tal, *A Case Study of Al Hajj Umar al Futi's Philosophy of Jihad and Its Sufi Basis* (McGill University, 1973). He too hails from Medina Serign Mass.

Alhaji Cherno Baba Jallow of Kerr Cherno, also in Niumi, was also a prolific scholar, as was the late Imam of Banjul, Alhaji Momodou Lamin Bah, a grandson of Maba Jahou. The late Alhaji Babou Samba and Alhaji Tamsir Demba Mbye of Banjul also were distinguished scholars of Islam. A young crop of Islamic scholars includes Imam Baba Leigh, who, unlike many of his contemporaries, is a strong critic of the current regime and is watched closely by it. Imam Leigh is president of the Sheikh Umar Futiyou Taal Foundation in The Gambia, which holds an annual *siyareh* (pilgrimage) in Gunjur to mark Umar's visit in the 1840s to the site where he was said to have prayed and meditated for a month.

Many more Gambian Islamic scholars, past and present, who have authored works will remain obscure because their works either could not be produced en masse or were destroyed by the elements. Yet many scholars writing in Fula, Arabic, Wolof, and Mandinka have left behind manuscripts, possibly for their disciples and children, that remain largely unknown to the public—Imam Badra Faye being a good example. The absence of a vibrant printing press and scarce readership due mainly to the relatively low levels of literacy in Arabic compared to English have limited the circulation of these Senegambian and Gambian scholars' works. In 2007, following an almost decade-long process of translation, an edition of the Qur'an in Mandinka, Wolof, and Fula was published in The Gambia. In sum, Islamic scholars have made important contributions. Lamin Sanneh's book, *The Jakhanke Muslim Clerics: A Religious and Historical Study of Islam in Senegambia*, attests to this fact.

Birth of Gambian Creative Writing Literature in English

Gambian literature in English reflects the rich cultural and historical diversity that is The Gambia. While the use of a foreign language, such as English or French, has been debated for decades by scholars and writers such as Chinua Achebe, Wole Soyinka, and Ngugi Wa'Thiongo, the fact remains that English was bequeathed to Gambians and is part and parcel of Gambia's cultural toolbox—a legacy of British colonialism and Western missionary education. Yet its use remains a hotly debated issue. However, like Gambians who use Arabic to write beautiful poetry in Fula or Wolof that reflects sensibilities that are part of The Gambia's cultural landscape, others use English as a medium of expression to accomplish the same ends. Therefore, the use of English does not make Gambian literature any less Gambian, indigenous, or authentic.

Dr. Lenrie Peters and William Conton are generally regarded as the pioneers of Gambian literature. Peters, who died in 2010, was a surgeon, pan-Africanist, and humanitarian. He was born in Bathurst in 1932 to Lenrie Peters Sr., an accountant, who once was an editor of *The Gambia Echo* newspaper, and Keziah Peters, who was raised in England and later moved to The Gambia from Freetown, Sierra Leone. The young Peters grew up in an intellectual and print-rich environment, an environment that would help lead him into publishing his first novel, *The Second Round*, and two books of poetry, *Satellites* and *Katchikalli*. Peters' works as a creative writer were also undoubtedly shaped by his Aku background and his studies in the United Kingdom. Understandably, one major theme that crops up often in his body of work is his incessant search for his roots and identity.

The Second Round was very much a by-product of its times, coming as it did in the heyday of African nationalism and independence. Like Chinua Achebe's *No Longer at Ease*, it vividly captures the trials and tribulations of a young African medical doctor who returns to his native Sierra Leone but finds himself torn between an African culture from which he has been alienated and a country caught in the throes of Westernization. Dr. Kawa, who like Obi in *No Longer at Ease*, is a civil servant in the colonial administration, is under immense pressure to marry and live up to high family and societal expectations—those befitting his education and rank in society. Under pressure, Dr. Kawa enters a relationship doomed to failure and rather than seek solace from a new wife, as his mother had expected, plunges himself and his energies into a provincial hospital. *The Second Round* is essentially autobiographical, capturing Peters's own search for roots.

Peters's sensibilities as a novelist were also very much shaped by the political philosophies of the day, not by negritude as professed by president and poet Leopold Senghor, but by a pan-African fervor. This enabled Peters's characters in his novels and later in his poems to indulge in political soliloquy, a terrain in which he felt more at ease than in the day-to-day and organic experiences of ethnic Africans. Therefore, for Peters pan-Africanism served as a platform from which he could lament and interrogate the dilemmas of independence, the state of the black world versus the European, and the enduring negative effects of colonialism—all written in beautiful prose and poetry. Peters's poems reflect a similarly abstract disposition, one that is often at odds with its surroundings. Renowned Gambian poet and World Bank senior economist Tijan Sallah, one of Africa's leading poets, captures eloquently the thematic continuity from Peters's novel to his poetry.

> In much of Peters's poetry, there is a serious groping for self which manifests itself in the exploration of images from different traditions, African-European, American and Asian—and this self-search is sometimes intellectual, sometimes political but always sincere. The poet's sophisticated musings bristle with names such as "Kafka," "Sunjiatta," and "Samori." But they remain at that level—intellectual musings; the poet is rarely involved in these characters, either through a mastery of the related traditions or through strong instinctual identification. The poet remains largely cool-headed, aloof, almost like a scientist poet—lacking the passionate involvement which makes poetry more than just the product of intellectual labor but also a social commitment.[6]

According to Sallah, *Katchikalli*, a book of poems, establishes the organic foundation for a national literature with Peters as its primary architect.

Born in Bathurst in 1925, where his father served as a clergyman, William Conton was educated in Bathurst and Freetown before completing his studies at Durham in England. He returned to Sierra Leone, where he became principal of a high school. Conton would come to international fame following the publication in 1960 of his novel *The African*. Among these pioneers of Gambian literature must be included Augusta Mahoney Jawara, the wife of The Gambia's first president, whose work injected into this emerging national literature a womanist/feminist sensibility—a tradition that today is carried on by writers including Sally Singhateh, Mariama Khan, and Amie Sillah, even though they may label themselves differently. They nonetheless follow and build on Augusta Jawara's prescient concerns over the rights of women and girls in Gambian and African societies.

Credit is also sometimes given to Phyllis Wheatley, the enslaved African girl from the area that is present-day Gambia who was mentioned earlier in this chapter. Also, U.S.-born Alex Haley, an African American, is sometimes credited as contributing to the early beginnings of Gambian literature. In 1976, Haley published a fiction novel, *Roots*, that was partly based on the capture and enslavement of his ancestor, Kunta Kinte, from Niumi, Juffureh, in modern-day Gambia. The epic miniseries *Roots*, which was an adaptation of this novel, remains by far the most-watched miniseries in U.S. television history, following as it did on the heels of the civil rights movement of the 1960s—a turbulent period in U.S. race relations. Both the miniseries and the novel focused international attention on The Gambia, which was barely over a decade old. However, whereas Haley's work references The Gambia, it focuses more on the African American experience, and on family saga, like Wheatley's.

THE N'DANNAN ERA AND ITS GENERATION OF GAMBIAN LITERATURE, 1971–1976

N'Dannan was The Gambia's first literary magazine, founded in 1971 by a group of young Gambian writers and aspiring writers. It would become the catalyst for the rise of a second-wave generation of Gambian writers. Derived from the Wolof word *dan*, which literally means to fell, a *n'dannan* is one who is a consummate griot or of high social status who is acutely familiar with the folklore, values, and history of his or her people. Lenrie Peters served as an advisor to the young publication and its mixed group of mostly aspiring writers, having published a novel and several short stories himself. Among its founding members were Suwaebou Conateh, a renowned Gambian journalist, Hassan Jagne, Charles Jow, and Marcel Thomasi, all educators; former civil servant Hassoum Ceesay Sr.; and Dr. Wally Ndow, among others. Peters, as a seasoned elder statesman would have a major imprint not only on *N'Dannan* as a nascent publication but also on young writers such as Tijan Salla, as well. According to Dr. Cherno Omar Barry, a former lecturer at the University of The Gambia and one of the most noted chroniclers of Gambian literature,

> *Ndannan* existed for seven years and was able to produce seven volumes during this period. The first volume came out in March 1971, and two volumes were published in 1972 and in 1973: in both years, it will release an issue biannually in March and in September. However, in 1974 only one volume was produced due to several difficulties including mainly financial and the lack of readership. *Ndaanan* will not release any publication in 1975 but in 1976, a bulky and final publication will be published—Contribution to the magazine was opened to everybody: students and teachers; civil servants and private employees; Gambians and non-Gambians; men and women alike. There were 69 contributors to the magazine and of these were 10 women 9 of whom were Gambians. Of the nine women, three were studying at the local high schools, two were housewives and the rest were composed of a student at Fourah Bay College in Freetown, an ex-school teacher, a government civil servant and a senior clerk at

the central bank. The non-Gambian, Kwela Robinson, was a housewife living in The Gambia. Her nationality was not established.[7]

The *N'Dannan* era in Gambian literature, which spanned the period between 1971 and 1976, was a significant historical development in The Gambia's literary history and tradition. First, it saw the beginning of a truly national literature predicated on themes that reflected Gambian traditions and culture. Rather than groping for self-definition and identity or being alienated from cultural traditions, as was the case with Peters, this crop of writers was for the most part deeply shaped and informed by their respective ethnic and pan-ethnic cultural backgrounds and landscapes. Novels, poems, and short stories explored themes, plots, and characters to which the writers had an organic connection. Just as important, the readership could easily identify with the material they read: colonialism, the conflict between the old and the new orders, and stories that evoked a sense of pride in Gambian tradition and culture while at the same time instilling grounded moral values.

Take, for instance, the work of the late Ebou Dibba, who was born in Bathurst. His father's family was from Baddibu, Kanikunda, a Mandinka area upriver, but his mother was Wolof. He grew up in the prevalent Wolof culture of the capital, with recollections of that urban life influencing his first two novels, *Chaff on the Wind* and *Fafa*, both written in the 1980s. In a moving tribute to Ebou, world-renowned writer Kaye Whiteman wrote in *The Guardian* on April 3, 2001, following Ebou's death:

> Both convey a strong sense of period, with an awareness of African culture confronted with colonial reality. *Chaff*, in fact, is set in the 1930s, before Ebou was born, but it has an almost psychic feeling of what it was like at that time. His third, short novel, *Alhaji*, was set in a contemporary Gambia of tourists and conmen, in which everything is changed. Unfortunately, this exploration of new subject matter was never followed up.[8]

Chaff on the Wind tells the story of Pateh and Dinding, two young men whose destinies could not be more starkly different. Pateh, the more outgoing of the two, has an affair with Charle's wife, Isatou, and both flee to Senegal, where Isatou gives birth. Dinding finds success as a trader after he comes into an inheritance following his father-in-law's death. Pateh is then hired by his friend Dinding but dies at the hands of French colonial police. *Fafa* contains some of the same characters and recounts the efforts of four friends who confront life head-on. Fafa wishes to marry Kombeh, who will not pay him any attention. The friends conspire to have Kombeh marry Fafa.

In another fitting tribute, Cherno Omar Barry succinctly sums up the life and contribution of Ebou Dibba, who as a Gambian novelist was deeply anchored in Gambia's social political, colonial, and economic milieu:

> Ebou Dibba is without doubt the first Gambian author to have used the Gambian setting in his writing. In his two novels, he succeeded in not only including some of the social and cultural setups of the 30s but equally used some of the local language in his novels. There is also a strong presence of historical events such as a plane crash in Jeswang, the approaching Second World War and the festivities marking the anniversary of George VI. It should also be noted that in both novels, he set up a rich mixture of cultures: Sidi Masood (Moroccan origin), "Guerre Quatorze" (Paterson from the Bahamas), Fafa (a fanafana probably from the Saloum region) and Charles (Portuguese origin). Issues of complexities surrounding marriage and love dominate the two novels.[9]

Like Dibba, Nana Grey-Johnson has also contributed immensely to the furtherance of Gambian literature with plots and characters that are deeply informed by Gambian traditions. He has self-published more than eight books, and like Peters he is an Aku/Krio of a yet younger generation. In his *A Krio Engagement and Other Short Stories*, Grey-Johnson gives his reader a good glimpse into Krio life and one story in particular, "The Man Who Came to His Own Requiem," is especially telling, as it is a mélange of myth, religion, magic, and death and their hold on a community. A victim of a boating accident is presumed dead by relatives, and friends shows up at his funeral three days later. What ensues is a complex interplay of the beliefs surrounding the other world and the protagonist's efforts to regain acceptance and live a normal life.

In *The Magic Calabash*, Grey-Johnson decisively turns political. Erubani, an office worker, is laid off from his job because of the government's efforts to curb spending—a World Bank–imposed structural adjustment policy in the mid-1980s. Erubani must now make a living to support himself and his live-in girlfriend. As financial and other social problems mount, a magic calabash offers respite for the financially strapped young man. The calabash in Gambian or Senegambian mythology and magic, like the chicken egg, occupies a special place, as a vehicle capable of magically resolving daunting challenges. Magicians use the calabash as they entertain crowds; just as the calabas, in Gambian mythology also provides sustenance in times of hunger. In some tales calabashes miraculously replenish with delicious foods for all to eat, never running out. Here, Grey-Johnson blends intractable modern-day economic challenges and magic to produce a novel that is deeply Gambian and entertaining, borrowing from the reservoir of folk beliefs that Peters could not in his book, *The Second Round*. Thus, for Johnson, and unlike for

Peters, his Aku/Krio background serves him well as he liberally appropriates from his rich Gambian cultural heritage.

Sheriff (Samsudeen) Sarr's *Meet Me in Conakry* remains an interesting read, especially among the young. Sarr taps into a long-cherished spirit of adventure among Gambian youth culture—the quest for one's fortune elsewhere than in the comforts of home, with its safety of country and a mother's doting. As in Dibba's *Chaff on the Wind*, which focuses on the adventures of two young men, Sarr's protagonists are three recently graduated high schools students who travel to Conakry via Senegal. The story unfolds with the challenges they face and overcome on their way to this seemingly mythical city. The story continues to resonate with young and older readers alike and is deeply anchored in tales of travel, hardship, and triumph.

One of the first dramatists who brought worldwide attention to The Gambia, as well as acclaim to himself, was Gabriel J. Roberts, a noted educator, former director of education, and, earlier, principal of Armitage School. A founding member of *N'Dannan*, Roberts published the only play in the first issue in 1971, entitled *Mandingerio Outwitted*. Yet it was *The Trial of Busumbala* for which he won an award that earned him international acclaim following its performance by the BBC. Not surprisingly, *The Trial of Busumbala* is set against an Armitage School campus backdrop in 1962, when Roberts was principal of the school. In the play, Maxwell Armitage, principal of Armitage School and a member of the House of Representatives, takes Marafang Busumbala to court for allegedly stealing his radio set, which Maxell had played loudly with little regard for the inconvenience it caused others. In the end, Marafang is acquitted, in large measure because the value to the campus and larger society of bringing the loud music to an end as a result of the theft of the radio trumped Maxwell's right to play his radio loudly.

Written in 1988, *The Goosieganderan Myth* begins where Roberts's 1971 play, *A Coup Is Planned*, ended. The former is a tale of two fictitious countries, rewritten as a play-Goosie (Gambia) and Ganderan (Senegal) whose leaders enjoy mutual respect and friendship. Owing to personal military ambition and likely frustration over the Ganderian president's failure to forcibly annex Goosie, the Ganderian military leaders take over Goosie. This novel is decidedly political, clearly a criticism of the Senegambian Confederation that was established in 1982 following the 1981 aborted coup. Here, Roberts is also evoking a deep-seated fear that many Gambians harbor—that of being taken over by Senegal. This is a recurrent theme in Senegalo-Gambian relations dating back to 1870, as we saw earlier, when it was proposed that in exchange for other colonies in the region Britain would cede The Gambia to France. This proposal was opposed by the Aku/Krio community at the time,

Gamtel House, Westfield Junction, Serrekunda, is a branch of Gambia's main Gamtel, the country's major provider of phone and Internet services. (Courtesy of Buharry Gassama)

the community to which Roberts belongs. In a sense, *The Goosieganderan Myth,* though not a literary flashback, nonetheless flashes back on a sensitive and thorny issue in The Gambia's political history and its relations with Britain, France, and Senegal. Roberts is also a widely published and accomplished poet and former chair of the Independent Electoral Commission, an agency charged with supervising elections in The Gambia.

Swaebou Conateh, also a founding member of *N'Dannan,* is a veteran journalist and former director of information and editor of the widely respected magazine *The Gambia Report.* Like other founding members of *N'Dannan,* he too has published in this literary magazine. In addition, he has published two collections of poems: *Great Wrinkles Up the Sky's Sleeves* in 1981, about day-to-day life in rural Gambia, and *Blind Destiny* in 1982, which deals generally with the promise as well as the challenges of independent Africa.

In the genre of poetry, Dr. Tijan Sallah stands out as a luminary in both The Gambia and in Africa. He is by far the most prolific Gambian literary figure, having written several books of poetry and essays on Gambian culture. He is recognized internationally as a leading poet and has numerous publications to show for it. His works have been the subject of graduate theses and Ph.D. dissertations, and he is regarded as one of the most important African poets and writers following the generation of Nobel laureate playwright Wole Soyinka and novelist Chinua Achebe.

Sallah's deep understanding and organic connection to Gambian and Senegambia cultures, and its delivery through poetry and prose, is always refreshing. This is partly because of the collective cultural memory that he evokes, especially for readers of his generation but also for younger and older readers. In literary essays and criticism, his analysis is sharp. His coauthored book, *Chinua Achebe: Teacher of Light*, remains the definitive scholarly work on this iconic African and internationally renowned writer and activist. Tijan had his start as a poet at St. Augustine's High School and in the early years was mentored by Lenrie Peters. He later published "The Princess Who Would Not Marry a Man on Whose Body There Was a Scar" in the 1973 issue of *N'Dannan*, one of the few high school students to have appeared in that publication. Njogu E. W. Bah, a former student at Armitage High, also published a moving poem in the 1972 edition of *N'Dannan*, dedicated to his late friend and classmate Katim Touray: "Sleep Without Dreams." Sallah is coeditor of *The New African Poetry: An Anthology* and author of *When Africa Was a Young Woman, Kora Land*, and *Dream of Dusty Roads*, among other books.

The following two subsections are primarily intended as a survey rather than a full-fledged analysis, critique, or review of their works. The last decade or two has witnessed the rise of a new generation of creative writers who can legitimately be described as the post-*N'Dannan*/postindependence generation. Born shortly before or after independence in 1965, they are as varied as can be in style and subject matter. Also included in this category are creative writers who were born in the 1940s or 1950s, yet whose creative endeavors came to fruition or national, and sometimes international, attention only in the last decade or so.

THE POST-*N'DANNAN*/POSTINDEPENDENCE GENERATION OF CREATIVE WRITERS

Baaba Silla best exemplifies this category of post-*N'Dannan* creative writers. Born in Banjul in the 1950s, Sillah came to national and international attention following the publication of his first book, *When the Monkey Talks*, in 2005. Baaba launched two other books in 2010, *Daabali Gi* and *Pencum Taakusaan*. *Daabali Gi* is a sequel to *When the Monkey Talks* and is set in colonial Gambia against a backdrop of acute economic changes and dislocated lives. In *Daabali Gi*, Silla vividly captures the sharp internal divisions and cleavages that arose between and among political leaders in the quest for national flag independence. The protagonist is none other than Edward Francis Small (Edu Fara Mundaw). *Pencum Taakusaan* is a collection of poems.

Among the postindependence wave of creative writers are Baba Galleh Jallow, Foday Baldeh, Essa Bokar Sey, Alpha Robinson, Yankuba Mambureh, Momodou Sawaneh, Essa Colley, Bala Saho, Ebou Gaye, Sally Singhateh, Mariam Khan, Dayo Forster, Aisha Saidy, Rohey Samba, and Amie Sillah, a longtime women's rights advocate. Baba Galleh Jallow is one of the more prolific among this generation of writers. His *Angry Laughter* (2004) is a biting critique of a repressive African dictatorship, and *Mandela's Other Children: The Diary of an African Journalist* (2007), as the subtitle indicates, is a diary of a Gambian journalist who was a witness to the 1994 coup in The Gambia and was thereafter caught up in the tumultuous political events that followed. It is a vivid chapter in the saga of a military and quasi-military regime in The Gambia. *Dying for My Daughter* (2004) tackles the issue of female circumcision, a common practice among many Gambian ethnic groups. Now in exile in the United States, Jallow completed a Ph.D. in history at the University of California–Davis and teaches at a university in Nebraska.

Foday Baldeh's book of poems, *A Fate of an African President*, was written while he was in detention following the 1981 aborted coup. It is an indictment of the Jawara regime and conditions under detention that was published only after the successful 1994 military coup. Essa Bokarr Sey was Gambia's former ambassador to the United States and a former military officer in the Gambian army. Like Baldeh's work, some of his poems and writings have been very critical of his former boss, Yahya Jammeh. Sey has published a book of poems, and some of his writings also appear in online Gambian newspapers. Alpha Robinson is an able poet in his own right and has written in both Wolof and English. Yankuba Mambureh's *In Search of a Lost Brother* (2009) is about the author's own search for his brother in what was then war-torn Liberia, along with its attendant risks and challenges, and Momodou Sawaneh's *Dangerous Love* (2010) is an intriguing love story about Mary, a young woman caught between tradition and modernity. Mary rejects a traditionally arranged marriage and chooses the man she truly loves.

Another post-*N'Dannan*, postindependence-generation writer is Essa Colley. Born in 1962, Colley's novelette, *If I Am Right or Wrong* (1993), tackles the much-discussed topic of bullying. Buka, the protagonist, is serving a long prison term for the murder of his tormentor of many years, whom he kills in self-defense. Another writer of this generation is Bala Saho. Born in 1963, he has also published a novelette and a collection of poems. *The Road to My Village* captures a deep-seated conflict that Musa has over pursuing his dream of going to Europe or staying in his ancestral village with his girlfriend, Majula. Saho taps into a recurrent conflict that many young Gambians, and all Africans, have had to face and continue to face. In the end, Musa decides to stay home but under different sets of expectations. *Songs of a Foraging Bird* (2000) is more reflective of life and its challenges, love, and other human emotions. Ebou Gaye's *Patience Is Accompanied by a Smile* (1999) is an autobiographical novelette, tracing the challenges the author faced as a child, in his marriage, and in his studies abroad.

This postindependence generation of male writers are also deeply engaged in The Gambia's social, political, and economic milieu and grapple with contemporary issues of love, life abroad, political repression, exile, and female circumcision—all very important issues to Gambians. Few if any of these male creative writers have yet to attain international acclaim, partly because their works remain predominantly local, except for those of Jallow, Mambureh, Sey, and Colley, who have had the opportunity to self-publish abroad.

Creative writers in The Gambia face numerous challenges, the most daunting of which is getting their works published. Unlike other former British colonies, The Gambia still lacks a dynamic publishing industry that could serve as an outlet for resident creative writers and scholars. Only a few resident creative writers have had their works published by major publishing companies like MacMillan and Heinemann. This means that the bulk of resident creative writers do not receive the attention and financial stability that often accompany fame. Consequently, most are forced to self-publish, which generally deprives them of an international readership and its financial rewards. Also, a small population of readers makes life in The Gambia all the more challenging.

Lady Augusta Jawara, wife of The Gambia's first president, is widely considered a trailblazer for women, as well as for many male writers, in The Gambia. Like Lenrie Peters, Lady Jawara (formerly Augusta Mahoney) was of Aku/Krio descent and David (later Dawda) Jawara's first wife. Her book *Rebellion* was published in 1968 but she is perhaps better known for *The African King*, a play that was staged at the Negro Arts Festival held in Dakar in 1966. *Rebellion* chronicles the dilemma many fathers faced in Gambia in the 1960s between educating their daughters beyond elementary and high school—in Nysata's case, university—or marrying them off to suitable suitors. In the end, Nysata receives her father's support to pursue her education abroad. This was perhaps the first avowedly feminist, pro–girl child book in The Gambia's literary history and tradition. It tapped into the social debates of the day and later, following as it did The Gambia's independence only three years earlier. Mrs. Jawara was at the time president of the Gambia Women's Federation.

Janet Badjan Young has also published and produced several of her plays to rave reviews in The Gambia. She is easily one of the most prolific playwrights. Her plays tackle, among other issues, the practice of wife inheritance (a traditional practice, although dying, in which a younger brother, following his older brother's death, marrys his widow) as a possible conduit for HIV/AIDS; *The Ultimate Inheritance* entertains as much as it educates audiences about the disease. *The Battle of Sankandi* revisits the conflict in 1900 in the village of that name in which several villagers along with traveling commissioners Sitwell and Silva were killed. *The Dance of Katchikali*, like Peters's poems, is about a sacred pond around Bakau, home to several sacred crocodiles. The play highlights the delicate ecological balance between humans and these crocodiles. Many young Gambian women writers followed in the trail of Jawara and Young. Mention must also be made of Ralphina Phillott-Almeida, a contemporary of Young, who in 2007, published a rich collection of poems, stories and proverbs, entitled, Poems, Stories and Krio Proverbs. Together, they capture her life growing up in colonial Gambia.

Born in 1977, Sally Singhateh is a young poet and author of *Christie's Crises* (1988) and *The Sun Will Soon Shine* (2004). In general, her protagonists are young people who face social, political, and economic challenges. *Christie's Crisis* is a mystery adventure in which Christie and her friends try to solve various social and economic crimes, such as drug trafficking, against a backdrop of bizarre family entanglements. *The Sun Will Soon Shine* tackles the challenges and courage of a young woman, Nyima, who, following female circumcision, seeks to rise above her calamitous beginnings to rebuild her life triumphantly. Nyima is still haunted by her past but must forge along. Singhateh is also the author of *Baby Trouble*.

Like Sally Singhateh, Mariama Khan was born in 1977. She is a Gambian poet who has received much acclaim nationally and is gradually building an international reputation. For Khan, poetry is a vehicle through which she seeks social justice for women, the voiceless, and the oppressed in society. It is also a vehicle through which Khan expresses her disappointments, loves, aspirations, and triumphs. She follows in the traditions of Mariama Ba and Aminata Sow Fall of Senegal. Khan came to national fame in 2010 following her appointment as secretary-general and head of Gambia's civil service. Before then, she was deputy director of the Policy Analysis Unit, Office of the President. Her tenure as secretary-general was short-lived, however, as she was removed a few months later and appointed permanent secretary at the Personnel Management Office (PMO). She continues to write poetry and is an aspiring filmmaker as well. She now studies in the United States.

Another promising young female poet of the postindependence generation is Isatou "Aisha" Saidy, whose poems grace several online Gambian newspapers such as *Maafanta*, a website dedicated to the views of women that is

owned and operated by Fatou Jow Manneh, a well-known Gambian journalist and critic of President Jammeh. Based in the United States, Isatou is
very much inspired by concerns that similarly inspire Singhateh and Khan.
To her, poetry also has to help liberate people under oppression. In her own
words, Isatou explained,

> Poetry is: liberating, a break away. It creates such an "un-limiting" universe
> for me, where I can express my emotions, my actions, anger, happiness and
> opinions about things that affect the world around me. It gives me that author-
> ity, such an unstoppable energy of freedom, and yet makes others feel liberated
> through the same medium, by giving it their own interpretation; imagine how
> limitless that is.[10]

Clearly, Gambian women writers are keenly aware of and sensitive to
the heavily dominated male environment in which they must function and
thrive. The works of Augusta Jawara, Young, Singhateh, Khan, Sillah, and
Saidy, to name a few, exemplify the continuous quest for justice and emancipation in what is clearly a conservative environment for women and girls.
Together, these female writers envisage a society in which women and girls
can grow and thrive to their fullest potential—enjoying the fundamental
right not to be circumcised or mutilated and the right to choose a partner
free of societal and family manipulation and pressures. Understandably, the
protagonists in these plays, novels, and poems are women of strength and
character who defy social norms and expectations and overcome tremendous
odds to succeed. Gambian women writers wish not necessarily to replace
the institution of marriage but to reshape the terms of marriage to make it
more equitable between women and men. They represent and embody the
strengths of Gambian women, making it in a profession that still remains
heavily male dominated. Their influence is being felt along with that of their
male counterparts, as many of their works are now part of the school curriculum, which results in both young and old being sensitized to gender and
women's issues. Together, Gambian writers, and particularly women writers,
have laid the foundation for succeeding generations of writers to succeed—
and this is a tremendous achievement.

It is good to note the contribution of Dr. Cherno Omar Barry, who created a website devoted exclusively to the documentation and preservation of
Gambian literature. The website, along with another called *Binda Gambia*
(writings of Gambia), are a rich repository for useful discussion and analysis
of Gambian literature. Formation of a Gambia Writers Association must also
be commended, as well as the reemergence of *N'Dannan* as a literary publication for current and future writers. Rosamond King has also done much in

her academic writing to promote Gambian literature and art. She is based in the U.S. The current and future epochs of Gambian literary production, the neo-*N'Dannan* era, promises to bring national and international acclaim to the growing number of Gambian writers, both male and female.

NEWSPAPERS AND MAGAZINES

The first newspaper in The Gambia was established by a British merchant and member of the Legislative Council as a vehicle to oppose the ceding of The Gambia to France. In 1871 Thomas Brown founded *The Bathurst Times*, and in 1893 Samuel Forster Sr. founded *The Gambia Intelligencer*. Brown used his newspapers as a political platform to oppose British policy out of fear that ceding The Gambia to France would result in huge financial losses to the business community. In the late 19th century, *The Bathurst Observer*, along with the London-based *African Times*, regularly covered events in The Gambia.[11]

In the early 1920s, Edward Francis Small established *The Gambia Outlook*, and *The Senegambian Reporter* was published for the first time in Dakar. Yet unlike newspapers of the previous era that were concerned primarily with business interests, Small's newspapers were decidedly against colonial policy. In 1934, *The Gambia Echo* was launched. Following World War II, several nationalist newspapers, including *The Vanguard*, emerged primarily to counter and criticize British colonial policy as well. Established by Kebba Foon and M. B. Jones in early 1958, *The Vanguard* became the official mouthpiece of the Gambia National Party. Dixon Colley, another luminary journalist in the years before and after independence, established *The Nation* in the early 1960s.

Following in the tradition of *The Vanguard*, Colley used his paper to criticize government policy, while *The Torch*, a newspaper founded by Sana Manneh, later became a thorn in the side of the PPP government for highlighting corruption and government malfeasance under President Jawara. In fact, Manneh was sued by the government and later acquitted; his work contributed to the general loss of confidence in the Jawara government. It can be argued that the publication of Sir Dawda's per diem allowances and other expenses while on vacation in the United Kingdom in early 1994 and corruption at the Gambia Cooperative Union (GCU) were additional ammunition and justification for the military coup against him and his regime. *The Gambia Onward* was equally critical of government, and its hardnosed journalism resulted in the fall of M. C. Cham, Fafa Mbai, and several other ministers accused of corruption.

Party-based newspapers, at least during the first republic, were a common feature of The Gambia's political landscape. As in the 1800s, and up until

World War II, newspapers carried a strident political agenda. Similarly, the NCP's *The Gambia Outlook* (1975); PPP's *The Gambia Times*, (1981); and PDOIS's *Foroyaa* (1987) were explicitly political and, except for the PPP-owned *Gambia Times*, were critical of PPP government policy. *The Gambia News Bulletin* was established in 1943. It remained in existence until after the 1994 coup, having been renamed *The Gambia Weekly* and then *The Gambia Daily* and edited at different times by Saptieu Jobe, before her fallout with the AFPRC and the late Amadou Barry, respectively.

Kenneth Best, a self-exiled Liberian journalist, established *The Daily Observer* in the early 1990s, and Best, along with Deyda Hydara and Pap Saine, cofounders of *The Point*, helped train many young journalists in the 1990s. Following in the tradition of newspapers before them, both *The Daily Observer* and *The Point* were critical of government policy and President Jawara in particular. However, following the coup in 1994, Best was expelled from The Gambia by the new leaders of the July 22 coup, and on December 16, 2004, Hydara was assassinated by what many believe to be killers in the pay of Yahya Jammeh's government or his Green Boys, a vigilante group he supported before they were allegedly banned several years later. There is, however, no evidence linking President Jammeh to Deyda's death.

The post-1994 coup period witnessed a drastic curtailment of democratic rights in general, and of expression specifically. Ruling by decree, the AFPRC imposed numerous decrees, including numbers 70 and 71, which increased significantly the amount of money required to be deposited for newly established and existing newspapers. Specifically, decrees 70 and 71 raised this amount to roughly $10,000. A hostile environment for journalists ensued thereafter as journalists were routinely arrested, tortured, imprisoned, or all of these. Pap Saine, Halifa Sallah, and Sedia Jatta, owner-publishers of *The Point* and *Foroyaa* newspapers, respectively, were taken to court several times and charged with technical breaches that were later dismissed. In the years to come, more restrictions were imposed upon journalists, including the Media Commission Act of 2002 that imposed lengthy prison terms on journalists for writing newspaper articles that "threatened national security." It was repealed later by the National Assembly but not before a majority in the assembly enacted the Newspaper Amendment Act in 2002, a more punitive law against newspapers and journalists. The term "national security," at best a nebulous phrase, was interpreted widely to include stories, personal or otherwise, that the government deemed critical of its leaders and policies.

Baboucar Gaye's *The New Citizen* newspaper was forced to close in 1998, and a building housing *The Independent* newspaper owned by Alagi Yoro Jallow and Baba Galleh Jallow was torched by agents of the state. The disappearance since 2006 of Chief Ebrima Manneh, a leading journalist who is now feared dead, and Deyda Hydara's assassination in 2004 have effectively established a culture of silence and fear. Kanyiba Kanyi, who worked for an NGO, is also feared dead. Consequently, as many as 30 or more journalists live in self-imposed exile in Senegal, Germany, the United States, and the United Kingdom, where they have gone on to establish online newspapers that are critical of the regime in The Gambia. These online papers, which include *The Gambia Echo, The Gambia Journal, Freedom Newspaper, Jollof Newspaper, Gainako, Senegambia Newspaper, Gambia News, Maafanta,* and *allGambian.net,* just to name a few, have been vocal in their criticism of President Jammeh and his regime, policies, and supporters and have, for the most part, waged relentless and critical campaigns against the government at home.

To some degree, the onslaught against Jammeh and his policies, as well as his much less publicized alleged involvement in the separatist rebellion in the Casamance, have raised doubts about his credibility. The criticism of Jammeh has become all the more vociferous in the absence or silencing of once critical newspapers like *The Point,* and the sale since 2004 of *The Daily Observer* to Amadou Samba, one of President Jammeh's most ardent supporters and a businessman who has benefited disproportionately from state largess. Regrettably, but for good reason, the domestic press is reduced to reporting stories that are of little critical consequence. The Gambia Press Union (GPU) and its affiliates in the United States and Europe nonetheless hold talks and seminars in support of press freedom. The GPU has also shown solidarity with slain journalist Deyda Hydara and his family by holding peaceful demonstrations to which many dignitaries are invited to discuss human rights issues.

Predictably, President Jammeh has reacted against online newspaper journalists and editors. In 2008 Fatou Jow Manneh was arrested at the airport in The Gambia while attending her father's funeral. She was jailed in a mosquito-infested cell for six days, after which a yearlong kangaroo-court trial ensued. Manneh's only so-called crime was to have criticized President Jammeh in a 2003 online newspaper article. She was subsequently found guilty of treason and fined $12,000.[12]

Despite the severe repression, many newspapers also serve as outlets for aspiring Gambian writers who otherwise would remain unknown to the reading public. These papers also serialize longer academic essays and editorials. Online newspapers also provide similar services for Gambian writers in the diaspora as well. Few magazines operate in the country, and the few that exist are often limited to literary, cultural, and fashion-related issues. *The Gambia News and Report,* a weekly magazine, owned and edited by veteran journalist and poet Suwaebou Conateh, is also understandably circumspect in its coverage and is known for its annual man and woman of the year awards.

Radio and Television

Radio Gambia, the nation's first broadcasting facility, was established in 1962, just three years before independence. Yet its reach was by no means national because its audience was limited to Banjul and its environs. For entertainment and news before Radio Gambia's establishment, Gambians tuned to radio broadcasts from neighboring Senegal, Mali, Guinea, and Liberia, and from as far away as Congo Leopoldville and Congo Brazzaville. The British Broadcasting Corporation (BBC) and the Voice of America (VOA) were, and still are, important sources of news and entertainment. During this period, shortwave battery-operated portable transistor radio sets served as the only links between Gambians and the rest of the world. In time, however, and along with Radio Syd, Radio Gambia's reach improved, especially following the 1994 coup d'état.[13]

Paradoxically, the post-coup period has seen a significant increase in the number of radio stations in the country but without improved access to information for the population. This is because the Jammeh government continues to exert the same pressures on radio broadcasts as it does on print journalists. For instance, Baboucar Gaye's Citizen FM radio station was banned from broadcasting the news in local languages and was ultimately shut down by the authorities for Gaye's alleged failure to pay taxes. On February 5, 1998, Gaye was arrested, along with the station's news editor, Ebrima Sillah, and detained for several days at the NIA headquarters in Banjul. Gaye was subsequently charged under a 1913 telegraphic law for allegedly operating a radio station without a valid license. The 1913 act is an old colonial law.

Teranga FM, a private community radio station, was also shut down by the Jammeh government for no apparent reason other than its broadcast of the news in local languages. The station was reopened in February 2011 following critical concerns raised by listeners. There are roughly six FM stations, including West Coast Radio, City Limits, Sud FM, Paradise FM, Unique FM, and Radio 1 FM. Unlike Teranga, these radio stations, though privately owned, are not allowed to broadcast the news in local languages unless relayed from Radio Gambia, which is a propaganda arm of the government. Five other community radio stations are located in Brikama, Farafenni, Basse, Kerewan, and Sinchu Alhaji (Teranga). All these community radio stations, especially Brikama's, have had their run-ins with the law and were closed at one time or another in their operating lives. In sum, access to information via radio is severely curtailed by the regime in an effort to keep the citizenry uninformed and more easily subjected and susceptible to manipulation and control.

The Gambia's only television station is government owned. Established shortly after the 1994 coup, Gambia Radio and TV Services (GRTS) are generally were effective tools in the hands of Jammeh, enabling him to mobilize and win the 1996, 2001, 2006, and 2011 presidential elections. In all these elections, the opposition was given little access to the TV, which Jammeh used to vilify them. Jammeh's monopoly of GRTS precipitated a reaction among diaspora print journalists that led to the establishment of online radios in the United States and elsewhere—the most notable of which include GRTS International, owned by Momodou Lamin Sillah and Mbye Sarr, longtime democracy and human rights activists based in Silver Spring, Maryland, and Freedom Radio, owned by Pa N'derri M'Bai, proprietor of the *Freedom* newspaper in Raleigh, North Carolina. Raaki-Television, an online radio/television outfit, is owned and run by Momodou Buharry Gassama in Stockholm, Sweden. Raaki-Television also provides useful information, news, music, and historical material on The Gambia.

Following in the tradition of the *Freedom* newspaper, Freedom radio is just as critical of the Jammeh regime and the civil servants working for him. Both online radio services provide important news about The Gambia in all the major languages—Mandinka, Fula, Wolof, and Serahule—something unthinkable except in the government-owned and controlled GRTS. They also have valuable programs to inform listeners about topics that range from history to women's issues and health. Gambians at home who have access to the Internet subscribe heavily to these news and entertainment outlets from the diaspora as well as the major international networks like CNN. In fact, President Jammeh is said to read these papers and listen to the radio broadcasts emanating from the United States.

Notes

1. Sylviane *Diouf, Servants of Allah: African Muslims Enslaved in the Americas* (New York: New York University Press, 1998).

2. Allan Austin, *Muslims in Antebellum America* (New York: Routledge, 1997); Michael Gomez, *Exchanging Our Country Marks: The Transformation of African Identities in the Colonial and Antebellum South* (Chapel Hill: University of North Carolina Press, 1998); Paul Lovejoy, *Slavery, Commerce and Production in West Africa: Slave Society in the Sokoto Caliphate* (Trenton, NJ: Africa World Press, 2005); Daniel C. Littlefield, *Rice and Slaves: Ethnicity and the Slave Trade in Colonial South Carolina* (Chicago: University of Illinois Press, 1991).

3. Austin, *Muslims in Antebellum America*; Gwendolyn Midlo Hall, *Africans in Colonial Lousiana* (Baton Rouge: Louisiana State University Press, 1992); James Walvin, *An African's Life: The Life and Times of Olaudah Equiano* (London: Continuum, 1998).

4. Ivan Van Sertima, *They Came Before Columbus: The African Presence in Ancient America* (New York: Random House, 1976); Philip Curtin, *Economic Change in Precolonial Africa: Senegambia in the Era of the Slave Trade* (Madison: University of Wisconsin Press, 1975).

5. Bala Saho, "Appropriations of Islam in a Gambian Village: Life and Times of Shaykh Mass Kah, 1827–1936," *African Studies Quarterly* 12, no. 4 (2011): 1–21.

6. Tijan Sallah, "To My Late Friend Dr. Lenrie Peters: The Gambian Vessel Emptied of Its Poetry," *Binda Gambia,* June 14, 2009, p. 4. http://bindagambia. blogspot.com/2009/06/to-my-late-friend-dr-lenrie-peters.html. Also see, Stewart Brown, "Gambian Fictions," Wasafiri, Vol. 7, Issue 15 (1992): 2–7; Samuel Baity Garren, "Exile and return, The poetry and fiction of Tijan Sallah," Wasafiri, Vol. 7, Issue 15 (1992): 9–14.

7. Cherno Omar Barry, "Gambian Fiction: An Analytical Study," in *The Gambia: Essays on Contemporary Issues and Future Direction: 1965–2011*, ed. Abdoulaye Saine, Ebrima Ceesay, and Ebrima Sall (Trenton, NJ: Africa World Press, 2012), 478.

8. Kaye Whiteman, "Ebou Dibba," *The Guardian,* April 3, 2001; Gambia Guide, The Gambia Information Site, 2011, http://www.accessgambia.com/information/.

9. Cherno Omar Barry, "History of Gambian Literature Writing," 2008, http:// gambianliterature.blogpost.com/2004/11/history-of-gambian literary-writing.html.

10. Isatou (Aisha) Saidy, e-mail communication, February 28, 2011.

11. Arnold Hughes and David Perfect, *Historical Dictionary of The Gambia,* 4th ed. (Lanham, MD: The Scarecrow Press, 2008), 26.

12. "Gambia: Fatou Jow Manneh Is Given Prison Sentence, Fined and Released," *PEN International*, August 26, 2008.

13. Radio Syd was a station devoted to playing music from around the world, including rock 'n' roll, salsa music from Cuba, and music from a number of African countries.

4

Art, Architecture, and Housing

THE OLDEST KNOWN archeological discoveries in the area where modern-day Gambia lies were pottery remains that dated back to A.D. 500. These finds suggest that the peoples who occupied the area at the time used iron tools, which they themselves smelted. The next oldest artifacts are the *Stone Circles* near Wassu in the Central River Region. It is not known who the builders of the *Stone Circles* were, nor when they were built or for what purpose. The *Stone Circles* are, however, believed to have been built by inhabitants of the area some 1,200 to 1,500 years ago and may have served as burial sites or as places of worship for residents in the area.

The Gambia has a rich heritage in art and architecture, which is reflected in its sculptures, masks, textiles, jewelry, pottery, matte decorations, carved doors, and wood and stone carvings. These art objects have both ceremonial and entertainment value and typically have socioreligious functions in society as well. Economic shifts and the resulting changes and dislocation of people's lives and livelihoods have resulted in the growing commercialization of these cultural artifacts. Nonetheless, masks in days of old were revered. According to Claude Rilly,

The mask was traditionally used in Africa in the majority of ceremonies: fertility or initiation rites, religious or funeral celebrations, but also theatrical or comic performances often linked to the deepest ethnic myths. The mask confers on the person wearing it—for the duration of the ceremony—the essence and the powers of the spirits or ancestors it symbolizes. Secret societies, almost always composed of adult males, are simultaneously repositories and creators. The wearers of masks, sworn to secrecy, are subject to constraints and taboos which protect them from the dangerous magic powers of these objects.[1]

This may no longer be the case in most places today, including The Gambia, where both materialism and commercialization, in response to tourist dollars, is the norm. Financial reward has trumped quality and the preservation of culture in the quest for a quick sale. Yet in an environment where land that was once owned communally is being sold to the highest bidder and national treasures have become easy targets for sale to tourists, it would be unreasonable to expect artists not to follow suit. It used to be that pottery was the domain of Serahule women, whose beautifully decorated clay water jars, cooking pots, and pots for burning incense decorated homes. Serahule men were known for making multicolored bamboo mats, beds, and chairs that decorated homes and were also used during naming ceremonies and weddings. Serahule men and especially women supplemented their incomes from these off-season ventures when they were not tending groundnut and rice fields.

Many art objects have since disappeared or are on the verge of doing so. In urban settings, especially, they have been replaced by refrigerators, carpets, and modern Western-style furniture made of wood—a departure from traditional art whose materials often came from within the country. In the traditional arts, materials and their use reflected a fine balance between inhabitants and their natural environment. The making of straw hats called *tengado* by the Fula was an important skill, as was weaving that produced immaculate and intricately decorated cloth of considerable value. Called *serri rabal* in Wolof or *pano* in Manjago, it was once a medium of exchange, serving as part of a woman's bride wealth. These expensive pieces of cloth would be lavishly displayed during naming ceremonies or given away as gifts to griots.

The Laube, *ette* (woodcarvers) are also well known for their wood-carving skills that include making figurines, masks, drums, combs, and cooking utensils used in day-to-day household functions. The tie-dye and batiks, known for their bright cola nut–enhanced colors are an important specialty among all ethnic groups, especially the Bambara, who of late bring them from Mali to sell in urban areas. The products made by goldsmiths and silversmiths, while still part of a vibrant trade, are now being displaced by cheap imports. Cobblers continue to use animal skins to make beautiful bags, sandals, and amulets and other items for personal needs; these are skills one finds in all ethnic groups.

Tourist markets punctuate major towns, coastal hotels, and beaches where one is sure to see a rich display of paintings, masks, cloth, and jewelry. Prices

Statues on the grounds of Arch 22, a massive structure that commemorates the July 22 coup. (Courtesy of Buharry Gassama)

are negotiable, determined by the size and/or the complexity involved in the making of the art object itself. Four-foot-high or even taller statues and wooden chairs are major attractions for tourists. These are made from locally harvested wood that may include mahogany. Economic hard times have led to a glut in art objects, which drives prices down, resulting in good bargains for purchasers. On visiting a tourist market on the coast or in Banjul's Albert Market, one is at once treated to a panoramic and colorful scene that is likely to include tie-dye and batik cloth sewn into shirts, shorts, kaftans, skirts, and blouses. These materials are also used to make bedsheets, pillowcases, curtains, and napkins. Craft markets are typically a happy and festive place where one can potentially find wares to suit almost any taste. There are laundry baskets, baskets for grocery shopping, and baskets for fruit and other household items. Colorful calabashes or gourds are part of any display and, like the straw baskets, serve as household decorations. These calabashes are still in use in both urban and rural areas. Serer and Fula women use large calabashes to sell *cherreh* or sour milk, respectively. Large calabashes are also used to serve food.

In the last quarter of a century, woodcrafts have witnessed a boom partly because of tourism but also because of the growth in home construction

Albert Market, Banjul, is a bustling open market that offers shoppers an array of goods and services often for a good bargain if one is willing to negotiate. (Courtesy of Buharry Gassama)

in urban areas, where outside doors and internal doors leading into rooms are beautifully crafted by carpenters and adorned by visual artists. These European-style homes are decorated with paintings that have an African motif, as large baskets adorned with beautifully decorated gourds and masks hang on walls or are displayed in living rooms. Windows and doors are likewise fitted with colorful tie-dye curtains while heavy mahogany dining tables and chairs are decorated with placemats, napkins, and an assortment of dining utensils. Locally made stools and chairs tend to accompany a mostly European décor; bedrooms have both an African and a European ambiance.

A Brief Profile of Some Gambian Artists

Gambian society has historically privileged the spoken word, poetry and the griot, perhaps at the expense of visual artists. The absence of writing until the introduction of Islam and Western education meant that the history of The Gambia's various ethnic groups was preserved in oral form and thus narrated and passed on from one generation to another. Yet in the last three decades or more, Gambian visual artists have emerged to make their names known, both nationally and internationally. The most noted of these was Ebou Madi Sillah, perhaps better known as Comrade Sillah, who died in February 2006. He was a prolific painter who in the 1980s produced numerous graphic watercolor paintings. Following his death an exhibition that displayed his numerous works was launched in public places in the Greater Banjul area.

Momodou Ceesay is also a prolific artist who studied in the United States and enjoys a worldwide reputation. When he is not living in London, England, he lives in the coastal town of Bakau, where he has a studio and gallery. Ceesay's works adorn several public buildings in the United States, where he had lived for some time. Baboucar Etu Ndow, an art teacher, is now a lecturer at the University of The Gambia. Ndow is known for his use of locally occurring materials that add color to his work. Bubacar Badjie has built an international reputation for himself, having had several exhibitions overseas and in The Gambia. His works can be found in museums as far away as New Zealand. He has collaborated with Njogou Touray, another well-known artist, and the graphic designer Lamin Marenah to create the logo for the 2006 Banjul AU Summit, which was held in Banjul on July 1–2.[2] Njogu Touray

Statues at a roundabout on Kombo Coastal Highway adorn a park with bar and restaurant services against a backdrop of several banks in the area, a couple of miles from Serrekunda's teeming open market. (Courtesy of Buharry Gassama)

A sample of wood carvings found in all major markets and the tourist district; some can stand as four feet or higher. (© Ianlangley | Dreamstime.com)

uses paints extracted from indigenous plants to capture cultural landscapes and ruins. Basically self-taught, Njogu has distinguished himself by his many exhibitions in neighboring Senegal, the United Kingdom, and the United States.

Edrissa Jobe is also a well-known Gambian painter who was born in 1968 in Basse and now lives in Bakau in the Katchikalli area. After finishing secondary school education in 1985 he went to reside in Banjul, where he started painting in 1986 on canvas using watercolors. In 1989 he progressed to using acrylic and oils on canvas, which he still uses today. Moulaye Sarr is also a rising young artist who is building quite a reputation in The Gambia and neighboring Senegal. Sarr began by sketching cartoon characters. His works are created using acrylic paint, sand, charcoal, and fabrics. He is also accomplished in portraiture. Another artist who has won respect outside The Gambia is Pa Ousman Martin, who resides in the city of Atlanta, Georgia, in the United States. Pa Ousman's paintings are vivid depictions of rural life in Gambia, using bright acrylic colors to capture this landscape. Some up-and-coming talents include Mustapha Jassey, Abdoulie Colley, and Lamin Dibba.[3]

Modern visual art in The Gambia, like creative writing, as discussed earlier, is a relatively young enterprise, coming into greater national and international attention only in the last two or three decades following independence in 1965. For the most part, the crop of artists briefly highlighted in this chapter, except for Comrade Ebou Sillah and Momodou Ceesay, were born shortly before or after independence. They are distinguished by their desire to capture on canvas Gambia's cultural heritage and rich physical landscape, using color, texture, and personal sensibilities.

ARCHITECTURE

Architecture in The Gambia is a mélange of indigenous structures alongside Middle Eastern/Arab and European forms. The introduction of Islam in the 11th century and European contact in the 15th century influenced African and Gambian architecture as it did other traditional institutions or coexisted with them. Partly because of the country's location in the Sahel, Gambians, like other inhabitants of Senegambia Major, appropriated material in their local habitat to construct homes, storage facilities, and places of worship, among other buildings. As elsewhere in the region and The Gambia, and especially in rural areas, mud was until about a quarter century ago the usual material for building massive structures like mosques and homes. In less arid areas grass-thatched roofs provided not only shelter from the elements but also a cooling effect for residents. In the rural areas, building structures remained simple. Homes typically took a rectangular, sometimes elongated shape or were more commonly circular huts with a single entrance. The walls of these structures were often reinforced with grass at the mixing stage to make them more durable. In some cattle-grazing areas, cow manure would be used as plaster to make the outer layer of the wall stronger and impenetrable by rain. It should be noted in passing that dotted along the Gambia River during the 18th and 19th centuries were elegant European-style Portuguese and French dwellings owned by European factory owners and mulattos who grew rich from trade in slaves, wax, and other commodities. Albreda, one such factory town, was controlled by the French, and its dwellings at the time had a distinctive French flavor.[4] These dwellings now lie in ruin, yet remain poignant reminders of an earlier era in Gambian history.

While there have been European-style homes in Bathurst (Portuguese Town) following its founding in 1816 that were occupied by well-to-do European merchants, their mulatto wives, and their offspring as well as Aku, Lebanese, and Gambians of various ethnic groups, the traditional dwelling in the poorer parts of Bathurst/Banjul (Jolof Town and Soldier Town) was simple. Homes were made of *kiringting*, a bamboo material that provided the skeletal structure of the walls along with several windows to complete the rectangular-shaped houses. Cement was then used for plastering the *kiringting* walls, which were then whitewashed. Corrugated iron sheets would then be used to roof houses. It made for comfortable dwellings; a bedroom adjoined to a small sitting room was typical. Depending on its size, a compound in

View of Banjul north from the top of Arch 22, a massive structure that commemorates the July 22 coup. (Courtesy of Buharry Gassama)

Banjul could accommodate several longer structures with separate bedroom/sitting room units for family members or tenants. The kitchen would be at the back of the compound, with washrooms and toilets placed further to the back for privacy.

Space in Banjul generally and the poorer areas in particular has always been limited, partly because it is an island and its inhabitants have for the most part not been in a position to build upward for lack of resources. This has changed, however, as Banjul now boasts numerous modern two- and three-floor homes as well as bungalows. Increased investment in housing by the new well-to-do inhabitants and, in more recent years, investments by diaspora Gambians throughout the Greater Banjul area has resulted in the construction of huge homes with first-class facilities to rival any in wealthier countries. President Yahya Jammeh's government has also supported many housing schemes to help meet the growing housing needs of an expanding middle class. Also, because of the warm weather and relatively inexpensive land, Europeans, U.S. citizens, and diaspora Gambians are investing in homes there. For Gambians who live and work abroad, building a modern home in

The Gambia can save about a third, and perhaps more, of what one would otherwise spend in Europe or the United States. While building materials are comparable in prices to those in Europe, Brazil, and other countries, one can save on labor and locally manufactured materials.

Consequently, architectural styles now tend to be more European with distinctively tropical, Spanish, and Caribbean terra cotta colors and roofs. There is a French flavor or touch to these houses as well, owing to Senegalese builders and contractors who dominate the construction market. Ceilings in these houses are more stylish, with intricate molds made of white cement, which after drying are hung and supported by the roof frame. The style resembles Italian- and/or Moroccan-decorated ceilings and tends to have a cooling effect. Middle-class homes have also seen some innovation in ceiling construction. Rather than cardboard, many today use varnished plywood, which is quite attractive and less expensive than the white-cement molds.

Owing to the mix of styles in building types, coupled with the fact that many Gambians now travel widely for business to Europe, China, India, Brazil, the United States, and the Middle East, many residents tend to bring back materials, styles, and decorative pieces for their homes. In the last decade or so, proximity to Dubai, in particular, has resulted in an influx of furnishings from this region of the world. Visitors to the United States and Europe are sure to bring back with them ideas, furnishings, and sometimes building materials for their new homes.

In conclusion, art and architecture in The Gambia are vibrant and growing industries, reflecting diverse sensibilities and geared generally for the tourist market and personal taste, respectively. Much art displayed at tourist markets is created to earn a quick and high return whenever possible. The traditional meanings that were once attached to masks, specifically, are being lost to commercialism. Building styles and aesthetics reflect a growing eclectic taste with African, European, and Middle Eastern influences. Locally produced art is part of every home's décor, along with influences from other parts of the world. Victorian buildings, still in use in Banjul's commercial center and the colonial enclaves in the provinces, maintain their grandeur even if they are eclipsed by more modern buildings. This trend is likely to increase as Gambians travel abroad and return with new designs and materials for their new homes.

A favorable exchange rate between the international currencies (dollar, pound, euro, mark) and the Gambian dalasi will enable diaspora Gambians and Europeans to continue to build their dream retirement homes in communities that are on or close to the white-sand beaches. Thus, art and architecture will likely continue to have a symbiotic relationship well into the future. Even in the rural areas, the scene is changing; more houses are

Apartment building on Senegambia Highway, one of many such residences catering to a growing middle class and expatriate population, close to the beaches, hotels, restaurants, and the tourist district. (Courtesy of Buharry Gassama)

being built with cement blocks, slowly displacing traditional structures and materials. One drawback of cement-block houses is that they tend to retain heat, unlike the grass-thatched mud houses, called *banku-bungo* in Mandinka.

NOTES

1. Claude Rilly, WOW.gm, Gambian News Community, 2011.

2. Each year African heads of state, foreign ministers, diplomats, and invited guests (usually other heads of state of nonmember states) meet at an African capital to discuss important policy issues facing the continent of Africa.

3. Gambia Guide, The Gambia Information Site, 2011, http://www.accessgambia.com/information/.

4. For a detailed study on this subject, see George E. Brooks, *Euro-Africans in West Africa* (Athens: Ohio University Press, 2003).Statues at a roundabout on Kombo Coastal Highway adorn a park with bar and restaurant services against a backdrop of several banks in the area, a couple of miles from Serrekunda's teeming open market. (Courtesy of Buharry Gassama)

$$5$$

Cuisine and Traditional Dress

Cuisine

GAMBIAN CUISINE IS as diverse as its peoples, with each ethnic group contributing to the national menu while simultaneously retaining distinct dishes and flavors. Given The Gambia's abundant marine life and rich tropical cornucopia, the typical Gambian diet is, in general, rich in seafood and vegetables, fruits, and fruit-based drinks and juices. Groundnuts, once the key export of the country, is understandably a key ingredient in many national dishes, the most important of which is variously called *domoda*, or *maffe*, the latter used generally in Senegambia Major. Because groundnuts are grown throughout this region, the dish itself may have diffused from ancient Mali to its periphery, including The Gambia. Thus, the term *maffe*, which is a Bambara word, is used widely; *domoda*, which is a Mandinka word and is also used by the Wolof (its literal translation is eat-mouth), is the local name for this delicious dish.

With a peanut butter base, *domoda* is a mixture of spices that include salt, pepper, onions, and seasonal vegetables that may include okra and bitter tomatoes. It can be beef, chicken, lamb, or goat based; *domoda* may also include morsels of dried fish and sea snails for flavor. Served over rice or *findi* (*findo* among the Mandinka), a couscous-like grain, *domoda* has a smooth and rich nutty flavor and today is one of The Gambia's national dishes that is enjoyed globally. Another dish is *kutcha*, which is a rich blend of green vegetables and seasonings that is eaten with fish over rice. Variants of this are *naa'da* and *nama' durang*, which are vegetable-based but with a more generous dose of okra and sap from a local plant that gives the latter dish its smooth and slippery texture. It too is served over rice and often eaten with fish. The Jola also have similar dishes; this may be due to the give-and-take between Mandinka and Jola ethnic groups. Yet unlike *domoda*, *kutcha* and *naa'da* have not conquered the palate of Gambians at the national level.

Benachin or *thiep* (Senegal) is also known popularly outside Senegambia Major and Minor as Jolof rice. A Wolof (Jolof) dish, *benachin*, is a blend of rice, tomatoes, tomato paste (if desired), black and red peppers, onions, cooking oil, and an assortment of seasonal vegetables cooked in one pot—thus the name *benachin*, which in Wolof means "one cooking pot." It is always a hit during major religious feasts and naming and wedding ceremonies. *Benachin* closely resembles Chinese fried rice, although many Gambians consider it to be tastier. Another popular national staple is *supakanja* or okra soup, which is palm oil–based and often cooked with fish or beef and eaten with rice, *findi* or *fufou*, a cassava paste that resembles mashed potato, only more rubbery. *Nyami'nolo* is a variant of *supakanja* but is different from *plassas*, a peanut and palm oil–based meal that uses beef or fish and is served over rice or *findi*.

Lighter variations of *domoda* often include beans, chicken, or dried fish, or a light tomato-based sauce (*baseh* in Wolof) served over *cherreh*, a millet-derived couscous at dinner. *Cherreh* and fresh cow's milk often conclude a dinner of *cherreh* and greens (*mboom* in Wolof) or *cherreh* with *baseh*. *Cherreh* and milk or *cherreh* and *mboom* are popular combinations among rural Fula, Tukulor, and Wolof households and among some affluent urban dwellers. These variations could also be served for breakfast along with the earlier sauces and soups. The meal of *cherreh* and milk is reflective of the symbiotic relationship between Fulani herders and their rural Wolof and Mandinka peasant-farmer neighbors. In exchange for their millet, Wolof and Mandinka peasants receive fresh and sour milk (fermented). *Cherreh*, however, is typically associated with the Serer. There is yet another version of *domoda*, which is not peanut butter based. Its base is *sang' hal* (Wolof), which is millet flour; where this is not available, regular white flour is used as a substitute.

Mba'hal (similar to dirty rice served in Louisiana) is yet another favorite of many Gambians. It is a simple dish with ground peanuts, dried fish, and locust beans, a pungent ingredient added to many sauces and stews for flavor. All the ingredients are steamed over cooking rice and later mixed to give the dish a grayish look and nutty taste. This is often served with butter or ghee, which in small portions is strewn over the rice, giving it a buttery taste. A popular side dish called *rang'ha* in The Gambia and *baegeuch* in Senegal made out of fresh sorrel (or spinach leaves in the diaspora) is ground into a paste and flavored with locust beans, lemon juice, salt, and hot pepper. It adds a hot and zesty taste to *mba'hal*. Another variant of *mba'hal* is one that does not have ground peanuts or groundnuts. In this case, the rice is left to simmer in a tomato paste, onion, and lemon juice mixture while absorbing all the flavors therein. For protein, beef or fish is used, but this version of *mba'hal* is not often eaten with *rang'ha*, though it can be spicy hot. *Yassa*, which has gained quite an international reputation, is fish or chicken marinated in lemon juice or mustard and cooked with spices that include black pepper, salt or *jumbo* bouillon cubes along with sautéed onions, eaten with rice or French bread for dinner or breakfast.

For many Gambian households, however, breakfast includes porridge with sugar and fermented milk, or a groundnut-based version, which the Mandinka call *teah'kerreh churro* or *churra gerteh* in Wolof. This is eaten with *kossam* (fermented milk) in Fula. The latter could also be eaten for dinner. Pap made out of the local millet or corn, and known variously as *mono* (Mandinka) or *rui* (Wolof), or *laah* (Wolof) with fermented milk is a favorite. In more prosperous households, especially among the Aku, bread, butter, jam, and eggs are preferred. *Accarah*, a bean cake, is often eaten with bread and a spicy onion sauce. Liver and onions is also a common breakfast item, especially among those on the run in the morning. These foods are often taken with tea, Ovaltine, cocoa, or local herbs called *kinkiliba* or *mbor'mbor,* with generous servings of sugar and canned milk.

Unlike in the United States and Europe, in The Gambia having dessert after a meal is uncommon. In most Gambian households, a meal, especially lunch, can be followed by the fruit in season—mango, guava, plum, papaya, orange, or other fruit. Because Gambians do not generally drink while eating, a soft drink or other fruit-based juice, and increasingly juices and drinks derived from hibiscus (sorrel)—called *wonjo* (Gambia) or *bisapp* (Senegal)—tamarind, and other local fruit and berries could serve as a dessert. These local juices are generally flavored with vanilla and lots of sugar. Among the Christian Akus, beer or wine may accompany or follow a meal. Some older Gambians may chew kola nuts, a bitter stimulant also used in cola drinks, after a meal. At times bitter kola, an oblong-shaped nut just as bitter as the kola nut, is eaten after a meal, sometimes to wash down the aftertaste of not so good palm oil.

Increasingly in recent times, *chakri,* or what was traditionally called *dang' ask-sow,* also made from millet, is eaten with fermented milk and flavored with vanilla and crushed pineapples. Other sweet desserts or snacks include *mbudake*, which is a mixture of dried *cherreh,* peanut butter, and sugar. *Dempeteng* is particularly popular, following the harvest of the new rice crop. The new rice is roasted while still in its husk and then pounded in a mortar using a pestle. The pounding removes the husk while flattening out the grains. It makes for a good snack when soaked in milk and sugar. Cassava and beans or beans and bread with a zesty palm oil–onion sauce is a popular snack for schoolchildren and for some a breakfast fast food or a mini-meal before lunch.

Ebbeh is also a popular food among youth and increasingly, adults in urban centers. It too is palm oil–based, with cassava and seafood, mostly shrimp, all mixed together to give it a tangy and spicy taste. This is a recent addition to the Gambian menu, arriving possibly from Sierra Leone or Ghana in the 1980s. Donut holes and donuts, locally called *pankett,* a name derived from pancake, are a sweet snack of deep-fried dough dusted with sugar crystals. They are also a favorite among schoolchildren and are also served at naming ceremonies. In earlier times and especially in the rural areas *mung'ko* (Mandinka for rice cakes) would be served at these ceremonies.

In the days before the growth in urbanization and relative affluence among The Gambia's ethnic groups, Gambian cuisine was simple, consisting mostly of low-fat, nonfried foods such as *cherreh, domoda, mba'hal, naa'da, kutcha,* and *bundi' neke* among the Serahule, and lots of fish and vegetables in season. The rural areas, especially, were known to have a simple and healthier lifestyle, with foods that were fresh and inexpensive. Today, however, Gambian cuisine is high in saturated fat with meat and chicken. Add to this the ubiquitous fast-food joints that offer the locally made *dibi,* beef or lamb cooked in an oil-based onion stew; *affra,* grilled (imported) chicken or lamb; and *chuwe' diwlin* and *chuwe' diwtirr,* rich stews that are vegetable or palm oil-based. In The Gambia, as in other countries, the cuisine is undergoing rapid change, coupled with the increased use of automobiles, taxis, and buses and declining labor on farms. This has exacerbated the incidence of hypertension and diabetes in the population.

There are many dietary restrictions among Gambian Muslims. Pork, though not a taboo animal meat among Christians, is most definitely *haram* (forbidden) among Muslims, and few, if any, consume pork or pork products. Islam also forbids the consumption of meats that have not been prepared according to the Islamic or halal way. Consequently, all carnivorous animals, birds, or fish that were not harvested along lines dictated by the Qur'an are not halal or kosher. Alcohol is a much trickier issue, however. While Muslims are not supposed to drink alcohol, many do, especially the young (and not so young). Palm wine or its distilled derivative, gin, locally called *kana,* is consumed by some Muslims, who drink even though it is *haram.* This could be a reflection of Gambians' *cheddo* or *Soninke* past.

The Gambia has one brewery that makes a beer called Julbrew. The brewery was a source of much controversy before it was established in the early 1970s. For Christians these drinks are not taboo. Pre-fermented palm wine (*chongkom*), though having low or no traces of alcohol, is also eschewed by

Muslim Gambians. Gambians, both Christian and Muslim, also do not consume beasts of burden—horses, donkeys, elephants, or giraffes—or primates. Crocodiles, along with hippopotamus meats, are consumed by some but not all Gambians. These restrictions have not by any means diminished the variety of foods available to Gambians. In fact, many Gambians brag about having the best and most varied menu in West Africa.

Globalization has also contributed to a rise in restaurants that cater to an increasingly cosmopolitan and multicultural clientele. Today one can find Indian, Chinese, European (British, Italian), and Lebanese restaurants in addition to Gambian restaurants that appeal to Gambia's upper crust and the expatriate community. There are also the local restaurants that cater to the average Gambian clientele. Eating out at restaurants is a recent trend dating back perhaps not more than two decades. Typically, most Gambians eat at home with family members, friends, and visitors. It is cheaper and the quality is often better, capturing the local flavors, smells, and hot spices that highbrow restaurants are likely to omit lest they offend their international clientele. Among the more affluent and Westernized, meals are served at the table, while the more traditional and perhaps less well-off sit on mats or low stools and use their hands or spoon.

Westfield Junction, Serrekunda, a busy intersection from which buses and trucks travel to different parts of the country and neighboring Senegal, Guinea Bissau, Guinea, and Mali. It is named after Westfield Clinic, founded by the late Dr. Palmer, who jointly operated it with the late Dr. Lenrie Peters. (Courtesy of Buharry Gassama)

There is a protocol to eating collectively from a large communal dish. First, one must wash his/her hands before and after a meal. One must eat with the right hand because the left hand is reserved for bathroom-related cleansing. In less affluent and more traditional homes men and women are generally separated during meals, with the younger children eating with the women. Older children eat from the same dish as older men but must keep their gaze focused on the dish and must wait to be served pieces of the fish or meat while eating or eat it after the meal. Older children must also anchor the vessel from which the food is eaten by pressing a finger or several fingers, sometimes including the thumb of the left hand, on the rim of the vessel to protect it from moving. The belief in more traditional times was that if a vessel shifts while the meal is being consumed, it can result in gastro-related problems. While eating is a social activity, only adults may speak, but they too risk not having enough to eat.

Children seldom engage in speaking or conversation while eating. It is also considered impolite for a child or adult to rummage through the vessel or consume morsels of food beyond one's proximity to the vessel. Children or adults who immediately go for the fish or meat, usually in the middle of the vessel, are considered rude or impolite. Children must wait to be served. While using one's right hand, one takes small mounds of rice mixed with some sauce, vegetables, and fish and use only four fingers, not the thumb, to deliver the food into one's mouth. Stuffing one's mouth or eating hastily is also considered impolite. However, an audible burp or belch following a meal is a complimentary gesture to the cook and is not considered impolite or out of place. Children as well as adults thank those who prepared the food for the meal—this is considered cultured.

If a visitor chances upon a family having a meal, the polite thing to do is to have a handful or two of the food and retire to a part of the room to avoid looking at those still eating. It is the polite thing to do even if you initially declined the invitation to partake of the meal. It is considered good manners to avert one's gaze from watching a person eat. Averting one's gaze is mostly out of respect and modesty but may also have something to do with the once widely held belief in witchcraft or sorcerers who are believed to have the ability to use their evil eye to cause havoc during meals.

Ceremonies are never deemed successful or complete without abundant food and drink for the guests. Unenviable is the patron who falters in this endeavor or is perceived to be a miser or food hoarder. Patrons can easily become the brunt of jokes from their *jeli* or *gewel* and among those with whom a patron enjoys a joking relationship. First cousins can also use this as a pretext or reason to extract articles of clothing as concession. Similarly, forgetting an article of clothing, shoes, or a watch, termed *pissal* in Mandinka and *challit* in Wolof, is cause for teasing and laughter, all in good spirits. In order to retrieve the forgotten article, one must offer a gift of money or the forgotten item itself as appeasement to ward off future jokes. As noted earlier, interethnic jokes based on food at naming and marriage ceremonies, especially among Baddibunkas and Kiangkas, Fulas and Serers, Nuiminkas and Jarangkas, Futa Fulbe and Jahankas, and Jolas and Serers, are occasions to engage in lighthearted merriment to defuse social tensions and enhance the fun at these events.

In sum, Gambian cuisine is diverse and delicious, and in spite of the country's small size, it offers Gambians and adventurous visitors a delectable array of dishes, snacks, and drinks. Lying on both sides of the Gambia River, which empties into the Atlantic Ocean, The Gambia offers a variety of seafoods complemented by groundnuts, rice, and various vegetables and legumes that are used creatively to produce rich flavors. As in other cultures, eating communally is a social activity that is steeped in etiquette and custom. A growing expatriate community that work for nongovernmental organizations, foreign embassy personnel, and students from abroad, among others, have contributed in no small measure to the mushrooming of an international cuisine that caters to them and wealthy Gambians. In the main, most Gambians prefer to stay at home for their meals, but on occasion they indulge in street foods or fast food. And a meal at home would be deemed incomplete without the usual green tea brew to wash down the meal. In fact, rather than dessert, green tea after a meal suffices adequately. A special set of skills is required to make the tea, and in the hands of an able tea maker one is assured of the right mix of sugar, tea, and mint leaves.

GAMBIAN CUISINE IN THE UNITED STATES AND EUROPE

Contemporary Gambians and Senegalese immigrants, like other Africans, have brought to the United States their foods, flavors, and cooking styles. This is not a new phenomenon because enslaved Africans had similarly brought with them considerable knowledge of food cultivation and preparation—such as okra for gumbo, black-eyed peas, rice, and desserts. On arrival to these shores, Senegambians had to improvise and seek substitutes for ingredients that could not be readily found in their new surroundings. For instance, in the absence of palm oil, they used substitutes like tomato paste to thicken soups and sauces. A visit to the Southern part of the United States and the Caribbean, specifically Cuba and Jamaica, easily drives this point home. In Jamaica, one finds the *churra gerteh* sold in fast-food restaurants—only that in Jamaica it is smoother and more liquid than the thicker Gambian version.

Most major cities in the United States have an array of African restaurants, one or two of which is likely to be Gambian or Senegalese. The city of Cincinnati, a Midwestern city of less than a million, has two Senegalese restaurants and several shops that are stocked with food items from home or their substitutes. The restaurants cater to a Senegambian and increasingly African, African American, and Euro-American clientele. Africans who visit these restaurants typically do carry-out or when they cook at home easily find the needed ingredients in adjoining grocery stores. The stores, in addition to selling groceries, also provide numerous services that include wire transfers, travel arrangements, and a meeting place to hear the latest news from home, watch television such as wrestling or comedies, or listen to the latest hit songs.

Recipe for Domoda/Maffe (Peanut Butter Stew/Sauce)

Ingredients

1 lb. chicken (can also be prepared with beef, lamb, or beans and vegetables), cubed into bite-size pieces, about half an inch.
1 clove garlic, minced
1 medium onion, chopped fine
Salt, black pepper, and/or cayenne pepper (add more or less depending on your tolerance for hot spices)
2 tbsp lemon juice
Half jar smooth, creamy (medium) peanut butter (*Do not* use crunchy peanut butter)
3–4 large carrot sticks, chopped into 1-inch pieces
1 bag whole okra, frozen
2 medium-size potatoes cut into half-inch cubes
One can tomato paste

Directions

1. Wash chicken (or other main ingredients). In a shallow bowl combine garlic, onion, salt and pepper, and lemon juice; add the chicken and marinate for 15 minutes.

2. Place marinated chicken in a deep cooking pot and fill pot halfway with water.

3. Bring to boil and then add peanut butter. Mix well and cook until mixture begins to thicken.

4. Add potatoes, carrots, and okra. Reduce heat to medium and simmer for another 20 minutes. Then add entire can of tomato paste. Mix well.

5. As the mixture thickens, thin layers of peanut oil will simmer to the top. At this time, you can add more spices to suit taste.

6. Serve on brown or white rice or couscous.

Peanut butter stew/sauce is a popular dish throughout West Africa. And, like its cousin (Jolof rice) it also is enjoyed globally.[1]

TRADITIONAL DRESS

Clothing styles in The Gambia are an amalgam of traditional African, Arab, and Western forms. What one wears, however, is influenced largely by religion, gender, class, age, ethnicity, or a combination of these. Partly because of the shifting social identities and roles that individuals play in society, be it at work, a naming ceremony, or a funeral, Gambians will dress appropriately to fit these specific occasions. Among the professional class and office workers, Western-style clothing would be the attire to wear from Monday through Thursday. On Friday, most Gambian Muslim men wear kaftans or gowns made from the locally produced tie-dye, with a skullcap made from the same material. These gowns typically cover down to the heels or extend a little below the knee to expose baggy trousers made of the same material.

Other young Muslim men may wear imported silky-white kaftans and pants and may or may not wear a skullcap. Older, middle-aged, and sometimes more prosperous middle-class Muslim men may be outfitted with flowing gowns of expensive *mbassen* cloth with elaborate embroidery that makes the tie-dye version seem very plain by comparison. Boys will generally dress like their fathers with sandals or Moroccan moccasins, while the less well-to-do wear plastic sandals or slippers. Muslim men in general who have performed the hajj often dress in expensive silk, muslin, or cotton gowns accompanied by the traditional headdress of a golden rectangular rim resting on a white head scarf. Moroccan moccasins are the preferred footwear for the Friday (*Jumma*) prayer. Well-to-do individuals are also distinguished by their use of expensive cologne for the main Friday prayers at 2 p.m. Dress in this case may also reflect a more somber, albeit colorful, atmosphere. One will also find the occasional person of means who dresses down but, as at Sunday church services in the United States, most are smartly dressed for the occasion. At a naming or wedding ceremony many elders might dress down by wearing less rich cloth or embroidery. Younger men with less means may dress just as they do for *Jumma* prayer. Funerals, on the other hand, are an occasion for the long-sleeved, sometimes collared white kaftans and skullcap. Understandably, clothing at this ceremony is less ostentatious.

Women, depending on their age and class, dress more conservatively, with flowing gowns that cover the entire body down to the heels and sleeves that cover to the wrist along with a head scarf—*tiko* (Mandinka) or *mussor* (Wolof). The *grand' mboba* (flowing gown) does the trick even for middle-aged and younger women, but of late the *kaba*, an oversized gown often worn with a head scarf, is more fashionable for weddings, naming ceremonies, and house parties. The *kaba* is new in name only, however, as it was preceded by the *marineer* and before it the *kamissol*—both similarly oversized gowns worn by middle-aged and pregnant women. At work, most women wear Western clothing and like the men revert to African/Islamic clothing on Fridays. In nightclubs Western clothing is more common. At home, women might wear a T-shirt with a wrapper, perhaps with an exposed head or a *tiko* or *mussor*.

Younger women also wear the *daggit ack mallan*, a wrapper with a tight-fitting blouse, sometimes with a head scarf. The *mallan* (wrapper) is often accompanied by another lighter, sometimes decorative *mallan*, or *becho* (Wolof), especially when the top *mallan* does not have a lining. Urban Senegambian women are renowned for their excellent taste in dress and fashion, blending with seamless ease African, European, and Islamic dress. A growing fashion industry headed by Gambian women has seen many innovative designs suited to all the categories outlined earlier. These designs target a growing international market as well as a local clientele. What one sees displayed at craft markets tends generally to be less well cut and tailored and is mass produced. In The Gambia and in Senegal, it is still the practice that both women and men have their clothes sewn by a favorite tailor, who takes precise measurements and in a few days produces a beautiful and well-fitting dress.

Like many women in other parts of the world, urban Gambian women, especially the young and married middle-aged ones, pay much attention to lingerie, both African and European. In fact, there is a tradition of locally designed lingerie among urban Wolof women that, like lingerie elsewhere, is sexually suggestive. This tradition has now become more common, irrespective of ethnic distinction. Yet there used to be, and still is, special clothing worn by newly wedded women, especially among the Mandinka and Fula. The fabric is often made out of cotton, has a thicker feel, and is often dyed in blue and worn as a mini *grand' mbuba* and wrapper, *fano* (Mandinka) or *wude reh* (Fula).

Brides also wear special clothing following their wedding or shortly beforehand. They are often adorned in similar clothing to that mentioned earlier, along with silver and gold earrings, bangles, and foot bracelets. Young circumcised girls also wear specially made cotton dresses, the lower part resembling a skirt called *kulembeng*. The Fula and Serahule have similar garments as well. In fact, *kulembeng* may very well be a Serahule word, but it has been appropriated by other groups. During extended droughts older women will wear male clothing to mock the gods into showering them with rain. This is clearly a pre-Islamic tradition, which is accompanied by drumming and dancing and much fun and lightheartedness. However, this is a dying practice, seldom seen these days except at staged festivals. Wolof and Fula women are also given to wearing the traditional horn-shaped wigs called *kalla*. This traditional wig often accompanied the practice of gum and lower-lip tattooing during which a nimber of needles are used to induce bleeding in the gums and lower lip—the practice termed *n'jam or timii soo* in Mandinka.

Gambian men also have an assortment of traditional clothing that once was very common but is being eclipsed by more modern clothing. The *dabakurr'to* (Mandinka) *chayya* or *jata* (Wolof) are baggy trousers that fall just below the knee. What is distinctive about the *chayya* is its baggy bottom, which in the hands of a skillful Fula dancer is very entertaining. The more elegant *sabadorr* and *turki*, both kaftans with rich embroidery, were also once very common, and the *jalabia*, a more common and recent addition, is essentially a sleeveless and open kaftan that allows air to flow in and out with ease during the hot summer months and is also used during regular prayers. Today, the more elegant *nyetti-abdou* is more commonly worn by young and middle-aged men. The *nyetti-abdou/morrso* is essentially a three-piece suit with a sleeveless embroidered kaftan worn on top of an oversized shirt that falls below the knee. The pants, while resembling the *chayya* at the waist, are a thin-legged trouser cuffed with more embroidery. The *nyarri morrso* (two-piece suit) is worn by men but more by the young and middle-aged. It is a kaftan that reaches to the heels and has beautiful embroidery and thin-legged trousers as in the *nyetti abdou/morrso*.

Unlike Americans, who have gender-specific colors even at birth, Senegambians, and Gambians in particular, do not have such designations. Color is an individual choice, and men wear pastels and violet. In fact, men often do wear the imported wax, a multicolored cloth that women also wear. These days the wax cloth is worn by all, but more so by the less well-to-do, as it tends to be too colorful for many of higher means, who today prefer the imported or locally produced Malian tie-dye or batik. Growing prosperity and improvement in locally manufactured clothing has resulted in further taste refinement among Gambians, even among the not-so-well-to-do. The once ubiquitous *samba' kuka* or *kassi konnoh*, cheap European imports, are seldom if at all worn these days. Gambia's professional class, like their counterparts elsewhere, wear rich and expensive traditional clothing at important meetings with officials of international institutions or when they travel abroad for conferences. Given the variety in taste, many also wear expensive suits at these functions and gatherings.

A discussion of Gambian dress and clothing styles would be incomplete without a brief discussion of adornments. Locally made and imported jewelry features prominently in the dress of Gambian women, especially the-well-to-do. Ceremonies, especially weddings and outings, are occasions to show off or flaunt them. With more Gambian businesswomen traveling to China, Dubai, India, the United States, and the United Kingdom to purchase goods that they then sell in The Gambia and elsewhere, the choices available to men and especially women have increased tremendously. For the less-well-to-do, domestic innovations in jewelry design, among them leather, means greater access to accessories of good quality at an affordable price. In such instances, a young woman of modest means only requires a few choice or designer jewelry imports. Add to this the new hairdos, the elaborate Nigerian-style head scarves, expensive shoes, and fabric from overseas markets, specifically China. Diaspora Gambians, who for the most part are better off materially than the bulk of Gambians, are regularly targeted by Gambia's women's business class, where higher profits can be earned and reinvested for new purchases from Dubai and China.

It is the laces and synthetic fabrics from these countries that well-to-do women in the Gambia and women in the diaspora now wear. The cost of these fabrics could easily run into hundreds of dollars or more, depending on the kind of outfit one wants. A *grand' mboba* is simply out of the question, except for the very wealthy, because its flowing and oversized quality will take more material to make. Thus, the choice of dress often falls between the *grand' mboba* and a *kaba*—a midsize kaftan and wrapper and a head scarf to match. Imported jewelry and handbags complete the attire. Also, while braids are still in fashion, long, silky hair, wigs, and prefabricated long Rasta hairdos are just as fashionable.

A long-standing dress form among Gambian women who belong to the same social or sometimes religious organization is the *asobi,* or uniform. Women and sometimes men who belong to such organizations will settle on a fabric type and pattern for the *asobi* that is to be worn on a special event or at the Independence Day celebrations. The latter is a colorful mosaic punctuated by music, drumming, and dancing amid long-winded political speeches. Almost all schools in The Gambia require uniforms and add to the color and pomp on national day celebrations. Even Islamic schools require uniforms, with girls covering their heads while donning long dresses.

In sum, both Gambian men and women take pride in how they appear in public and will dress appropriately depending on the occasion and circumstances. Fashions change frequently, perhaps yearly or less often, but the *grand' mboba, kaba,* and kaftans will remain permanent fixtures in Gambian wardrobes for some time to come, changing perhaps only in name. While Gambians and Senegalese are themselves trendsetters (many, but not all tailors are Senegalese), they are also influenced by regional trends from the subregion and globally. American jeans are a favorite among young women and men alike, and so are the T-shirts and Nike and other designer shoes and sneakers. In fact, American fashion has so infiltrated clothing tastes among the young that it may have taken over, except perhaps in formal wedding, naming, and other ceremonies. This has been made possible by the growing availability of secondhand clothing and relatively cheap imports and travel to the United States and Europe by Gambian businesswomen and businessmen.[2]

Also, given the large Gambian diaspora in the United States and Europe, many who visit The Gambia are sure to bring gifts of these choice clothing items even though they are readily sold, perhaps at lower prices, locally. Islamic clothing also continues to influence both young and old, men and women alike. Here too, fashions change, influenced by regional and global trends. Veiling (*ibadu*) is today more common among young Muslim women. This may well be a reflection of a growing religious orthodoxy or fashion, or perhaps both.

Thus, fashion in The Gambia is a dynamic industry that is influenced by local and global trends, travel, television, and the Internet. The baggy jeans nestled on lower posteriors among young men and clothing that is a size or three too large are common. Yet this is not new because this trend was common and fashionable among young Gambian men some 40 years ago—the style was then called *uttal*. Young people everywhere, it seems, dress alike, taking their cue from urban Americans who set the fashions. The choices in clothing and their availability, especially for the young, are unprecedented. Today, like many Africans, Gambians generally and Gambian youth in particular are comfortable in their native African, Islamic, and European dress styles. Chinese imports are also making important inroads into The Gambia and are slowly overwhelming the local tailors, who previously were the main clothing suppliers. The influx of Chinese-made goods is likely to ease access for the poor to these mass-produced goods and is slowly displacing tailors. The well-to-do are, however, likely to hold on to their rich *grand' mboba* and laces. Notwithstanding, fashion, jewelry, and the clothing industry will remain dynamic and will likely remain so into the foreseeable future.

NOTES

1. This is but one version of *domoda/maffe*. You can replace the chicken, dry fish, beef, or lamb with tofu for a vegan or vegetarian dish. Recipe is author's own.

2. Secondhand clothing businesses are very common, especially in the big markets of Banjul, Serrekunda, and Brikama. These clothes come from the United States, the United Kingdom, and Scandinavian countries. There are also secondhand markets for house furniture, cars, and car parts, among many more.

6

Gender Roles, Marriage, and Family

GENDER ROLES, MARRIAGE, and family systems are the building blocks of societies and lend coherence to cultures and communities the world over. The norms that undergird them are often a reflection of a people's religious and social beliefs regarding how different units within a society, such as the family, should interact, rear children, and provide sustenance for its young and old alike. Thus, traditional African belief systems, as well as Islam and Christianity and a changing socioeconomic and global landscape, all affect gender, gender roles, marriage, and family in The Gambia and elsewhere.

The Gambia is a deeply male-dominated society where women, in general, do not enjoy equal social, political, and economic equality. This male-dominated culture is so deeply ingrained that many men and women take their gender-specific roles and expectations as a matter of course, seldom questioning their basis. Because of its insidious character, male domination of social, political, and economic institutions are taken for granted. In fact, women and girls are so heavily socialized into their constructed and subordinated roles that ideas, beliefs, actions, and expressions of self-doubt and denigration, such as "women are like infants," "women should be guided by their husbands because they are not as gifted intellectually," or, from a religious point of view, "women enter paradise by how happy they make their husbands and how well they follow their lead" are frequently expressed.

Family, among Gambians specifically and Africans generally, remains the most important social unit in society. Families trace their origin to the same ancestor or set of ancestors. It is typically the source of one's last name, a marker of a person's social origin and ancestry. Thus, individuals are related by blood, marriage, or adoption. Family also is an important marker for location and residence in a village and affords its members a sense of self-worth and identity. Families provide safety nets and assistance in times of grief, for example, following deaths, and in happier times, during ceremonies, such as welcoming the arrival of a newborn, a wife, or a husband.

Family structure in The Gambia includes the nuclear as well as the extended family, and a compound, a constellation of houses fenced by a wall or some form of demarcation, is typically populated by aunts, uncles, cousins, grandparents, and others who, in fact, may not be related by blood or marriage. This is unlike the Anglo-American nuclear or conjugal family system of Mom, Dad, siblings, and pets. Some relatives are termed fictive. They could include individuals or families who because of many years, perhaps generations, of mutual support and association are elevated to the status of family. Neighbors, for instance, often earn this status. These relationships are further reinforced by the general practice in The Gambia of calling individuals older than oneself by family kinship terms—uncle, aunt, father, mother, brother, or sister. It is, in fact, considered rude for a younger person to call an elder by their first name, except during a light moment with grandparents or elders with whom they have a grandparent-grandchild relationship. Joking relationships, as discussed earlier, allow one to call an elder by their first name. The African American family structure takes on many of the qualities of the African or Gambian family system and structure, and it can, like its African counterpart, be multigenerational. Mutual assistance and sustenance for individual members, including the young and old, are functions that justify the existence of multigenerational residences and compounds. The family, its social organization, and the various roles it members play permeate all Gambia's ethnic groups. Among the Mandinka, in particular, an extended family can be a constellation of compounds called *kabilo* that is located in a particular part of a village or town, most, if not all, of the residents related by blood or marriage and most times bearing the same last name.

The compound constellation is often called *kunda*, which is further defined and specified by a last name—Manneh *Kunda*, Ceesay *Kunda*, Touray or Janneh *Kunda*, as in Kaur, in the Central River region. In fact, the latter have grown to constitute large towns. Disharmony among brothers in the same compound, pressures over agricultural land, the need for greener and more abundant grazing lands, or the quest for independence could lead to a sibling moving out to establish adjacent villages or migrate further afield. This practice is common among all The Gambia's ethnic groups, and more so among the Mandinka and Fula. In fact, the Fula are often teased by the

Serer that every Fula aspires to be a village head, and such ambition has driven many motivated Fulas to found villages of less than a dozen people—called *sarre* (village). The village, in this case, often bears the name of its founder—Sarre-Alpha, for instance. Among rural Wolof, a similar development also occurs, with each village bearing the name of the founder and termed Keur-N'derri, Keur-Masamba, and so forth.

Lineage

Family in The Gambia, unlike in the United States, is often broadly defined, and the larger it is, especially in rural areas, the better, as this can mean more hands to produce abundant cash and subsistence crops—groundnuts and rice, respectively. Family members are related by blood or by marriage and enjoy consanguineous or affilial relationships, respectively. Descent, in general, is traced along the patrilineal line, that is, via male ancestors, to reveal intricate family ties, origins, and relationships between and among current and previous generations. Today, almost all ethnic groups in The Gambia trace their descent on the father's/male line even though in pre-Islamic times, the Wolof, Serer, Fula, and Lebou practiced a matrilineal kinship system. Today, because of high rates of intermarriages across ethnic groups, many Gambians acknowledge or identify with both sides of their ancestry. Yet a child or individual will always bear his/her father's last name, even if conceived out of wedlock. This is so because in a patrilineal system, an individual could only inherit land or other properties from his/her father, whereas in matrilineal systems one inherited property from one's maternal side of the family. While women and girls enjoy inheritance rights, they normally receive a smaller portion, and married women may receive even less. Shari'a law is generally followed closely when it comes to inheritance, with men often receiving double the share of women and girls.

A slight extension of patrilineality/matrilineality is seen in tracing descent from both the grandfather's and grandmother's sides of the family (a bilineal or duolineal system). However, when *jeli* or griot sing songs of praise to his or her patron, they are likely to trace descent from both sides of a person's grandparents, both male and female, even though the grandfather and great-grandfathers enjoy more prominence. Thus, members of a group who can trace their origin to a common ancestor constitute a lineage, and if descent is traced to two ancestors, then they are a clan. Owing to intermarriages and migration among Gambians, the clan, though still maintaining an ancestral *kabilo*, may see some of its members dispersed throughout The Gambia and surrounding countries, with each branch of the clan maintaining close ties through intermarriage and naming, wedding, and funeral ceremonies.

Conversions to Islam and Christianity have together deepened male kinship systems. Yet several social matrilineal practices persist to this day. A very close or special relationship is often known to exist between a male and his sister's children, resulting sometimes in the privileging of nieces and nephews over one's own children. This is changing, however, with growing urbanization, because families may be smaller. Yet relations between first cousins, especially the offspring of two sisters, is special, as both sets of children deem either sister a mother figure. It was also once common for an uncle to marry a niece, or even for first cousins to marry; while this practice still exists, it is dying rapidly. Thus, descent affects one's identity and inheritance, and where one may reside and farm. It can also set one in a caste, rank, and profession in traditional society and can influence the choice of a marriage partner and where one is buried.

MARRIAGE

In large rural Muslim Gambian households or compounds, polygyny, that is, a man marrying more than one wife, commonly termed polygamy, is common. Muslims in The Gambia, as well as in neighboring countries, can marry as many as four wives, with the strict proviso that the husband treat them equally. Invariably, many men fall short of this expectation. The rationale for keeping many wives was that with more children to work on farms, one's wealth and prestige would grow.[1] Not only would men and boys grow the cash crop, but women and girls would focus their labor on rice and vegetable cultivation. Thus, a man's prestige and wealth depended on how large his workforce was as well as his ability to support them. In reality, it is the wives and children who support the husband by their labor, but because these societies are or were deeply patriarchal, the proceeds from such labor went to the husband. Marrying more than one wife in rural Gambia ensured to some degree that each woman potentially stood to have a husband and children. High infant mortality, coupled with childhood diseases and a relatively riskier lifestyle than that of girls, meant that the supply of marriageable men was always less than the number of girls. Bride wealth and gifts to a wife-to-be could involve high monetary costs, which could then delay a couple's plans to establish their own household. Therefore, many young men wait to accumulate enough money or cows, perhaps until they are in their 30s, to marry. Today, marrying more than one wife is seen as a status symbol among urban young and middle-aged men. However, with a shrinking economy and smaller urban dwellings, having more than two wives is difficult to sustain.

Marriage is also a social and economic affair that is contracted between two extended families and the community and involves gift exchanges and goodwill. It used to be that elders or a *jeli/gewel* would begin the marriage proposal process after a young man took a liking to a young woman and expressed his feelings to his father or uncle. Negotiations then began, which ended in marriage at a mosque or church. In Muslim weddings, the bride and groom do not have to be present for the marriage to take place. In fact, it is often the case that they are in their respective homes or different locations, possibly in Europe or the United States, unlike in Christian weddings, where the bride and groom must be present. Once the marriage is concluded and consummated, the new bride moves in with her in-laws or stays at her parents' home until the necessary arrangements are made for her to move in with her husband. The newlywed wife could also be "on loan" to her husband until such time that all the required ceremonies and gifts are given to the bride's family. Thereupon, the last rite of the wedding, *murr* (covering) among the Wolof or *Manyoe bitto* (Mandinka), is undertaken. This involves an elaborate ceremony at the wife's compound during which her head is covered amid singing, advice, and incantations by older women while the wife holds on to a ladle or calabash—symbols of domesticity. Following this, the wife is then transported to her husband's compound or home. It once was common for less-well-to-do grooms to move in with in-laws to perform labor on their farms before moving out with his wife. They may elect to stay in the compound until such time that the husband is able to establish a household of his own. This may require having a farm of his own, engaging in some kind of trade, or moving away to accumulate enough resources to take his wife.

Given that marriage is sometimes elaborate and expensive, divorce is never condoned, as it could result in the wife's family returning gifts that were given earlier to the husband's family. Consequently, families and elders work tirelessly to keep the marriage from breaking, except in instances of excessive abuse or the wife's supposed inability to bear children. In the latter case, a husband may or may not divorce his wife but is at liberty to do so. Instead, many marry another wife. Given The Gambia's male-dominated culture, it is always believed to be the woman's fault, not the man's, if a wife does not conceive and bear children. In more traditional families and rural settings, contracting a marriage was simple and straightforward. A maximum of 10 dollars would be all that was required (*niet' ack transu*) from the groom or his family, along with several pounds of kola nuts. Elopements, though not unheard of, seldom occur.

Christian church weddings are also elaborate among the Aku and can be expensive. These tend to resemble European and American weddings, with a wedding gown, tuxedo or expensive suit for the groom, *asobi* for the bridesmaids, cake, and drinks.[2] A reception often follows, with dancing and food for guests. Among other ethnic groups weddings and gifts can be quite expensive as well, and these are also accompanied by singing, drumming, and dancing. Depending on the social status and professional standing of the groom or bride, more is often expected. A well-to-do groom can shower his wife-to-be with gifts that these days may include a car, home, or parcel of land. Gift giving can increase significantly if a young lady is courted by two suitors. A competition can ensue between the two men, and the suitor who gives the most typically wins. This is seldom heard of these days but may still occur. It once was the case, and still is, to some extent, that a young wife-to-be who is a virgin could receive many more gifts and a bigger bride wealth. In instances like this, the morning after the first night of a honeymoon would reveal whether the new bride was a virgin or not. If she was a virgin, the white bedsheets bearing the evidence would be ostentatiously displayed for all to see. Such an outcome was often greeted with more gifts, dancing, merrymaking, and praise singing. However, as many young women are sexually active before marriage today, this is now a dying practice and expectation.

Arranged marriages also used to be common among all ethnic groups in The Gambia. However, this is also not as common as it once was, especially among the young and educated. Today, young Gambian men and women choose their partners, irrespective of caste or ethnicity. Social status, now based on education and income, have to a great degree eclipsed caste and ethnicity. The closest thing to arranged marriages occurs when families marry off their children to each other as a matter of historical ties and tradition. This too is less the case today. Marriages, irrespective of religion and ethnicity, are freely entered into and occasioned by festivities. It is a time when griots/*gewel* and *jeli* stand to make money and receive expensive gifts. It is also a tradition among all ethnic groups, especially those in urban settings, for friends and relatives to give gifts to the bride or groom's family to assist in what typically is an expensive financial undertaking. Reciprocity is key here, as gift givers at a wedding or naming ceremony will be the recipients of gifts when their own child gets married.

Urban Gambians, especially the educated, are more romantic than their parents' generation and are more likely to express love to one another, kiss, hold hands, go to movies or parties, and engage in premarital sex. Unlike their mothers' or grandmothers' generations, young women today are less dependent on men for their daily existence. They are also less likely to enter into a relationship with a man who has another wife, except if they were once married or have children and hence fewer options. Other women in a similar situation may very well reject such a marriage. Typically, unmarried young women still live at home and there is no pressure for them to move after a certain age. In fact, an unmarried young woman who elects to live on her own will be suspected of illicit sexual activity and is frowned upon, except perhaps in exceptional circumstances, such as when quarters are tight and social conflict is unavoidable with a parent or co-mother (stepmother). Yet even in these cases, a young woman will rent in a compound where she can blend in as a daughter or niece.

As men elsewhere do, Gambian men often partner with younger women, sometimes young wives whom they can potentially control, leaving many older women their age without partners. This is an issue among highly educated, urban, and professional women, who hold important jobs and own beautiful homes but remain single also because of the so-called intimidation factor. Consequently, successful and high-achieving women may unwillingly accept a younger lover or become a second wife to an older man, or they may remain single, hoping to find a suitable partner. Some may enter a long-term liaison with a married man. It goes without saying that many young and middle-aged Gambian men may have girlfriends in addition to their wife or wives. Conquest and machismo, though not peculiar to Gambian men, is alive and well, even if in decline because of the threat of HIV/AIDS. So-called sugar daddies are also common, and young women, especially high school girls, become prey to these men. In sum, Gambian men, in general, are not very different from their counterparts elsewhere.

Wife inheritance, or marriage between a widow and her deceased husband's younger brother, though once very common, are less so today. Older brothers typically do not marry a younger brother's widow. In rural as well as in urban settings, this practice ensured that both the widow and her children were cared for. With growing options for women these days outside the home, many women undergo the mandatory period of mourning and seclusion before entertaining the interests of a suitor. If she is middle-aged with a son or daughter living abroad, she could move into her own place or perhaps a compound built by a brother or sister or one of her children in the urban area. Though HIV/AIDS is not a major problem in The Gambia, as it is in eastern and southern Africa, it may dissuade many Gambians from this practice.

Globalization and urbanization have caused an increase in interracial marriages and liaisons, alongside an illicit sex industry built around tourism. Interracial marriages, which were once looked down upon, have become more acceptable among Gambians. Such marriages could be a lifeline and source of family support from a child who lives abroad. And as economic conditions have worsened in The Gambia, with fewer job prospects for those graduating from university and for high school seniors, there has been growth in sex tourism as well as marriages between young Gambian men and aging European or American women tourists, as well as between older European men and younger Gambian women. There are reports of pedophilia. Unsuspecting parents, often lured by money and promises of school fees being paid for their young children, may unwittingly be casting their young ones into the hands of predatory sex offenders who frequent these shores as tourists. Some have been apprehended and are now serving prison sentences. In efforts to curb prostitution, police routinely conduct raids of women suspects along coastal beach bars and hotels. So-called bumsters, young men who frequent beaches to solicit money or befriend tourists for sex, are also targeted for arrest by the police. The Jammeh government has vigorously prosecuted Europeans accused of such crimes, leading to several Europeans being handed stiff sentences in The Gambia or their country of origin.

BRIDE WEALTH

Bride wealth in traditional African or even contemporary marriages is important. The giving of bride wealth, not dowry, is often misunderstood as the sale of the bride to the groom and his family. Nothing could be further from the truth. Bride wealth is not considered the sale of the bride or compensation for the labor that the bride would have otherwise rendered to her family. Importantly, it not only legitimizes the marriage in the eyes of the community, it also places children from this relationship in a position to inherit property following their father's death. Bridewealth is the seal to a socially contracted agreement between a bride's family and that of the groom, and rather than taking away from the bride's self-esteem and pride, it builds both and places her in a position of respect and sometimes envy among her less-favored peers. The bride wealth, especially when it involves large quantities of money and goods, helps anchor a marriage on a stronger footing because a divorce could result in having to pay it back.[3] This, however, is a double-edged sword, as many women likely remain trapped in marriages they find abusive and unfulfilling. Christian marriages do not often require bride wealth but include the giving of gifts. In instances where a Christian turned Muslim marries a Muslim wife, he too would have to pay bride wealth to the young woman's family.

Marriage ceremonies, especially the time before a wife joins her husband, provides an occasion on which to advise a woman on how to become a good wife, which includes, among other things, obeying her husband, not talking back to him, and pleasing him at all costs. Patience is a virtue emphasized above all else, with respect for in-laws and hard work following closely. How many children a woman bears is often the measure of her success and value. The success of her children is also a measure or reward of exemplary behavior—an embodiment of listening to one's husband. Today, however, many young women and professionals expect a relationship based on relative equality or parity. While bride wealth may be given in these marriages, it is seldom returned when a marriage fails.

Relatives and well-wishers or even strangers can attend and pray for the newlyweds and partake of the food and drink thereafter. Tying or contracting of a marriage at the mosque is preceded by several stages that include the sending of kola nuts as an expression of interest and intent to marry. In instances where cows constitute part of the bride wealth, it often takes careful and protracted negotiations to arrive at the number considered fair by both parties. Greed and covetousness are socially decried, even though some families have been known to marry off their daughters to the man who offers the most bride wealth. In the end, marriage is a sacred and joyful occasion among Senegambians. It brings families together and builds new social, economic, and community relationships. While variations of this ceremony may occur across ethnic groups, these groups share more in common than the differences between them. Islam and Christianity continue to serve as unifying forces. Even among traditional believers, of which there are very few today, marriages perform similar functions.

FAMILY AND GENDER ROLES

In The Gambia, as in many African societies, family is important and is the source of a person's social identity. Whether a couple is monogamous, or, put another way, whether a man is married to only one woman, as is the case in Christian homes, or polygynous, as in Muslim households, men are still the heads of households. Consequently, men in general play a more substantial role in decision making than women on a daily basis. This is not to suggest, however, that women do not exercise power. In fact, in many households women exercise considerable power in decisions at the household (private) and public levels. Decisions by men are often taken with substantial female input, especially in these hard economic times when many women have become de facto heads of households or head families on their own without a husband.

It would be unthinkable for a husband to make decisions affecting his entire family without input from his senior (first) wife—*musu follo* (Mandinka) or *awo* (Wolof)—even when a husband wishes to marry another wife. In fact it is sometimes the senior wife who encourages her husband to marry another wife. This may sound counterintuitive, but it is generally done for strategic reasons. In large compounds gender-specific roles for women and girls include cooking, cleaning, fetching water, laundry, and child car, as well as rice and vegetable garden cultivation. These tasks could easily overwhelm a wife or two wives, and a third or fourth wife could provide additional hands to meet

Large ferries transport passengers, cars, trucks, and animals daily from Banjul to Barra, crossing the Atlantic, and smaller ferries do the same for major towns and trading posts lying on both sides of the river. (© Susan Robinson | Dreamstime.com)

this growing workload and potentially ease a senior wife's workload considerably. First wives who have not given their husbands a child or son may also encourage the husband to take another wife. Yet in some instances, a senior wife will resist any additional wives, but in the end, it is a man's prerogative to take a second or third wife. The practice is dying out slowly in urban areas where living quarters are rather restricted and the cost of living is high.

Many Americans and Europeans find such an arrangement amusing and too often focus on sexual matters and, importantly, whether the wives get along. While sex is an important part of a polygynous household, and sometimes the reason for tension between a husband and his wives, the division of labor and the economic considerations appear to be just as important. However, love and sex are never absent in a man's considerations for an additional wife, as the institution persists even when there is no need to have additional hands to help cultivate larger tracks of land, at least not in urban areas where polygyny is common. However, a husband who has several wives is careful to keep a strict schedule of visits to each wife in her house within the compound or in another compound, town, or village. In the best of circumstances, generally the wives get along and share their daily tasks of cooking, cleaning, and the like on a two- or two-day rotational basis. Child care is then shared or performed individually, and in some households children grow up cared for by their biological mother, sisters, or co-mothers. Consequently, in general children grow up feeling loved and attached to their co-mothers well into adulthood and sometimes for life. In such instances, co-mothers, unlike biological mothers, tend to be more doting and are less strict and more likely to spoil their co-wife's children. In fact, in instances where a co-wife does not have biological children of her own, a husband may assign her the full responsibility of rearing a co-wife's child as her own. This, it must be emphasized, is in the best of circumstances and points to the heavy emphasis on harmony and pressures placed on women to bear many children, especially boys. This is also the case for men because a man's worth, his so-called manhood, is measured in general by how many children he has. In other instances, competition between and among co-wives, though muted, is always present, as distinctions are made between children who are sometimes pitted against one another to do better than their half-siblings.

In the households described previously, conflicts do invariably occur. In such instances, the husband and elders in the compound, and sometimes neighbors, step in to address the causes and concerns of the parties in conflict. Jealousy or violence may also occur at times between co-wives over their respective children, and over what a co-wife may perceive as preferential treatment by the husband of another wife. This often calls for immediate resolution by elders. Elders, including grandparents, mothers, and fathers in the compound, play important roles in seeking to keep things under control. While an older son will invariably assume the role of household head, his parents still exercise considerable influence and power in the daily affairs of the compound. Yet in a male-dominated society like The Gambia's, a woman who is perceived as difficult and not able to get along may be divorced and replaced by a more compliant wife. However, women are not without recourse, especially over a routinely abusive husband. A woman in such circumstances will often return to her father's compound to protest her husband's abuse (*fai* in Wolof or "a borr' ta le," (Mandinka)). It will take several weeks or even months before she finally returns, but not until generous inducements of new clothing and/or money have been offered and promises made to end the abuse. It is fathers, more so than mothers, who are unsympathetic to the concerns of their daughters who have decided temporarily to leave a husband's home. This may be due to the father's unwillingness to return the bride wealth should his daughter's abandonment of her marital home end in divorce. Impotent husbands, or husbands who keep been away for years without communicating or providing material support for a wife, are reasons for a wife to seek a divorce. When a wife leaves her husband for another man, the bride wealth is supposed to be returned to the husband; sometimes it is, sometimes not.

As noted earlier, a household includes not only the mother, father, and children but uncles, aunts, grandparents, nephews, and nieces as well. Thus, compounds are full of activity, with child care typically shared by parents and grandmothers. Roles are well defined by gender and age, and there is often a sense of mutual obligation to one another—call it family corporate responsibility. Harmony rather than conflict is also emphasized, and in general, common enterprises such as fishing, farming, or long-distance trade, as well as a common religion, are the ties that bind family members. Children generally grow up feeling secure in the love of their parents and relatives. The old adage that "it takes a village to raise a child" remains true to this day, especially in the rural areas. In urban areas, this is also true but to a lesser extent. Grandparents, as elsewhere, are only too eager to spoil their grandchildren. For grandparents, grandkids are always a source of pride and a sign of having arrived. It wins them new and increased social status in the community.

While grandparents have often retired from grueling labor on groundnut or rice farms, grandmothers, in particular, are active in child rearing and child care. As a result, children build strong relationships with their grandmothers and grandfathers. Grandmothers also may serve as traditional midwives and nurses to ensure that daughters-in-law seek the right protections from those who have the "evil eye," drink herbs during and after pregnancy, and learn how to care for their newborn child. Following the birth of a young woman's first child, grandmothers serve as coaches to the young mother. The new mother will refrain, generally, from sexual activity with her husband—a method of birth control until her child is weaned. This period could last up to a year or longer. Sexual abstinence by men for periods lasting many months to a year has been a justification for many men to marry a second wife. Nowadays, however, young mothers in urban settings are unlikely to abstain from sexual activity for long periods because of the growing availability of modern birth control devices.

Fathers in Gambian society serve, along with their own fathers, now often retired from arduous physical labor, as coadministrators of the compound. A son who heads a household generally consults with his father on the day-to-day running of the compound, and if his father is deceased, his mother plays this role. Fathers in rural settings also train their children to become good farmers and hunters and to perform so-called manly tasks such as clearing farmland in preparation for the planting, harvesting, and sale of the groundnut crop. As his parents age, the son takes care of them and sees to their comfort and well-being, as he does also for the rest of the household, including his wives, children, younger siblings, and their wives. The father, along with his brothers in the compound, will initiate or deliver marriage proposals of their sons and likewise receive them on behalf of their daughters. Discipline is generally the purview of fathers, mothers, elders, and older siblings. Fathers also have the sacred responsibility to have their boy initiated or circumcised in the "bush," where they learn traditional lore, survival techniques, songs, signs, and symbols of communication (*passin* in Wolof). It is here, too, that new initiates learn to sing songs of old that are related to male circumcision. These are sung at the *kassak,* a ceremony marking the end of the boys' training.

Mothers in Gambian society generally take on the brunt of household duties, as mentioned earlier, and child rearing as well. Mothers focus on their daughters more, to bring them up as hardworking, respectful young women who will behave well in the future. In rural areas, where the average age for marriage is 14 for girls, there is considerably more pressure for these young women to bear children, causing potential long-term negative medical complications and consequences. This is changing, however, especially in the urban areas, where the average marriage age can be in the early 20s or higher.

In the case of young urban women, school attendance, starting in a new profession or job, and ambitions for further education abroad may delay marriage even further. Educated urban mothers are more likely to encourage their daughters to go further in life, but there is a point at which they begin to worry if the daughters remain single. Then the pressure is on them from all angles to marry and have children—many children. However, the pressure to have more children seems to be declining among young urban women, partly because of hard economic times and partly because of the desire of many young women to have smaller families. In the rural areas, on the other hand, the situation is the reverse, even though there is growing realization by mothers and young women about the dangers of early marriages and female circumcision, a controversial cultural practice that is opposed by a growing number of nongovernmental organizations such as The Gambia Committee on Traditional Practices Affecting the Health of Women and Children (GAMCOTRAP). Before this, it was the mother's responsibility to prepare her daughters for this rite of passage, which, thanks to the works of many organizations, is on the decline. The more common practice in rural areas is the ritual without the cutting of female genital parts.

Sons are raised to look up to their fathers and male relatives in the compound. From an early age boys are socialized to be hardworking and brave, to bear pain and hardship. By the time they are eight or nine, if not earlier, they are taught to be engaged in sports, such as soccer or wrestling, and to live at least for somet time an almost carefree existence. As teenagers, boys are encouraged gradually to let go of their once-close ties to their biological mother or co-mother and are encouraged to have interest in the opposite sex. One important role that grandparents in particular play is the socialization of their grandchildren along sex and gender lines. Grandmothers become pretend "wives" of their young grandsons and grandfathers become pretend "husbands" of their granddaughters. These couplings further help define and reinforce gender roles, and grandparents will likely call their grandchildren "my husband" or "my wife, with each party playing their roles, albeit in a lighthearted fashion. The message is not lost on the grandchildren, however, as to how a man or woman is expected to behave, especially after marriage. Where there are no grandparents, older men or women in the village or close relatives will take on these roles. Experimenting young men and women will now try to play out these roles with one another.

Formerly, in pre-Islamic matrilineal homes, maternal uncles often rivaled fathers in their roles and responsibility for nieces and nephews. In that era, nephews and to some degree nieces could inherit from their maternal uncles. Uncles could in turn arrange marriages for their nephews and receive gifts from a niece's suitor and preside over negotiations for the bride wealth. Today, in a mostly Islamized society, fathers play this role, sometimes in collaboration with maternal uncles. To this day, maternal uncles continue to play important roles in the lives of their nieces and nephews, especially regarding education and choice of marriage partners. Paternal uncles play roles similar to those of fathers. These uncles too can help in marriage negotiations and stand in place of a deceased brother as a father and, if younger, can marry his deceased brother's widow.

Maternal uncles also are often doting, especially with nieces. A niece could in the future be the source of gifts to him after marriage—thus the term jarr-batt (Wolof) or mb'aring'ndingo (Mandinka), suggesting that someday her voice and positive response to a marriage proposal could earn him some presents for himself. Aunts, like uncles, play a similar role to that of mothers in preparing their nieces, especially for marriage. They may also be expected to assume the sole role of mother, raising a niece even when both parents are alive, but especially after a parent dies. Paternal aunts, bajen or mb'aringba (Mandinka), can raise nieces and prepare them for womanhood. A paternal aunt enjoys considerable power over children because of her relationship to their father, and especially if she is an older sister. She too plays an important role in the compound, whether she is resident in it or not. During naming ceremonies and weddings paternal aunts feature prominently in the activities and dole out gifts and money to the gewel.

Gender roles in The Gambia, as in Senegal and much of Senegambia Major, are shaped by Islam and Shari'a, specifically. The cadi is responsible for adjudicating matters that pertain to inheritance, divorce, marriage, and sexual rights or frequency in times when there is a conflict over this issue. *Cadi* base their decisions on rules and traditions based on the Qur'an and Haddith. Gender roles overlap considerably with those of Islam, and both constructed roles reinforce male supremacy and domination. Therefore, domination over women and girls by men gets its justification from both the Qur'an and customs.

Clearly, while there is a feminist movement as well as a growing presence of women in government, women continue to face many cultural challenges daily and have taken very small steps to enhance their status. Women seldom speak in public gatherings and typically remain in the back at such functions. Village *bantaba* or *datte*, meeting places for men, usually a platform under a shady tree, remain a preserve of men who meet there to talk about everything of interest. Girls also receive, on average, fewer years of primary, high school, and university education, which then reinforces the gender gap. Women, by contrast, have their own spheres of influence that include clubs and societies (*compin*s in Wolof and *kafolu* in Mandinka) that women run. Women may also own vegetable gardens and support one another during times of harvest and cultivation. Many women, as noted earlier, control money derived from these farms. Women in many communities in The Gambia also have their own so-called credit associations, *asusu*, from which they collect money every so often. It is useful to mention that in the past Mandinka women (such as Fenda Lawerence of Kaur) could own land (rice fields), and some had slaves they inherited, bought, or that were given to them as part of their bride wealth. These situations give women space within which to exercise authority without men. Men in general keep away from these organizations. Women also support one another during bereavement, pregnancy, and moments of joy. Many own businesses and also travel widely. Thus women in The Gambia are not passive onlookers to developments in the country.

Yet long hours for expectant mothers working in rice fields and vegetable gardens for extended hours, often without adequate nutrition, and limited pre- and postnatal care leave infants vulnerable to childhood diseases. While there are many more hospitals and clinics in The Gambia today than there were some 20 years ago, death rates per 1,000 births remain alarmingly high. There is also a lack of drugs to treat the most basic of childhood diseases. While vaccination for children has improved some, dehydration, dysentery, whooping cough, and other childhood diseases, as well as malaria, remain continuing challenges. In sum, The Gambia is ranked very low in the Human Development Index, a United Nations measure of well-being in countries throughout the world.[4] While The Gambia's ranking has inched a couple of notches upward, these childhood afflictions continue to claim many lives annually.

Female circumcision is yet another traditional practice that can potentially have negative physical and medical consequences.[5] Girls as young as five are circumcised, meaning that their clitorises are excised, which sometimes results in profuse bleeding, infections, and even death. A rite of passage, young girls are lured into the "bush," where they undergo cutting under conditions that are less than sanitary with instruments that are not sanitized after each use. This further exposes young girls to potentially more harmful infections and complications. Many remain in shock following cutting and some do not recover from it emotionally. Following the cutting, young girls' wounds receive minimal care, and those who survive the experience are treated to a ceremony where they are showered with gifts and delicious meals.

Some conservative Gambians, including Muslim clerics and the women who perform excision on girls, are supportive of the practice and justify it along lines of cleanliness and curbing female sexual appetites. Some argue that it keeps women chaste and is good training for girls who are destined for childbirth—a more painful ordeal. Many argue that rather than curbing sexual appetite in girls and women, it blunts it totally. Yet without it, a woman is considered a child, uninitiated (*solima* in Mandinka, *solijo* in Hallpullar), regardless of how old she may be. Being called a *solijo* among the Fula is perhaps the worst insult one could possibly inflict on a woman. It used to be the case that a *solima*'s marriage prospects were significantly lower for having failed to undergo cutting. Thus, women who went through the process were welcomed into a sorority, as the ritual bestows initiates with a sense of pride and self-confidence, qualities unattainable to the uninitiated.

Fuambai Ahmadu, a scholar at the University of Chicago who has gone through female circumcision herself, is critical of Western feminists whose aversion to the practice, she believes, rests on their assumptions of Western femininity and sexuality. Isatou Touray, a Gambian scholar and activist and founder of GAMCOTRAP, is one who is opposed to the practice in The Gambia and elsewhere and has worked along with Amie Bojang Sissoho and like-minded women and men to end the practice in The Gambia. Many women and men who support the rights of women see it as a flagrant violation of human rights, and girls' rights in particular. Many young women who fled their countries out of fear that they would be forcibly circumcised have sought and been granted asylum in the United States and in several other countries in Europe.

In some African countries, like Kenya and Senegal, the practice has been banned through legislation, but many argue that banning rather than stopping the practice may in fact promote it. Some cite evidence from colonial Kenya, where after colonial authorities banned the practice, rural girls fled to the "bush" to be circumcised or circumcise themselves in defiance of colonial laws.[6] Others believe that medicalization of the procedure under sanitary hospital conditions could be the way to eradication. Others advocate education and medicalization instead. Still others maintain that the practice will be eradicated only when women and young girls are empowered enough to gain access to opportunities that they are otherwise denied.

Not all ethnic groups in The Gambia practice female circumcision. Neither rural nor urban Wolof practice it, and the practice is believed to have diffused culturally from Asia, possibly the Middle East. Alternatively, it may have developed independently within the Senegambia region itself. Others argue that it predates Islam and may represent one of those traditions that have continued in spite of its potential negative effects. Some scholars contend that because it has existed this long, it indicates human adaptation to the practice. This will not be the last word on this controversial practice, and it is likely to fuel further debate in The Gambia and elsewhere for many years to come.

Isatou Touray and Sylvia Chant have together and individually written specifically on this topic in The Gambia, as well as other important issues relating to women and girls. Betina Shell-Duncan and Ylva Hernlund in 2000 edited a book titled *Female Circumcision in Africa: Culture, Controversy and Change*, and Ahmadu's chapter in this volume in particular is a must-read for those interested in an alternative view on this controversial subject. Many Gambian men, especially those in the diaspora, oppose female circumcision.

VIOLENCE AGAINST WOMEN (WIFE BEATING)

In the United States and in Europe, where laws against girlfriend and spousal abuse are stringent, there have been reported cases of wife beating/battery in the homes of Gambians in the diaspora.[7] This practice is normalized and pervasive, though not unique to The Gambia. It is a universal phenomenon, and in spite of the many human rights instruments of which African states and The Gambia, specifically, are signatories, the practice of wife beating in The Gambia, and in Gambian households in Europe and the United States, has reached epidemic proportions. While there are many Gambian and non-Gambian men who do not physically or emotionally abuse their wives, these men go against the grain. Why do men, generally, and Gambian men, specifically, batter their spouses? Why is wife beating so entrenched in Gambian and other cultures? In The Gambia, as in other countries, wife beating involves the physical abuse/battery and attack on wives by husbands, boyfriends, or relatives of the husband or even the abused wife's for perceived transgressions. As such, women and girls often suffer serious physical injury as well as psychological scars, which remain long after the physical injuries have healed.

For many men in The Gambia and elsewhere, wife battery is a proof of one's manhood, a testimony to male power and control over women and girls. It earns many Gambian men bragging rights and is a practice that is often admired and emulated. Cruelty toward women and girls by men is pervasive and culturally sanctioned universally, and The Gambia is no exception. It is most often justified by the belief or rationale that women, even mature women, are children or childlike and need discipline periodically to keep them in line. Consequently, many women and young girls in The Gambia are socialized into accepting a subordinate status, which male domination, a universal phenomenon, has sought to perpetuate. In turn, many women accept this construction, while at the same time just as many resist it by hitting back, seeking redress in traditional courts, or divorcing their abusive husbands.

Some Gambian men, particularly among the so-called enlightened in the diaspora (and in The Gambia), batter their wives often and typically bark orders to be served meals and provided other services as if the women were maids. Along with these obligations, wives try to anticipate and meet every need their abusive husbands may have, while stroking their egos. When it comes to helping around the house and with the kids, many Gambian men still hold onto age-old traditions of long-dead ancestors—that when it comes to raising, feeding, and dressing the kids, cleaning, and cooking, it is a woman's job. Again, this is not unique to Gambian men. Often, women perform these tasks while holding down a full-time job and paying bills. A wife's perceived poor performance in the domestic realm and in the bedroom is often justification for verbal abuse, battery, or threats of taking a second wife.

The problem is often more acute in The Gambia, where women, especially poor and rural women, work from dawn to dusk and still are expected to provide dinner and sex when men return home from work or other ventures. However, such abuse is not limited to rural and poor women. Professional women also suffer indignities—emotional and sometimes physical abuse for not bowing to a husband's demands, or their perceived failure to stroke fragile male egos. And human rights instruments and national laws offer little to no protection or recourse to wives and women who suffer such abuse from husbands and other males, including relatives. Add to this the numerous unreported cases of rape, sexual harassment, and sexual imposition, sometimes committed with impunity by men in positions of authority against women professionals. Many young girls are sent into prostitution by family members, or family members look the other way as young girls engage in (sex tourism) prostitution to support aging parents.

Gambian culture in general perceives women and girls as commodities that are traded or bargained for by their families, trained for the marriage industry

Supreme Court building on Independence Drive, Banjul. (Courtesy of Buharry Gassama)

(*rang'be*, line of unmarried women) and groomed to fetch high monetary returns and become good wives. Being a good wife means bearing male children, being submissive, pleasing husbands to the extent of tolerating verbal and physical abuse, cooking well, and looking good.

Also, many diaspora Gambian men remain clueless when it comes to the construction of gendered roles and practices and their consequences. Diaspora Gambian women and those at home, including professionals, have now begun to question the gendered roles into which they were born and socialized. Both men and women, especially in online Gambian newspapers like *Maafanta*, are addressing self-esteem issues, such as why many Gambian women continue to use skin-bleaching products to feel attractive, and why many men similarly prefer bleached light-skinned women over their darker-hued sisters.

Frequently, prejudice and violence against women and girls are sanctioned or justified along lines of religion in The Gambia as well as in the diaspora. Many *Dairra* (Islamic religious associations) rigidly replicate societal gender roles and divisions, with men dominating the key leadership positions women generally reduced to domestic roles and concerns. Clearly, many of these *Dairra* are driven not by a desire to promote women's rights and equality, despite their religious pronouncements, but rather by a desire to control and keep women in their place.

Men in these religious clubs are likely to defend themselves against accusations of sexism or bias against women by evoking their admiration for Prophet Muhammad's first wife, Khadijah, who was reputed to be an independent and wealthy entrepreneur and a model for modern-day Muslim women. With this, many feel they are absolved. The truth is that many of these men use religion, and the Qur'an, as discussed earlier, to justify power and gender inequality in society and when the occasion favors or suits them. They are also more prone to batter their wives, support female circumcision, and ostracize all who dare oppose them and these practices. Many Imams, including Abdoulie Fatty, have frequently labeled efforts to empower women as ruinous to society. He issues threats and spews invectives against women who dare to stand up to him and his ilk.

Take, for instance, the current homophobic environment that pervades in countries like Malawi, Zimbabwe, and The Gambia, where homosexuality is being described as unnatural, un-African, and a Western invention foisted on Africans. The situation is exacerbated by President Jammeh's homophobic views. He believes homosexuality is Western in origin and has promised to kill (cut off the heads of) gays if they are ever found out. These attitudes, like those toward wife beating, are rooted in the same socioreligious and cultural practices that violate and subordinate women and girls and justify wife beating. They are driven by fear of difference and, more importantly, by a desire to control and define what sexual acts are considered normal and natural. President Jammeh's diatribe against gays drew much international criticism because of the punishments that were attached. This is another instance in which Jammeh's views on social issues coincide with the strident position of the Islamic Council's, and they then become the basis on which state policy is built to criminalize the "other."

THE COLONIAL IMPACT

Female Africanist scholars, in particular, have long argued that colonialism had an overwhelmingly negative impact on gender relations in African societies. Not only did colonialism restructure traditional political and economic institutions and bring them under colonial control, it also reconfigured gender relations to give men more power and influence in society. A growing body of historical literature, however, argues exactly the opposite, namely, that colonial rule empowered women in a number of different ways and helped them challenge male structures of domination. Luise White's *Comforts of Home* shows how women in colonial Kenya were able to acquire wealth, become landlords, and even pay the bride price for their siblings back in the village. The works of Richard Roberts and Kristin Mann, among others, show how the invention of African customary law gave women access to the courts, where they could challenge abusive husbands, lay claim to landed property, or seek divorce.[8]

Scholars who contend otherwise suggest that armed with Victorian values, colonialists and missionaries before them, through tradition and policy, privileged African men over women. Before this, women and men in Africa generally enjoyed relative equality—women cultivating crops for their sustenance on land they owned or that was communally controlled. Men cleared the fields for planting and labored together with women to meet their daily needs and bartered or exchanged whatever was left after saving seedlings for the following year's crop. This soon ended with the introduction of cash crops—groundnuts, cocoa, coffee, and other crops for export to support European industrial and consumer needs. Colonial policy, especially the hut tax, reinforced further the divide between men and women.[9] This, in addition to Victorian values of the day, slowly relegated subsistence agriculture to women while men focused on the production of cash crops, from which they now had to pay taxes.

At a beach in a coastal fishing village, a woman and her child enjoy the calm surroundings and watch a beautiful sunset on the horizon, just as the sun's rays are reflecting on the ocean. (© Ferdinandreus | Dreamstime.com)

With the support it received in the form of credit, fertilizer, roads, training, and subsidies, cash crop agriculture quickly overtook subsistence agriculture, and in time valuable and fertile land were reserved for cash crop production. This gave men higher incomes relative to women, and in time income and wealth inequality began to take root. The gradual segmentation of labor along gender lines also meant that the private household and nonpublic functions became the purview of women. By contrast, men's roles were elevated and rewarded in the public sphere and in time, through education and favorable colonial policy, became dominant. While this critique is generally accurate, it fails to recognize the spheres in which women exercised power and control.

Nonetheless, it is generally agreed that colonial policy sought to reproduce family and gender relations similar to those in Europe. Even after independence in the 1960s, men's roles became more dominant, and increasingly so with Western developmental and lending policies. The development enterprise for a long time remained a male preserve, and women did not feature into development policy until the 1980s. In southern Africa, where mining was prevalent, especially in South Africa and Zambia, men migrated to the cities and mines and left the women, children, and elderly to fend for themselves. Through seasonal employment in the mines they became increasingly enmeshed in the global economy through wage labor, while food production dwindled for lack of labor and government support. Hunger and famines became notoriously common, but African-run governments could or would not alter the patterns of trade in favor of Africans or the distribution and redirection of resources in support of cash and food production. In time women were displaced and kept at home to service the men, who worked to generate higher crop yields for export.

Only since the 1980s have governments in Africa under programs supported by the International Monetary Fund (IMF) and the World Bank begun to address women in the development process. It became increasingly apparent that African countries could not make significant development strides unless women were part of the development agenda—not as an afterthought but as integral players. Since then, no development program was approved unless it included a women's component assessing potential impact, cost, and benefits. Financial institutions and universities then began to institute studies in women in development (WID) to sensitize their graduates to the centrality of women in the development process. Some gains have been made in the empowerment of women since, and feminist movements in Africa generally and The Gambia specifically are stoking the fires for greater equity.

Two women and boy walking home after a day's work in a rice-field is a common scene in rural Gambia, where transport services, though improved, may cost a few dalasi. (© Susan Robinson | Dreamstime.com)

In the end, most countries established women's bureaus or ministries for women's affairs, and increasingly African women were included in policy think tanks or headed important ministries to improve the lives of women and girls. It would be easy to blame gender inequity completely on Victorian values and colonial policies, but that would be both unfair and inaccurate. Clearly, as our earlier discussion shows, Islam, as well as African traditional values, had long conspired to keep women subordinated. Which values or combinations had the most decisive effect is open to debate. Some scholars argue that colonialism and neocolonialism remain the major contributors and are today aided by the current-day neoimperialism of the IMF and World Bank. Others look to African ruling elites for the causes of current African underdevelopment and by extension women's as well. Yet the fact remains that while many women have made significant strides, and enrollment of girls in elementary schools is rising, women and girls continue to suffer both institutional and tradition-based gender discrimination. Educating boys over girls remains a cost-benefit decision, especially in rural areas. This phenomenon is changing, however, partly because of external funding to support education for girls, making education almost free at the elementary level in The Gambia.

Socialization

Socialization in The Gambia remains an important vehicle by which values and mores are passed from one generation to another. Young girls from an early age are expected to help their mothers with child care, cooking, and laundry and to emulate good behavior. Respect for elders, and deference to male elders in particular, reinforce male supremacy in society. Domesticity and catering to men are learned at an early age. Gender bias is further reinforced by Islam and Christianity, which, while professing equality for all, explicitly privilege men over women. The two combined make life difficult for young girls and women. Boys, similarly, look up to their fathers and uncles on how to become men. At an early age, they are taught to perform tasks that are considered masculine—hunting, farming, collecting firewood, and activities that mold them to exhibit bravery and endurance.

As noted earlier, life is generally more carefree for boys than for girls in Gambian society, and almost all boys, especially among the urban Wolof, go through a period of being a *ndongo* (literally means student, but in this case defines a carefree period in a boy's life around the teenage years to early adulthood—about age 20, perhaps older in some cases). Many boys never graduate from this developmental stage. *Kambaniya* among the Mandinka encourages similar traits in men at this age. It is a time to experiment, learn how to fight, flirt, smoke cigarettes or marijuana, and have girlfriends. *Ndongos* and *kambanos* are encouraged to be outgoing and sometimes defiant of adult authority, especially that of their father. Girls may have room to experiment and socialize with boys before marriage. They learn how to flirt and to hold their own with boys but must avoid pregnancy at all cost, as that would bring shame to the family and significantly reduce the bride wealth a suitor may potentially offer. The double-standard message to girls is clear.

Children are all socialized to take care of their parents in old age—they serve as security nets for parents who become too old to fend for themselves. Children grow up seeing their parents take care of their own parents, and they grow up with a similar expectation. Older siblings are also socialized to help bring up and take care of younger ones. Thus, the firstborn (*dingfollo*, Mandinka, *taw,* Wolof), especially when they are male, steps in for his parents when they no longer can support their kids or when they no longer are alive. Thus, in large compounds, especially in the rural areas, a man's worth is measured by how well he provides for his immediate and extended families.

Naming ceremonies, weddings, and funerals are also occasions to send subtle messages of socialization to both young boys and girls, each emulating the same-sex parent. Naming and wedding ceremonies are times to

Bijilo village is a rural setting that captures the changing architecture from grass-thatched huts to houses make of cement bricks. (© Susan Robinson | Dreamstime.com)

demonstrate generosity, especially to the griot, a time to flaunt what wealth one has, even to the extent of incurring heavy debt. This is more common among urban Wolof, who often empty their wardrobes as they lavish expensive gifts and jewelry following songs of praise in which names of ancestors are recited and deeds of bravery recounted for generations. This too is a common practice among other urban ethnic groups in The Gambia, except the older generation of Aku. Funerals were once more austere but have in recent times become expensive. A funeral, especially during the 40 days and nights following a relative's death, is now used as an occasion to flaunt one's wealth. This is demonstrated by the amount and quality of food and drink served and the dignitaries who attend.

In more traditional settings, socialization also took place along age sets or age groups, as they are commonly termed in The Gambia. These are social organizations based on sex, that is, boys and girls who were born within a few years of each other or who may have "entered the bush" or been circumcised (*llel* in Wolof, *kassai'o* or *kuun'yao* in Mandinka) the same year. These age sets or age groups go through a common socialization process in which they are secluded and taught the lore and values of their specific ethnic group—signs and symbols for communication unintelligible to the uninitiated. This rite of passage includes rituals and ceremonies, following which the new initiates assume adult responsibilities or try to act as if they do.

Often, these new graduates grow to be very close, and as they mature, marry, and have children they maintain symbiotic and mutually satisfying social and sometimes economic relationships. They look to each other in times of need, name sons and daughters after one another, and are part of a self-help organization (*kafo* in Mandinka, *mbotai* in Wolof). These social organizations, for both males and females, are places where leadership roles are learned. Through elections, a president, a treasurer, and other officers are chosen. Some may assume villagewide roles as policemen, health inspectors, or judges and may impose a fine on a guilty party over a dispute; this is in preparation for their future roles as village elders. Women too have their own organizations in which roles and responsibilities, just as with the men, are assigned. In time, they will assume the roles and responsibilities in society that their age and gender demands. Domestic work often defines women's work at the village level.

As young people have left their villages in search of fame and fortune in the urban centers, these social organizations have slowly weakened, even though many do return home during religious holidays and for naming and wedding ceremonies. However, as they take to the lifestyles of the city and marry sophisticated urban wives—or at least that is the perception of the villagers left behind—their outlook changes. Yet many individuals from the same village and sometimes ethnic group may still form village-based organizations, just as they did in the village, to support newcomers to the urban centers in which they are now located and in time replicate a similar self-help organization.

Members of organizations may at times support development projects in their ancestral villages or host relatives who visit the city along with high school students who may not have kin in the city. While in the city, the newly arrived from the village bring their hosts a hen, several pounds of newly harvested rice, and other provisions to ease the financial burden that hosts are likely to incur. These village-based organizations are also increasing in the diaspora. Thus, while the link between relatives in the village and city may weaken to some extent, it is never completely severed. In fact, some in the city who are seasonally employed may on occasion return to their villages to cultivate a groundnut farm and return to the city after the harvest. Others, now accustomed to city life and no longer suited to long hours of backbreaking labor on farms, remain in the city, performing odd jobs to get by while sending, when they can, little gifts, including money and food supplies to aging parents.

In recent years, however, urban Gambian society has become more extravagant and showy and less given to moderation, a quality that defined social relations some 30 years ago. This trait may very well be old and enduring. Changes in social class status, higher incomes or remittances, and sometimes corruption have enabled many people to live comfortably amid deepening poverty. This new social class has in many respects trumped traditional social stratification and caste and owes its wealth to state jobs, the private sector, or control over state resources. Children therefore grow up assimilating these values and as adults try to live up to parental and societal expectations. Doing well, or the appearance of doing well financially, is highly valued. This may have unsavory consequences, such as living beyond one's means and indebtedness. Those who suffer these consequences are often said to be living a false life, especially when they seem to be able to afford expensive clothes and date the most sought-after young ladies. In sum, Gambian society, though always materialistic, to some degree has become more so due to growing affluence in some circles.

Modern education and globalization have slowly eclipsed many social organizations, even if they remain in some modified form today. Age sets are today replaced by social professional organizations; sporting clubs; and *attaya* (green tea) *vous*—that is, loosely organized tea clubs, some constituted by professionals but for the most part by unemployed youth. Gender-based organizations are today more common, and so are religious organizations among Muslims called *Dairra*, often led by men. Some female organizations serve only a social and financial function and may maintain the *osusu*—a pyramid scheme into which members contribute a set sum of money each week that is then allocated to one person. This is then repeated until each member collects. This practice has given some women degrees of independence and solidarity.

SOCIAL CHANGE

The collectivist ethos that once was prevalent in Gambian and other African societies has been eroded somewhat by education, rural to urban migration, and shifts in the national and global economies. While large compounds with a mix of cousins, uncles, grandparents, and parents still remain in all urban centers, families are becoming increasingly nucleated, especially among the well-to-do, who often are better educated and higher income earners. The collective ethos that was once emphasized primarily for purposes of survival under harsh economic conditions is now replaced by government safety nets such as pensions for some government workers. Thus, ethnic groups, clans, or families that would otherwise have pooled their resources in order to survive a famine years ago now rely not on their extended family, but on immediate nuclear family members. Despite these changes, however, many roles and family obligations persist. A civil servant with a nuclear family will still be expected to support aging parents, pay the school fees of a niece or nephew, and give occasional cash gifts to an aunt or aging uncle or other extended family members. Increasingly, these roles and family expectations have fallen on the shoulders of diaspora Gambians, who juggle resources to help support their nuclear families in their host countries alongside aging parents in the mother country.

Employment for women, though still of low and unskilled status compared to men, enables many women to engage in moneymaking endeavors to help support their families. Highly skilled professional women who enjoy higher salaries tend to marry men of similar socioeconomic status and are therefore more likely to move out into the new urban settlements, such Kerr Serign, Kotu, and Bursubi, with their children. Even in this context, the family is still likely to be extended, albeit modified in that a niece or another relative may still reside within the family home. Thus, the increase in nuclear families or modified versions of this institution exist side-by-side with the extended family, and as newly married couples opt to establish their own household the extended family and its traditional role of providing security for its members also weakens. The growing emancipation of educated urban women and the passage by the Jammeh and Jawara governments of key laws to protect women from discrimination and to grant women 12 weeks of maternity leave with pay without job loss following delivery are important strides and achievements for Gambian women. The passage of the Women's Bill in 2010 by The Gambia's National Assembly is an important instrument that augurs well for women and must not go unacknowledged by individuals interested in women's rights, feminists and nonfeminists alike. The act is an expansive document that brings together international as well as domestic covenants and laws aimed primarily at improving and protecting women's and girls' fundamental rights. Unlike in neighboring Mali, where a similar bill was watered down, in part because of substantial and sustained protests from Islamist groups, Gambians have reason to be proud of their National Assembly members (NAMs) as well as the APRC government for the overwhelming support the bill received and particularly for spearheading it in the first place. This does not mean that there weren't the expected protests from the usual suspects of rabidly sexist men and conservative Islamists.

Passage of the bill and women's empowerment more generally were battles long fought for by women activists, women's organizations, and many men. The rationale is that women and girls in The Gambia and elsewhere deserve proactive state policy and legal intervention to protect them from discrimination and other forms of poor treatment that they are often subjected to. This makes a lot of sense because regrettably, much talent and potential go unrealized and untapped—trapped by centuries-old mores and values. Therefore, this is an important first step. By lending legal muscle to bear on women's empowerment, the APRC demonstrated a degree of commitment to both

St. Therese's Upper Basic School, Kanifing, is one of many schools in the area and country catering to students dressed in their school uniforms, a relic of British colonialism that has been retained. (Courtesy of Buharry Gassama)

women and girls, and Gambian society stands to benefit in numerous ways—including economic, social, and political, to name just a few.[10]

The herculean challenge, many supporters argue, is enforcing the bill's provisions. Perhaps a more challenging task is to sell the law to different actors in civil society, especially conservative Islamist clergy. APRC government officials and security agencies, specifically, must also be brought on board. This will require considerable retraining as well as awareness raising to transform once-repressive agents and agencies into defenders of human and women's rights in particular. The APRC must also go beyond the typical rhetoric, some argue, to impress on everyone the seriousness it attaches to issues concerning women's emancipation—a daunting task at best. Undoubtedly, educating both men and women as well as civil society remains crucial to acceptance of the law and to furthering the promise of a genuine march toward women's and girls' empowerment. Yet, while these are important markers for success, we should not underestimate the many cultural and religious residues that remain to threaten and undermine the Women's Bill.

This is because too often, progressive bills and laws such as The Gambia's 2010 Women's Bill remain unenforced, are sometimes unenforceable, and die a slow death or at best decorate bookshelves where they collect dust and mold. In the end, these laws become soundbites to embellish flowery policy papers and speeches. Therefore, while the 2010 Women's Bill is a welcome development that bodes well for all Gambians, women and girls specifically, it must be enforced with reasonable benchmarks. Because, in the end, it holds out hope for justice for thousands of women and girls in The Gambia who suffer violence, female circumcision, and other forms of gender discrimination, including employment that severely limits freedoms as well as the opportunities women in other parts of the world readily take for granted.

In sum, while Gambian women have made important gains since independence in 1965, a lot more remains to be done. Under President Jammeh, many women have been promoted to important positions of power, including Isatou Njie-Saidy, who has served as vice president and secretary of state for women's affairs since 1997. Jammeh also boasts several women secretaries of state in his cabinet, even if he is sometimes criticized for his support of female circumcision. Under Jammeh's rule enrollment of girls at the primary education level has also improved. Therefore, The Gambia under Jammeh has also made significant strides in providing access to education at the elementary, high school, and university levels. His government's continuing efforts to bridge the education gender and regional gap and disparities in the country is praiseworthy. Importantly, that The Gambia today has a university is a major developmental achievement. These achievements are likely to have long-term positive effects on The Gambia's current and future development. The task now remains to improve the lives of rural and poor urban women, who die disproportionately from childbirth. Women in general still carry the overwhelming burdens of child rearing, cooking, and cleaning, except for the well-to-do who can afford maids since grandmothers have slowly been displaced. And in place of communal farms, the well-to-do have their garden boys and hire help to tend their fenced gardens and orchards.

In the last two decades, perhaps longer, The Gambia's family structure has changed significantly, resulting in the further growth of nuclear families. This has not replaced the extended family entirely but has somewhat eroded its centrality in society. Increasingly among the well-to-do, children are not seen entirely as future safety nets for aging parents because children move out of the large family compounds to establish their own households, in the past but even more so now. Yet relations with extended family members remain important and are, in large part, maintained. Government pension services, schools, and hospitals have grown in importance but have not totally eclipsed the role of the local healers and *cadi*. While traditional authority patterns coexist with modern political institutions, the former have also been eclipsed somewhat.

Society as a result is increasingly divided between the haves and the have-nots. Access to education or the lack thereof seems to make the major difference. And while the middle class is expanding, many more Gambians are left struggling to eke out a living from an inhospitable economic environment. As noted earlier, Gambian women are resourceful, assertive, and independent, contrary to widely held perceptions. And in these days of severe economic crisis, globally and nationally, many women provide for their families by engaging in petty trade, selling vegetables to take care of aging husbands who no longer work. And women-headed households seem to be on the increase; sometimes they are supported by remittances from children and relatives abroad.

Notes

1. Vincent Khapoya, *The African Experience* (Upper Saddle River, NJ: Prentice Hall, 1998), 35.

2. *Asobi* is a garment made out of fabric of the same color and pattern worn by children and adults at weddings and special occasions. It is also worn by persons belonging to a social or political organization to distinguish members from another organization.

3. Khapoya, *The African Experience,* 51.

4. Since 1990 the United Nations Development Program (UNDP) has used this measure to assess well-being in "developing" countries in favor of the more traditional Gross National Product (GNP), income per capita measures. See, *Gambia, Country Profile: Human Development Indicators* (New York: UNDP, 2011), http://hdrstats.undp.org/en/countries/profiles/GMB.html.

5. Betina Shell-Duncan and Ylva Hernlund, *Female "Circumcision," in Africa: Culture, Controversy and Change* (Boulder, CO: Lynne Rienner Publishers, 2000), 119.

6. Ibid. See Fuambai Ahmadu's chapter 14 in Shell-Duncan and Hernlund, *Female "Circumcision,"* 283–312.

7. See Abdoulaye Saine, "Violence against Women (Wife-Beating): A Bastion of Male Domination that Must End," *The Gambia Echo* (Raleigh, NC), March 2010. www.TheGambiaecho.com. Used with permission.

8. Luise White, *The Comforts of Home: Prostitution in Colonial Nairobi* (Chicago: Chicago University Press, 1990); Kristin Mann and Richard Roberts, *Law in Colonial Africa* (London, Heinemann, 1991).

9. The hut tax was a levy imposed on Africans by British colonialists to raise revenue to support administration of the colonies and to push African peasants into wage-labor and export-crop production.

10. See Abdoulaye Saine, "The Gambia Women's Bill 2010: A Promise Yet to Be Realized," *The Gambia Echo* (Raleigh, NC), May 2010. www.TheGambiaecho.com. Used with permission.

7

Social Customs and Lifestyles

GAMBIAN CULTURE IS fundamentally a tapestry of various ethnic-based sub-cultures, customs, values, and religious practices that have coexisted for centuries. While each ethnic group may exhibit slight variations in rituals—such as weddings or naming ceremonies, as well as burial rites—core rituals and practices remain pretty much the same. Islam serves as a unifying force and has introduced modes of worship, a unified belief system, and practices that are centuries old. Because over 90 percent of Gambians are Muslim, Islam is a way of life, with expectations and modes of interpersonal conduct derived from the practices and teachings of Prophet Muhammad—*Haddith*. Social and economic interdependence through intermarriage and joking relationships further cement an already fused cultural landscape.

Western culture has also had an important imprint on Gambian culture with the introduction of Christianity and Western education. These forces, along with those mentioned earlier, make Gambian culture a dynamic and ever-changing phenomenon. These national, international, and global forces have made The Gambia and Gambian society, unlike many other ethnically divided societies, a model of cultural harmony and diversity. This has engendered relative peace and tranquility for its peoples and neighbors. The level of ethnic tolerance that Gambians enjoy is perhaps unparalleled, regionally or even continentally.

This has been made possible by two tendencies: partial de-ethnization and Wolofization. As the former has increased due to cross-ethnic marriages, so has the use of Wolof as a lingua franca, especially in the Greater Banjul area. Both processes were further enhanced during the colonial era and thereafter by migrations of people of Mandinka and Fula stock from the provinces to the Greater Banjul area. In the process, succeeding generations of Fula, Serer, Mandinka, Jola, and Manjago became Wolofized, and in fact many speak Wolof as their primary language. Wolofization, however, is more pronounced in Senegal, where the Wolof are the majority, unlike in The Gambia, where they rank third in terms of numbers. In sum, these processes, along with Islam and Christianity, which are both Abrahamic religions, have fostered and maintained harmony and peace among ethnicities.

Some Gambians may take issue with a position on de-ethnization and may contend that Gambian society has become more ethnically divided, especially in the time since President Jammeh has been in office. They too can point to many examples to support their case. This, however, may be a new and passing phase or trend. Gambians have historically collaborated, especially after the tumultuous half-century of the Soninke-Marbout Wars. The rhetoric of peace, that is, the absence of war, has always served as justification, perhaps ideology, to maintain peace and the status quo. It seems to have worked but may have also blunted the will of Gambians to challenge secular and religious authority. More importantly, President Jawara had a deliberate policy of co-opting individuals from minority groups into his government and the bureaucracy. This ethnic balancing act also helped engender inter-ethnic harmony.

Gambians are a social and friendly people, albeit more reserved than their Senegalese cousins, and share the principle of *teranga* (or *tedungal* in Fula), which roughly translates in English to hospitality. This is highly cherished. *Tedungal* is the building block of all ethnic subcultures and is exhibited among Senegambians and all Gambian ethnic groups in particular. Willingness to meet the needs of strangers or visitors even when they themselves go without food, drink, or a comfortable bed is a case in point. Gambians, even under today's changed economic fortunes, will go out of their way to ensure that a visitor feels at home even if just for a short visit. Often, a meal is quickly prepared and soft drinks or green tea are served to welcome the visitor. In fact, it used to be the practice in most homes to reserve a good serving of the day's meal for a potential stranger or visitor who might arrive unannounced. The rationale for this was that one never knew for how long a guest may have traveled, sometimes under arduous conditions, perhaps arriving following days without food. Thus, a hot meal was always a welcome sight for such a visitor. Jokes abound among all Gambian ethnic groups, especially those who share a joking relationship, about visitors who were so eager to partake of a meal that they would scald their hands and throat with tears dripping from their eyes.

When asked the reason for the tears, they would feign happiness in seeing their host rather than admit to the hot morsel of food lodged in their throat.

SOCIAL RELATIONS

Social, and in particular interpersonal, relationships are important among all ethnic groups in The Gambia. Personal relationships tie an individual to family and family identity, and one way in which both are manifest is in greetings between people. While in the United States and Europe a quick "hello" or "hi" will suffice, in Gambia and Senegambian society in general, greetings can take up to five minutes or longer, among rural dwellers especially. All ethnic groups use the common greeting "As salaam mu alekum," which in Arabic means "peace be on to you." The response is typically "Ma lekum salaam," "peace be on to you as well." All ethnic groups have variations of the same greetings in their own languages and these greetings are often punctuated with the mention of one's last name—Sidibeh or Joof, and so forth. Greeters may inquire not only about health but about that of a wife or wives, children, other relatives, and even the farm animals and crops. In fact, conversations about important issues may revert once more to greetings to ease difficult negotiations or to ask about an individual who had not been inquired about earlier. Upcountry Wolof are known for their long greeting style.

Greetings are a sign of respect, and one greets elders by extending the right arm, with the left hand clutching to the wrist of the right hand. The left hand is never extended in greeting except when bidding farewell to a relative, visitor, or stranger, this to ensure good luck and as an expression of the expectation of seeing one another soon. Women and young girls greet both men and women elders by kneeling; young men or even elderly men, on the other hand, do not kneel but upon withdrawing both hands from the greeting handshake will place both hands on their chest as a sign of respect and goodwill. In fact, the mere offering of two hands in a handshake rather than one is a sign of respect to elders. These greeting styles, interpersonal speech, and social interactions permeate society at large and regulate social behavior among and between ethnic groups.

These days, a peck on each cheek or even an embrace or hug is increasingly common, partly in response to the growing adoption of this Arabic practice and Islamization. These practices may have taken root in the last quarter-century as a result of more Gambians performing the hajj, or pilgrimage to the Holy City of Mecca in Saudi Arabia, and returning students from the latter. Among the Aku, however, a handshake, a kiss, and a hug are defining elements of their cultural greeting style. They are also less likely to engage in long greeting exchanges, similar to other urban dwellers pressed for time. Urban exchanges are typically brief among relatives as well as friends— a quick *ee beh dee* (how are you) in Mandinka, *nakam* (how is it) in Wolof, *ah da saeli* in Fula, and *kusamia* in Jola. One greets people everywhere, and one may greet a person or a group sitting under a tree, for instance, or on the way to and from the market. One is seldom faulted for greeting too much. Instead, it is a sign of good etiquette, and hence one's upbringing.

Consequently, greetings are an important pillar of Gambian culture, and people who do not perform this rite and engage in conversation with another party or parties are considered rude or psychologically impaired. Conversely, Gambians in general express anger or disapproval by refusing to greet a person who offends them. Things can get worse when the aggrieved party refuses to speak to the offender for several days, but not exceeding three days of silence; Islam forbids beyond this. Offenders are just as quick to apologize for their mistakes or offenses, and one is further bound by Islam to accept an apology that is delivered with remorse; Christianity teaches the same principles. Children are quick to offer gifts of kola nuts to offended parents or elders, and so are husbands to wives and vice versa. Respect underpins social interaction and relationships. Elders receive respect from younger family members just as younger siblings accord respect to older ones. Respect for parents is a cardinal societal rule. One does not talk back to a parent—at least that is the expectation, though not always followed these days.

Disrespect is when one fails to observe these social codes. In fact, it is also considered rude to address elders by their first name(s), as noted earlier. The name(s) of an elder must be preceded by the title uncle, auntie, grandmother, doctor, pastor, and so on. Similarly, the young do not look directly into an elder's eyes while speaking with them—this is a sign not of dishonesty but of respect and good upbringing. Even at a time when cell phones are common, even in rural areas, face-to-face interactions and negotiations are preferred over those conducted over the phone. This was especially the case when communication and transport systems were poor.

A person's goodness is often measured by the degree of harmony and personal interactions he or she enjoys and cultivates with others. This pays off well in naming ceremonies, where a larger than normal turnout is the reward, or even in times of death. One would often overhear conversations about the crowds that attended an event on behalf of so and so: "There were so many people that one could not move an elbow without hurting or hitting another," someone might lament, joyfully. This is all the more important at burials. Large crowds at this event are the ultimate reward for good interpersonal relations. There is a Wolof proverb that has its equivalent in all other Gambian ethnic groups: *nit nitai garab'am*, roughly translated as, "The cure to a human or person's ills is another human." Other proverbs, such as "It takes a village to raise a child" and "I am because we are," underscore the centrality of good interpersonal relationships in Gambian culture. Reciprocity in gift giving or home visits quickly ends if not reciprocated because each ethnic group has a saying that roughly translates, "One foot does not sustain a family relationship," which underscores the importance of reciprocity. Among the Wolof, this saying *bena tanka du doh mboke*, and the Mandinka equavelent is *sin fuuloo lehka badinyaa deialtama*.

Humility is also a greatly valued personal attribute among Gambians. Persons who flaunt their wealth or overstate titles and accomplishments are often not looked upon with much respect. Yet Gambians also respect accomplished individuals and titles such as doctor, professor, *alhaji* (a man who has performed the hajj and *ajaratou* for women), sheikh, and other titles, especially scholarly ones. A good illustration of this is President Jammeh's many titles. Among these are *alhaji*, professor, doctor, and sheikh. He does not have an earned doctorate, yet he insists on being addressed using all these titles, which is a source of much amusement to his critics and even to some degree his supporters. You will hear Gambians praise individuals of achievement and high standing as "down to earth," or "simple," not as a simpleton.

Gambian culture or its various components also value oral expression and delivery skills—abilities so common among the *gewel* or *jeli*. The use of eloquently constructed sentences, or praises, proverbs, songs, riddles, similes, and metaphors and general self-expression in local and international languages, draws praise and admiration. Consequently, among many Gambians, the bigger the words used in a speech and writing, the more impressive. It is also a skill that is somewhat feared for social criticism when used by the *gewel* or *jeli* against patrons and others who may offend them. Similarly, praying for friends, family, and neighbors; the country; or even the head of state is common at formal religious gatherings and at informal settings as well. Just as greetings inquire about almost everyone and everything, so do prayers. At the top of the prayer list is peace—peace in the country, in the family, in households, between husbands and wives, and between friends—as well as prayers for a bountiful harvest. Following 2011's Arab Spring of unprecedented political uprisings in the Middle East and North Africa, President Jammeh, some say self-servingly, called upon Muslim elders to pray for peace in the country and to mark this occasion gifted elders with cows, sheep, and cash.

Prayers for peace, good health, and other concerns typically open and close every formal and informal gathering. The fixation over peace is attributable to turbulent political events in West Africa and the world, especially in the last two decades. *Kherre be* or *jamma' ngam*, which translates into "are you in peace," a more formal greeting than those mentioned earlier in Mandinka and Wolof, respectively, illustrate this well. As noted earlier, churches and clergy also perform similar prayers, and joint prayers are often held between Christians and Muslims, which underscore the excellent relations between religious communities in the country.

Social and interpersonal relations, specifically, are undergirded by moral as well as cultural expectations to behave ethically, the avoidance of social conflict, and desisting from behaviors that potentially foster conflict within family members and neighbors. Many Gambians try to live up to their religious obligations, and piety, or at least the appearance of it, is a highly valued attribute among Gambians, even if not all behave in moral ways. As in other societies, respect, honesty, fidelity to one's spouse, and good neighborliness define both individual and societal norms and expectations. A belief in God among both Muslims and Christians has deeply shaped Gambian culture and individual and interpersonal behavior. The consequence is a country, culture, and people that are shaped and deeply steeped, for the most part, in conservative religious and cultural traditions.[1]

CEREMONIES

Ceremonies and rituals are an integral part of Gambian life and culture. Among all ethnic groups in The Gambia, there are ceremonies to celebrate the stages of life, from birth to death. Children are always a welcome addition to a family, especially among newlyweds. The birth of a child helps cement a relationship and is the reason for much fun and entertainment. Weddings are also an occasion for merriment and celebrating the building of ties between families and the community. The ceremony bestows on the newlywed recognition of their union and their membership in a community. Funerals mark the transition from this earthly life to life among ancestors, spirits, and angels. Both Muslims and Christians believe in a life of rewards and luxury in heaven for those who have lived a life of goodness, and piety, and punishment for those who did not lead exemplary lives.

Ceremonies also mark rites of passage from childhood to adult status. Circumcision for both boys and girls occur along age sets or age groups when children of roughly the same age undergo this initiation. These rites of passage represent milestones in one's life—from childhood to adulthood. It is a period when these young adults begin to assume adult responsibilities and duties after having been taught the expectations, songs, rituals, and mores of a community. Ceremonies to induce rain were once very popular. Old women in tattered men's clothing sing songs accompanied by drumming to mock the sky gods to release much-needed rains. Rain dances are also occasions both to entertain the crowds and to poke fun at the gods to save wilting crops from the sun's intense gaze. Grandmothers in tattered European trousers and long-sleeved shirts, along with a wrap around the waist that serves as a belt, never fail to elicit roaring laughter from the audiences that accompany them.

It is routine among all ethnic groups in The Gambia that a naming ceremony is held a week following a child's birth. These ceremonies are a mixture of both traditional and Islamic rituals. In the intervening days, a child is nameless, even though a name has been chosen, known only to the father or mother. Both mother and child remain secluded and are attended to only by a traditional midwife or female relatives. Outside the door leading to the new mother's room are special leaves and several amulets displayed to ward off evil spirits. On the day of the naming ceremony, relatives, friends, and community assemble at the compound, sometime around 10 A.M. Dressed in expensive cloth, possibly a *serri rabbal*, an aunt, grandmother, or an elder female member of the family cradles the child, who also is wrapped in expensive cloth. With her head covered, she sits on a mat in the compound courtyard surrounded by the guests. With a bar of soap, a blade, and water in a bowl, the child's head is washed and shaved; nowadays, the hair is slightly nicked. The child's name is then announced by the presiding religious leader, preferably the village imam, who in Islamic tradition also whispers the name in both the child's ears, followed by prayers of long life and fruitfulness to both parents and family.

Following this, refreshments are distributed to guests. In some instances, especially for a first child, a name is given but the festivities are delayed to allow parents and relatives time to prepare for a big celebration, in which several sheep, goats, or possibly a cow are slaughtered, prepared, and served during festivities that can last two to three days. This is a time for parents, friends, and relatives to flaunt their wealth and give gifts of money to the griots who often help run these affairs. Many families of lesser means are known to incur significant debts to entertain guests to ensure that they are not outdone by a neighbor or a ceremony to be talked about for many years to come. As they grow up, children are reminded by a *gewel* or relative about their sumptuous naming ceremony. This brings satisfying smiles to the child and parents.

Names have immense significance in Gambian society. A child can be given the name of a living person or ancestor or the name of the Prophet Muhammad or other significant prophets or their wives. When named after an ancestor or a parent, a child will often have a preceding name, such as Ndey (mother), followed by the name, such as Amie or Fatou. For boys, the names Bai (father) or Mam (grandfather) are common and like those of girls show respect to the departed or living relative. It is a great source of joy and pride among Senegambians when a child is named after another person. It is also a sign of true friendship and respect when a child is named after a person. Individuals so honored are, as a matter of custom, are expected to shower his or her *tomma* or *tura'ndorr* (namesake in Mandinka and Wolof, respectively) with gifts. Some so honored could even assume partial or full responsibility for the child's upkeep and education. A child may, in fact, assume the last name of their namesake, to the extent that a father's own last name is almost lost. It is also a source and sign of prestige when an individual in society has many children named after him or her. It confers respect and recognition of an individual's success, goodness and achievement.

Unlike Westerners, most Gambians do not typically name their children after themselves. They are more likely to name a child after someone else in their family or community. Among some educated Gambians, including the Christian Aku, children could be named after a father and be called junior, the second, or the third. While fathers generally determine a child's name, naming a child alternates between a husband and his wife, with the first child named by the father and the second by the mother and usually from her side of the extended family. It is also believed that a child often assumes seven qualities of the person he or she is named after, making it all the more important to name a child after a person of high moral standing, achievement, kindness, industriousness, and bravery.

Young women in The Gambia, as in other countries and cultures, look forward to their wedding day—it is a woman's day of honor and happiness with friends, family, and community. She dresses in new clothes and changes attire as she sees fit. In urban settings especially, this is followed by a big party for the couple's friends and relatives at night, while the early evening is reserved for more traditional dance, music, and drumming. Depending on wealth or family income, these celebrations can last for days, and guests are always assured of good food and entertainment.

Burial ceremonies are a more somber occasion. Loss of a loved one, especially an elder, is occasioned by days of mourning by relatives, friends, and the community at large. When a woman of status dies, she is given a purification bath by her peers and as Islam dictates is shrouded. Islam also recommends burial within 24 hours. Only men accompany the dead to the cemetery. When a man of honor dies, especially after having enjoyed a long and prosperous life with many children, the ceremony is often more elaborate. Wives, dressed in black, enter a period of mourning and seclusion that lasts for several months. Forty days after death, another ceremony is performed. This allows family and friends to travel from afar to pay their last respects to the dead. Like naming and marriage ceremonies, burials and ceremonies following it are times to reflect on the good character of the deceased and pray for their entry to heaven and the forgiving of their sins by Allah.

Muslim ceremonies after death are less involved. Once the body has been washed and shrouded, the body is carried in a casket to the cemetery, where Muslims are buried facing the Kaba, a holy site in Mecca. Once the burial takes place and prayers are performed, individuals are required to leave the cemetery hurriedly and not look back as they exit the grounds. It is believed that it is then that an angel arrives to interrogate and assess the dead person's good deeds and sins on earth. If the good deeds outweigh the bad, the person is assured of eternal bliss in heaven. The not so lucky will suffer in hell but may at some point receive the mercies of Allah. Prayers of intercession continue to be made by the living for departed relatives. In fact, one of the primary roles of children to their departed parents is to continue to pray for them that their sins be forgiven by Allah. Friends do likewise for departed friends. It has become common practice that the entire Qur'an is recited at anniversaries or 40-day ceremonies as a way of intercession.

The dead, especially the elderly, become ancestors and are revered. They are not objects of worship, however, as some Westerners erroneously believe. Yet ancestors are believed to wield considerable influence over the lives of the living. Offerings of water, food, and even liquor (libations) among non-Muslim Jola, Serer, and Fula were once common—a relic of pre-Islamic times. Ancestors are also the basis for praise for the living. One's lineage and the grandparents that link the living to the dead are cause for such praise.

NATIONAL AND RELIGIOUS HOLIDAYS

National and religious holidays are occasions for Gambians to celebrate and commemorate dates and events that hold national and religious significance. Before Independence Day celebrations, there were Empire Day and Commonwealth Day, both of which celebrated Gambia's subservient colonial status. The Commonwealth is an international organization of former British colonies that included India, Ceylon (Sri Lanka), and other colonies. These celebrations, like that for their successor, Independence Day, were marked by sporting events, such as track and field competitions, and the giving of well-cherished prizes. Independence Day is celebrated February 18 each year, the day that marks the end of colonial rule by Britain in 1965. It once was characterized by pomp and circumstance—parades, receptions, speeches, and numerous cultural performances in Banjul and all regional headquarters. At the MacCarthy Square in Banjul, now renamed July 22 Square following the 1994 coup, amid tumultuous crowds the president of the First Republic, Sir Dawda Jawara, would give a speech imploring citizens to work hard and support the ruling party in its quest to develop the country. Schoolchildren were encouraged to take their education seriously, as they would become the country's future leaders. Civil servants were encouraged to work harder and to eschew partisan politics. Similar festivities also occurred at the regional capitals but on a smaller scale. There, provincial commissioners presided, giving speeches to inspire both the young and old toward virtues that contributed to national development.

Following the July 22, 1994, coup that ousted Sir Dawda Jawara from office, this date has now eclipsed the February 18 celebrations. It is today punctuated by military parades, receptions, and other entertainment once reserved for Independence Day. In fact, July 22 is now dubbed Revolution Day, when four young men risked their lives to save the country from corruption, tribalism, and nepotism, or so they claim. Today, these national festivities are often held at a large Chinese-built stadium outside Bakau, a coastal town less than 15 miles from Banjul. Gambians also celebrate most international holidays, such as International Workers' Day on May 1, International Women's Day, and many others. People often have a day off from work, and people typically spend these holidays at home entertaining friends and relatives or at beach parties.

By far the most recognized and celebrated holidays are religious. Being mostly Muslim, Gambians celebrate Eid Al-Adha, or Tobaski, the feast of sacrifice. The prospect of delicious food offerings and new clothes to wear for the celebration is always a cause of much anticipation among children. Following a late morning prayer at the mosque or square, worshippers return home to slaughter a lamb, and the cooking and grilling begins, culminating in lunch around 2 P.M. of *benachin*, and *cherreh* with lamb for dinner. Thus, Tobaski always elicits much excitement, especially among children. Elders are also happy, as it is an occasion when family members from near and far travel to their home-villages and towns to celebrate. In this sense, it is like Thanksgiving or Christmas in the United States. Every family that can afford it sacrifices a lamb, a portion of which is consumed by the household while another is distributed to neighbors and households that cannot financially afford a lamb. Tobaski was and still remains a time to indulge and stretch one's appetite for food and soft drinks. It also is a time for children to visit neighbors to solicit gifts of money, similar to Halloween in the United States, where kids go door-to-door soliciting candy from neighbors. Tobaski night is yet another opportunity to indulge in merriment. Music from clubhouses and house parties punctuate the night air, and everywhere one goes there is a true sense of goodwill and friendship.

The other religious holiday for Muslims is Eid-ul-Fitre (also called Korriteh), which marks the end of a 29- or 30-day fast, depending on the sighting of the new moon during the month of Ramadan. Though slightly more subdued than the earlier Eid, Korriteh is an occasion to strengthen community, build solidarity, and deepen faith. A lamb or sheep is often slaughtered, followed by much eating and drinking and festivities to mark the occasion. Both Eid celebrations are opportune moments to heap praises to the president and the the the secretaries of state, and they are a time to pray for peace and tranquility in the country. Like Tobaski, Korriteh is also a time for dances and much amusement, accompanied, as in Tobaski, with gift giving. These are truly national, as both Muslims and Christians take part in these celebrations.

Christmas remains one of the most popular holidays in the country despite the high number of Muslims in the country. Christmas Eve is celebrated at churches throughout the country only by Christians, but Christmas Day is celebrated by all with masquerades, drumming, and dancing with *fanals* and lanterns in Banjul and other urban centers. A *fanal* (a Portuguese word meaning lantern) is a wood or bamboo replica of a ship or house decorated with intricate hand-designed paper patterns that are glued to the wood or bamboo frame and lit with candles or small light bulbs wired to a radio battery. The *fanal* is then attached to wooden stilts and is handled by boys as it floats majestically in the air. Lanterns are typically small house frames made from bamboo that are just as well decorated, and like *fanals* travel the streets from one compound to another, soliciting gifts. At the end of the Christmas season prizes are handed out to the club or organization with the best *fanal*. Sometimes, a *fanal* or lantern may catch fire, and depending on the severity of the fire, it is repaired the next day in time for the nightly celebrations.

Christmas celebrations can last for weeks and culminate in presenting the *fanal* or lantern to a patron, who is expected to reward the club with a substantial gift. Often the best-decorated *fanal* also receives a much-coveted prize. The nights of *fanal* are an opportunity for young people to meet for dates. So Christmas night, just like Tobaski, is one for clubbing and fun, especially among the young, long after the church services end. Truth be told, Gambian Muslims celebrate and welcome the Christmas season less for its religious significance than for the fun that accompanies Christmas. Boxing Day is a day for soccer tournaments among the country's best soccer clubs as well as a day for Christians to visit family and friends, exchange gifts, and share meals and drink.

Easter or *Nan m'buru*, roughly translating into taking of the sacrament, as well as Good Friday and Good Monday are celebrated by church services and exchanges of goodwill between Christians and Muslims. The Imam of Banjul, just as the Christian clergy do on both Eids, sends messages of solidarity and friendship to all Christians, emphasizing the importance of Jesus to both Christians and Muslims alike. Sang Marie (St. Mary), the mother of Jesus, is greatly revered among Christians in the Gambia. Also known as the Feast of the Assumption, Sang Marie, which falls on August 15, is celebrated by Christians, and like Christmas Day is characterized by masquerades (*pakins*, *egugu*, *mamapara*), parades, and sumptuous meals and drink. Muslims indulge just as much in the festivities and typically receive gifts of food and drink from Christian relatives and friends. All these Christian holidays remain relatively vibrant to this day. However hard economic times along with growing immigration have dampened the enthusiasm that once greeted the Christmas season in The Gambia.

Among Muslims, *Maoloud'Nabi*, or, as locally known in all the languages, Gammo, like Christmas is a celebration of Prophet Muhammad's birth. It is marked by all-night prayers and recitation of the Qur'an, as well as sermons on the noble character of Prophet Muhammad. During this all-night celebration, tea, biscuits, and mints are served, culminating in the early-morning prayers at dawn and then breakfast of *cherreh* with a tomato-based beef or lamb stew. Today, Gammo is commercialized and is a platform to praise the political leadership. It is a venue to flaunt one's wares. It has come to resemble a naming ceremony during which each person of means is greeted with the expectation of a nice gift for the imam and his coterie of hymn singers. In recent years, *Gammo* has also become a place of self-promotion for men, and middle-aged widowers or singles in a society where men generally have more than one wife. Therefore, the seriousness that once graced these occasions has been greatly diminished and in some instances replaced by sheer entertainment and praise singing with little substantive discussion of the Qur'an or the teachings of Prophet Muhammad.

In sum, Gambians celebrate many holidays, both religious and secular, and these are occasions to indulge in fun activities. Music, masquerades, food, and drink are important in the success of all celebratory events. Though not a national holiday, Gambia's Roots Festival is a recent addition that showcases Gambian culture. It is a means to attract tourists whose dollars have become all the more important in a struggling economy. The more cynical see it as yet another opportunity for President Jammeh to party with his friends and supporters. It is an event or series of events in Banjul, Juffureh, and Kanilai, the current president's adopted home, for endless partying—a poor showcasing of Gambian traditional culture, some contend.

AMUSEMENT AND SPORTS

Gambians enjoy playing and watching all kinds of sporting events. Playing soccer for most Gambian males, especially as adolescents and young adults, is considered a rite of passage. Everyone grows up playing soccer, and local soccer stars and teams enjoy much popularity and an enthusiastic fan following. Wrestling is also a much enjoyed sport throughout the country and attracts both young and old spectators. It is by far the oldest sport, whereas cricket, golf, and tennis, as elsewhere, are played by elite urban Gambians. Basketball is also popular, due largely to the growing availability of television sets and access to global sport channels like ESPN and their European counterparts from South Africa. Thus, Gambians young and old are fans of European teams that include Manchester United, Chelsea, Liverpool, and Arsenal, to name a few. With the growing number of Africans, including Gambians, playing professional soccer and basketball in Europe, the United States, and even Mexico, sports have captured the imagination of young Gambians, just as they have elsewhere. This leaves many parents worried, as studying becomes less of a priority. As in the United States, many young Gambians aspire to play in the European or American leagues, and many talented young Gambian players do get a break and get recruited into the European junior leagues before making it to the big leagues. Yet for all those Gambians who do make it to the elite ranks, many more fail to make it. The Gambia's under-17 team has generally performed well internationally.

Also known as the smiling coast, The Gambia is home to beautiful beaches. Beach soccer, volleyball, jogging, swimming, fishing, bird-watching, and ecotourism make the beaches and environs attractive sites for visitors and tourists. Abuko, a nature reserve, is home to a variety of flora and fauna, while Tendaba Camp, about a hundred miles from Banjul, also provides interesting sites for the more adventurous. Some Gambians engage in wild game hunting, but it is not as popular a sport following the extinction of elephants, possibly before World War II; lions and tigers in the 1960s; and other wild game. The Gambia River also provides opportunities for recreational fishing and sailing, and because it is navigable by both small and large vessels almost throughout the year, it offers opportunities for travel upstream into the provinces.

Nightclubs have always been a big attraction for the young and not so old. Dotted along the coast and in major urban areas, one is sure to find a club that meets one's taste. Gambians have an eclectic taste as far as music is concerned. Music ranges from *mbalax*, a Senegambian music genre made popular worldwide by Senegalese superstar Youssou N'Dour, to reggae, dance hall, hip-hop, rap, salsa, salsa-*mbalax*, and much more. On the Gambian music scene, however, Jaliba (big *jali* in Mandinka) Kuyateh is by far the biggest music sensation, with a music genre that reflects a rich mélange of Mandinka or Manding-based *kora* percussion and songs.

Going to the movies or cinema is historically a popular mode of entertainment for young and old in both urban and rural environs. Indian films have always been popular in The Gambia, even though Gambians do not speak Hindu. Yet they once were glued to these films because of the song and

The majestic sunbird, one of many beautiful birds that make their home in Gambia—a bird-watchers paradise. (© Joan Egert | Dreamstime.com)

dance numbers and the occasional brawl that broke out between the good and bad guys. Chinese movies that are full of fights and action were popular until recently, when Nigerian movies took over in the late 1990s. American films, especially cowboy or Western movies, drew many crowds to cinema houses, partly because of the storyline of good versus evil, the pistol fights, and English, which many Gambians speak or at least understand enough to follow a movie. French movies were once popular in The Gambia but to a lesser degree, partly because of the language barrier.

With the VCR and the ready availability of other digital technologies, well-to-do Gambians can watch programs from Senegal or neighboring countries; certainly CNN and BBC. With the ease of travel these days, many Gambian households have a television and other equipment, as a result of which they are able to view the latest movies from the comforts of their homes. Many Gambians also invest in satellite dishes to escape the monotony of the government-owned television station. Thus, options for entertainment have grown for most Gambians. Before this worldwide media revolution, however, radio from Gambia, Senegal, and neighboring countries were the main sources of broadcast news and entertainment. The VOA, BBC, and Radio France International (RFI) to name just a few, also continue, as in the past, news and entertainment.

Today, CNN is a main source of news and information, and to some degree entertainment. Therefore, for Gambians who are wired, the volume as well as the variety of entertainment has increased tremendously. This environment is in contrast to the time in the early 1960s or before, when The Gambia did not have a national radio station. Then, entertainment was in large measure family-based by way of storytelling, village wrestling, or visiting a local jazz band like the Super Eagles and a few others. Local drumming was also a form of entertainment, especially during weddings and other ceremonies. Yet radio broadcasts from Mali, Guinea, and especially Senegal provided much of the entertainment at the time. The Colonial Film Unit also traveled throughout the colony, showing poor-quality and often degrading movies of Africans that were made for African consumption—part of the colonial enterprise. This was partly why Indian films became popular during this era.

The Gambia, unlike Nigeria, does not have a film industry to speak of yet several Gambians, including Johnny Secka, made it relatively big in Hollywood. Mbye Cham, a Professor of film and literature at Howard University, has made a big impact on both, and as a judge at African film festivals. Today, Nigerian films, known as Nollywood, have saturated the market, as they have in other African countries, the United States, Europe, and even Jamaica. Gambians rent these movies to watch at home, and as these Nigerian movies and actors have grown in popularity, so has The Gambia as a popular site to shoot Nigerian movies. This trend has undermined the once popular pastime of going to the cinema or movies. Yet plays, concerts, drama clubs, and entertainment by the national troupe and visiting artists from Senegal, the United States, Europe, and the Caribbean also provide additional entertainment. Gambia Radio and Television Services (GRTS) televises movies and runs several European and American soaps. Momodou Musa Secka was one the best known actors and entertainers on television, having sharpened his acting and writing skills, also as a journalist, at Armitage High. In sum, there is a lot more to do these days for entertainment in The Gambia than was the case a quarter-century ago, and there is enough variety to meet any taste.

OLD AND NEW: VILLAGES AND URBAN CENTERS

Despite several gains in education and physical infrastructure and growth in urban centers since independence in 1965, The Gambia remains distinctly rural. The bulk of Gambians, approximately 60 percent, still live in villages, eking out a living from agriculture. The structure as well as the social organization, though changing, is built around the compound, compound head, and village chief. Deeply religious, social hierarchy remains patriarchal, with social stratification based loosely on caste that for a longtime remained endogamous. Traditional values that include respect for family, family history, and hard work are still cherished in rural Gambia. Consequently, rural Gambians in general tend to hold both positive and sometimes negative views of their urban-based compatriots. They are likely to see urban Gambians as materialistic, Westernized, and less honest and hardworking than they are. Urban Gambians, on the other hand, see the rural folk as simple, uncivilized, and left behind by modernization. Yet the phenomenal shift in population from the rural to the urban centers of the Greater Banjul area suggests that rural Gambians are just as attracted to urban amenities and opportunities as earlier relatives. Rural Gambians in general are also more likely now than in the past to send their children to urban centers in search of an education.

Today, unlike some 30 years ago, provincial headquarters and major urban towns, such as Basse, Janjangbureh, Kaur, and Kuntaur, have lost their vibrancy and once-productive citizens to urban migration. What is left in many villages are the old, the women, and children as well as individuals who for lack of desire or means to migrate remain behind. Part of the reason for this phenomenal population shift is that most services remain concentrated in Banjul and its environs. Yet as infrastructure and services increase in the rural areas, and there have been many improvements, some urban Gambians may choose to go back home, especially given that living quarters in urban areas are often limited and expensive. The cost of living is also considerably higher in urban centers, unlike rural areas in Gambia, where one can still supplement the rising cost of living with farming, fishing, and seasonal work.

The urban settings, though larger in population, exhibit demographic and social structures similar to those of the villages. All remain compound based, social hierarchy remains largely unaltered, and unemployment and underemployment remain abysmally high. In fact, social relations between village and urban centers remain fluid insofar as travel between the two continues to flow regularly. It is also a fact that many villagers are being introduced to basic technologies, such as cell phones, and amenities that include piped water, electricity, and health care, which once were not widely available.

PASTORALISM, FARMING, AND VILLAGES

Cattle herding was once the traditional occupation of Bororoji Fulas in The Gambia. They traveled long distances in search of pastures for their flock. Originating from Futa, Bororoji Fula traveled far and wide and are today found throughout western and parts of central Africa, plying their occupation. As noted earlier, depending on the vegetation and water supply, these nomads may have settled temporarily in some location before moving on in search of greener pastures elsewhere. In The Gambia, most Fula are today sedentary, having abandoned their once nomadic lifestyles in exchange for farming groundnuts, millet, and sorghum. The introduction of schools, health clinics, and dispensaries in rural Gambia has provided the opportunity for education and upward mobility. Those not engaged in agriculture are heavily involved in long-distance or local trade endeavors and currency speculation and exchanges. Being the second largest ethnic group in The Gambia, the Fula have played important roles in The Gambia's political and economic development both before and after independence. They occupy important positions in the civil and administrative services and remain key players in the politics of the first and second republics, with Assan Musa Camara and Isatou Njie-Saidy, respectively, serving as vice president.

Farming is by far the largest industry in The Gambia, and while the percentage of peasant farmers has declined relative to the population, they nonetheless remain the largest occupational group. Persistent droughts in the 1970s, declining groundnut prices, and lack of government incentives and subsidies have combined to make farming relatively less lucrative than it once was. Farmers in The Gambia are nothing like farmers in the United States and Europe, however. They do not enjoy much political clout despite their large voting numbers, and they continue to bear the brunt of government mismanagement and various economic reforms, along with low-level civil servants in the mid-1980s. Typically they have very low incomes.

Slash and burn practices and shifting cultivation are the main methods of farming on small family-owned plots using rudimentary tools. The result is low agricultural productivity, never reaching the lofty national goals of food security or self-sufficiency. Partly because agriculture remains labor-intensive and backbreaking work, farming holds little attraction for the young, who flock to the urban centers to escape such a life. Land grabbing by the elite and government officials and its sale to outside investors make agricultural land all the more precious. Mechanization, as well as the consolidation of small farms through land reform, can go a long way in addressing these issues. Take the case of rice cultivation, for instance. Despite heavy financial investment during the first republic, rice farming has yet to reach its potential in either feeding a growing population or cutting a mounting import bill since independence. "Strange-farmers," a term used to describe seasonal migrant laborers from Mali and Guinea, once contributed immensely to the volume of groundnut yields in The Gambia. Land pressures and a decades-long drought in the 1970s have all but halted this flow of seasonal labor.

Low-scale fishing remains an important albeit undeveloped and underdeveloped industry. The potential for large-scale commercial fishing is good on both The Gambia River and the Atlantic; it remains underutilized. Porous and unsecured maritime boundaries have encouraged poaching or illegal fishing by large foreign fishing vessels that are now on the verge of depleting these vital marine resources. Small-scale fishermen in motorized dugouts ply the waters but remain uncompetitive and are reduced to harvesting small quantities of fish for their daily catch, part of which is consumed or sold. Again, the potential for large-scale commercial fishing remains tremendous, but it will take concerted and thoughtful policies and adequate financial investment to realize this potential. Coastal women, by and large, engage in the sale and/or drying or smoking of fish and oysters for the local market and regional export. This could potentially become both a lucrative and sustainable source of employment for women if the right investments and incentives are made in equipment and training.

Meanwhile, those who work with crafts that include carpentering, tailoring, wood carving, pottery, and jewelry making (gold and blacksmiths) carry out their trade to make a living under what are difficult economic conditions. They are engaged in potentially lucrative trades, but government disinterest or lack of policy, or perhaps both, keeps them relatively poor but better off than the unskilled. Owing to The Gambia's low and unsophisticated industrial base, manufacturing is limited to the production of plastic bowls, pans, and similar items and lacks absorptive capacity. This makes The Gambia a potentially attractive site for investments. The addition of factors such as a tropical climate; abundant land and labor; generous tax incentives; beautiful beaches, flora and fauna; close proximity to the United States and Europe; and the prevalence of English make The Gambia ideal for direct foreign investments (DFI).

In sum, The Gambia, in spite of its small size, has tremendous potential that remains untapped. Poor incentive structures for farmers, low investment in agriculture, and the absence of land and agricultural policy reforms leave many otherwise hardworking and productive citizens trapped in poverty. The river and the Atlantic Ocean within the country's maritime borders are by far the biggest assets The Gambia and Gambians have to develop the country. Both offer tremendous opportunity to boost agricultural productivity, the country's backbone, and propel the economy beyond subsistence. The potential synergy in damming the river to generate energy for domestic consumption and fuel agricultural and economic development, as well as for export to neighboring Senegal, must be tapped. Rather than being a liability, The Gambia's size could be an asset. Coupled with good interethnic relations the country's small size will likely provide, under good leadership, the momentum for growth and development.

Yet these goals are realizable only when Gambians are free or free themselves from a repressive political environment. While the current government prides itself on its economy policy strategy, Vision 2020, which aims at transforming The Gambia into a developed economy or a middle-income country through exports, the policy pronouncements are oddly at variance with the political landscape that thwarts free expression, violates property rights, and undermines the rule of law. For all intents and purposes state institutions are predatory, used by those in power to amass wealth at the expense of the people, and their policies will not likely advance The Gambia. Notwithstanding, The Gambia remains a dynamic country and culture that is constantly changing, influenced in no small measure by dynamic innovations in technology and communication from globalization. Many Gambians, especially the Western educated, are leveraging opportunities that globalization affords them to receive training and higher education, and hence higher incomes, part of which they invest in the domestic economy at home.

NOTE

1. Today, Gambian culture is deeply Islamic, and it is sometimes difficult to tell which is which. It is a mélange of traditional African belief systems, the sayings and practices of the Holy Prophet Muhammad, Christianity, and Western culture. Islam's initial attraction lay in its overlap with African traditional practices. Yet Islam has been modified and absorbed into African traditional institutions, giving Islam in Africa a syncretic outlook. See Bala Saho, "Appropriations of Islam in a Gambian Village: Life and Times of Shaykh Mass Kah, 1827–1936," *African Studies Quarterly* 12, no. 4 (2011): 1–21.

8

Music and Dance

EACH ETHNIC GROUP possesses a language and music tradition of its own that is, however, related to and influenced by music styles of other ethnic groups with whom they have lived and intermarried. The result is a rich and highly integrated mosaic that is linked to music styles performed in neighboring Senegal, Guinea, Mali, and Guinea Bissau—countries that are constituted by the same ethnic groups as in The Gambia. Yet to classify music played in The Gambia as "Gambian music," per se, is misleading, in large measure because it is part and parcel of a larger music constellation or tradition whose origins are traceable to Mali, Guinea, and Senegal, predominantly. The National Council for Arts and Culture (NCAC), as well as Gambia's National Cultural Troupe, like their counterparts in neighboring states, reflect the unity as well as the diversity in musical styles and traditions in the country and in the region.[1]

The twenty-one-string harp-sounding *kora* and the *balafong* (xylophone), which are music instruments played by Mandinka *jeli,* are traceable to ancient Mali, whereas the *xalam*, a four to three-string lute, is often associated with the Wolof and to some degree the Fula, Mandinka (*n'goni*), and Moors in Mauritania, where it may have originated centuries ago. The Jola as well as the Manjago also possess a guitarlike instrument, with fewer strings yet bigger and perhaps a cousin of the *xalam.* The *riti,* a one-string instrument, is played predominantly by the Fula and to some degree the Serer. Flutes also feature prominently among the Fula. Today, this instrument, with its melodious sound, is an important addition to both traditional cultural troupes and contemporary music groups throughout the subregion.

Drums of various sizes and shapes also feature prominently in music forms played in The Gambia and neighboring countries. All ethnic groups have within their traditions a variety of drums that are used for entertainment and in ceremonies. Among the Wolof, for instance, the *gorong, sabarr, lambe, junjung,* and *tamma* (talking drum) serve specific functions in an ensemble of drums. The *tabala,* on the other hand, is a single drum, which like the *xalam* may have originated from North Africa, or possibly the Middle East, as a result of cultural diffusion many centuries ago. It is an important instrument among the Narr of Mauritania, Senegal, and The Gambia. The *tabala* has both an entertainment and a ceremonial purpose.

Among the Narr, both men and women dance to the *tabala* accompanied by hand clapping, while in other instances the *tabala* serves as the prelude to a village announcement, sometimes signaling the sighting of the new moon that indicates the end or beginning of Ramadan, Islam's holy month of fasting. In the past it could also be used to signal the death of a village elder or a village meeting in days when the telephone and radio were not available. The Mandinka also possess a large repertoire of drums that are used for entertainment, with each drum playing specific functions in an ensemble of *sewruba* drums. Yet it is the *tamma* that has always drawn the greatest attention among drums, notwithstanding the *jimbe*'s current resurgence and popularity among Westerners. Partly because of its undulating and voice imitation, the *tamma* possibly originated from ancient Mali and was appropriated by many music traditions in West Africa. It is an important instrument among the Wolof and under the hands of an able or master drummer; it can mimic the inflections of the human voice, which often elicits amusement among audiences. Thus the *tamma* lends itself easily to *tassou,* a poetic expression among the Wolof that precedes a dance.

Music and dance are closely bound together in all the music traditions of The Gambia and the larger cultural landscape that is Senegambia Major and Minor. Within each music genre, be it *kora* or *xalam,* are different schools that may be distinguished by styles of playing, tuning, or singing. These distinctions are not necessarily localized but may, in fact, transcend artificial political borders, and it will take a seasoned listener to make these distinctions. With drumming, the mix is often complex, combining as it often does multiple rhythms that result in fast and often explosive performances, led by a lead drummer who with skill guides the other drummers and dancer(s).

Wolof women's dance performance, modern or traditional, unlike that of the Fula and Mandinka or Jola, is typically lewd. It is often inspired by the lead drummer, who encourages the dancer verbally, gutturally—leading to some sort of a duel between the two. In the process, the lead drummer, using short, quickened, and repetitive polyrhythmic sounds, prompts the dancer to dance just as fast as the rhythm, which ends in an explosive display of the woman's undergarment and some flesh. This is often followed by rapturous laughter from the audience. This kind of performance is generally restricted to young and often single women; married women's performances are more restrained. Thus, in most dance performances, there is often a dynamic and verbal interaction or communication between lead drummer and dancer, as well as with the audience.

Gambians in general have had an eclectic taste in music that ranges from Afro-Cuban music styles of the 1950s and 1960s to adaptations of that style that now include genres such as Afro-Manding, *mbalax*, jazz, salsa, reggae, hip-hop, and numerous others. Radio stations in The Gambia, especially in the urban centers, delight listeners with a mix of traditional music and modern tunes that are sometimes adaptations of traditional tunes as well as new creations. The Gambia is or was home to numerous *kora* and *xalam* virtuosos who travel the subregion entertaining patrons. Lalo Kebba Drammeh remains one of the best-known Gambian *kora* players. His mix of both traditional and modern improvisations earned him a regionwide and international reputation. While he sang mostly in Mandinka, during moments of improvisation he would include popular Wolof sayings. In one of his most listened to songs, called "Kano" (love in Mandinka), he intersperses this song with laments of a scorned woman—*wy'atchal suma ngegenai yaw ya maa terreh nelaw* (step down from my bed/pillow as you have deprived me of sleep thinking of you). His "Tutu Jarra," "Jimbeseng," and numerous other songs attest to his skills with the *kora* and his golden voice, which was silenced by death in 1974. His music lives on, however, in the West African subregion and the Senegambia diaspora in Europe and the United States.

Jali Nyama Susso, who died in 1991, was by contrast a traditionalist and sang the songs of old from ancient Mali and Guinea. His rendition of "Alla la ke" (Mandinka, it is God who did it or willed it), an old song with numerous interpretations, including Bembeya Jazz Band's version sung by the late Aboubacar Demba Camara, is a classic. Jali Nyama had a deep and commanding voice that held sway with the older generation, while his style was more tempered compared to Lalo Kebba's faster pace. Other virtuosos include Amadou Bansang Jobarteh and Alhaji Bai Konteh, who with several of his sons lived and performed in the United States and Europe. Now deceased, Alhaji Bai was perhaps the first Gambian *kora* player to attain international acclaim. Malamin Jobarteh and his son Tata Dinding, along with Alhaji Papa Suso, among others, have attained international acclaim and today also perform in the United States and Europe. Increasingly, some of these virtuoso *kora* players have teamed up with well-known African American, European, and Anglo-American musicians to produce a fusion of numerous songs and styles. Today, many *kora* players are resident abroad and travel to entertain diaspora communities and Western audiences. The great *kora* songs of old, including "Tarra," a song dedicated to Al Hajj Sheikh Umar Tal, is often performed by *xalam* players of Saloum in the Central River region of The Gambia and in Senegal.

These renditions very often include original Mandinka or Bambara verses, sentences, or words. It is believed that many Wolof *xalam* players, like their patrons in this region of The Gambia, especially in Ballanghar, Kaur, and Medina Sabach in Senegal, were from Mali and their ancestors were, in fact, Bambara or Susu. And their offspring, after several hundred years, became Wolofized, or Wolof both in culture and language. As they became more Wolof over the years, so did their songs of praise. The late Ebou Sosseh and N'derri Sosseh, both sons of Hayib Sosseh, grandfather of Professor Hayib Sosseh in the United States, were the griot (*gewel*) of the Touray dynasty in Ballanghar and Medina Sabach. Alhaji Sait Camara, perhaps better known in The Gambia, was a student of N' derri Sosseh, and the latter was a cousin of Ali Sosseh and Mammat Sossseh, all of whom hailed from Ballanghar and were the griot (*gewel*) of the Tourays of Ballanghar. The praise term "Manding-mori," often uttered after praising a Touray or Ceesay patron, alludes to their Bambara/Mandinka and Mali origins. (Sanneh, *ballamang*, is a term of praise for individuals who bear that last name.) There is also Ceesay-Ngari, which alludes to a Fula origin. In fact, given Alhaji Sait Camara's last name, his ancestors were either Bambara or Susu. And before the Sossehs assumed the Sosseh last name, they were Sissoho.[2]

This brief discussion points to the fluidity of ethnic identities and their construction. Today, Sosseh, Touray, and Ceesay families in Saloum identify as Wolof, yet their genealogy suggests that they are of Bambara or Susu heritage. Similarly, Mandinkanized Wolofs, having lived in Mandinka communities, have also shed, over time, their Wolof identity. In fact, the fluidity between Mandinka and Jola seems all the more apparent, as the surnames are similar and so are some of the traditions. The Fula, on the other hand, represent a conglomeration of different groups that assimilated into this large Fula/Fulbe group who are light-skinned Fula with Caucasian features.

Banjul is also home to several Wolof *gewel* families—the Mboob (Mboup in Senegal), Jeng (Dieng), and Mbye (Mbaye), whose ancestors hailed from Saloum in The Gambia, Sine-Saloum, and St. Louis in Senegal. Together, they have served as the repositories of Gambian Wolof/Manding and Fula cultures and today serve as journalists, musicians, and in other professions, some never abandoning their *gewel* roots and taking considerable pride in them. The *gewel* of Senegal are a much larger group than in The Gambia, and include the likes of Samba Jabbareh Samb and Al Hajj Mansour Mbaye, who is a gifted griot orator yet plays no musical instruments nor does he sing—he is a well-known television and radio personality in Senegal. His longtime brother, Al Hajj Samba Jabbareh Sambe, is a world-renowned historian and *xalam* player and singer. Aja Harr Mbaye Majagga is perhaps the best-known contemporary female singer in Wolof from Senegal. The incomparable Yande Codou Sene (Saine) sang in Serer and Wolof and was Leopold Senghor's griot. The more recent additions of Youssou N'Dour, Thione Seck, Baba Maal, and Kumba Gawlo Seck, especially, are each redefining what it means to be *gewel* or *n'gewel*. Their music, based in Wolof, Serer, and Tukulor traditional music and using percussion, has gone international in the last two decades, thanks to younger performers including N'Dour, his sister Abi, sister-in-law to Viviane, Masanneh, Titi, Abdou Thiouballo, the late N'dongo Low, and many more.

Among contemporary Gambian musicians in The Gambia, it is Jaliba Kuyateh with his Kumarreh Band that has received the most international acclaim. Coming as he does from a renowned Namina *jeli* family in the Central River region, Jaliba is a virtuoso *kora* player who sings in Mandinka and Wolof, performing new and old songs along with his own creations. His band, including an electric guitar, several Mandinka drums, a synthesizer, and a *kora,* relies on a traditional repertoire of praise songs, some of which he has modernized to capture a growing fan base in the United States and Europe. Perhaps one of Jaliba's greatest gifts, as with his *kora* predecessor, Lalo Kebba Drammeh, is his improvisational skills, especially at concerts at which he dazzles crowds.

As a *jali*, Jaliba also praise sings during his performances and is able to evoke among his listeners bouts of generosity seldom witnessed elsewhere. When he praises the Manneh, Sanneh, Touray, and other Senegambian surnames associated with gallantry and valor (*nyancho*), throngs overtake the stage, showering him with dollar notes and expensive gifts. While there are several promising young hip-hop, reggae, *mbalax*, and rap artists in The Gambia, none enjoy Jeliba's acclaim. Mam Tamsir Njie, though a good musician, has yet to take up his craft full-time, as he is a schoolteacher. Moussa Ngum, a Wolofized-Serer *mbalax* star, is Gambian and performs and lives in neighboring Senegal, where he has made a name for himself, but he has yet to make a name overseas. However, his style is unique, combining a repertoire that includes modern tunes as well as traditional *kassak* (circumcision) songs.

In the early 1960s, Laba Sosseh, a *gewel* whose ancestry is traceable to Banjul and Saloum in both Senegal and The Gambia, and who was by far the greatest salsa singer of his generation and perhaps of all time in Senegambia Major, also moved to Dakar, then the hub of the African music scene. While in Dakar Laba helped form the Star Band and later the Super Stars of Dakar before moving to Abidjan, and then to New York. Laba sang in both Spanish and Wolof and was a pioneer in the so-called *salsa-mbalax* genre, an infectious blend of African and Cuban percussion with Wolof lyrics. Some of his most famous songs included *Aminita*, a song of love to a young woman whose parents did not welcome him at their home. Dakar in the 1960s boasted great bands and singers that included not only Laba Sosseh but in addition Pape Seck, also of the Star Band of Dakar, and many other singers who later became part of Africando, a band based in New York comprising Senegalese and Cuban musicians. In fact, Laba sang one of his signature songs, "Suma Neneh" (My Baby), with them before he died in 2009.

A major Gambian band of the 1960s was the Super Eagles, previously known as the Super Eagles Band. Founded in Bathurst in 1967, two years after independence, the band drew its members from preexisting bands that included the African Jazz and the Black Stars, to which Ousu Njie, also known as Senor (singer) and Tom Cocker (singer and drummer) belonged. Along with Badou Jobe (bass guitar), Modou Cham (singer), Edu Heffner (singer), Pap Touray (singer), Malang Gassama (drums), Senemie Taylor (synthesizer), guitarist Marielle, a Congolese, and Sammie from Guinea, the Super Eagles went on to dazzle audiences throughout the West Coast of Africa and London. Photographer Malick Secka was their first financial sponsor but later parted ways with the band. Thereafter, a mixed group that included Nurainu Carew, Fisco Konateh, Rex King, and Modou Cham were among the Super Eagles Band's major supporters. It was a businessman, Solo Darboe, however, who bought them their first set of instruments.[3]

In its initial phase, the band played popular R&B, rock, Beatles songs, and salsa, along with Congolese rumba and *pachanga* tunes but later metamorphosed into a truly Afro-Manding band. Subsequently called Ifang Bondi, the band sang in all The Gambia's major languages while incorporating their different music styles. The outcome was truly revolutionary because for the first time Gambians could listen to music played and derived from Senegambia and The Gambia, specifically. The Super Eagles were loved throughout the subregion and Europe. It could be said that the Super Eagles and later Ifang Bondi made The Gambia better known through their music. Both the Super Eagles and Ifang Bondi were major competitors to the Dakar-based Senegalese bands and always attracted big crowds whenever they performed there. One of their most popular songs at the time was "Mandal Li" (roughly translated as Oh my, this), of which there were several versions performed by Senegalese bands; however, their own was simply irresistible and by far the best version. In July 2000, Ousu Njie (senor) released a CD, *Best of Faateleku* (Remembrance), in which he remixed old Super Eagles and Ifang

Bondi tunes. The result is a truly captivating, irrestible, danceable mélange of rumba, salsa, and other songs of decades ago, enhanced this time with the benefits of new recording technologies.

There were also several Gambian bands of lesser regional acclaim but with a national reputation. Gelewur, under the leadership of Bai Janha and Abdel Kader Ngum (Lie Ngum), dazzled audiences with their superb guitar-playing and singing skills. Just like Ifang Bondi, they contributed in no small measure to West Africa's and Gambia's contemporary music landscape. Together, they formed part of the changing waves of Gambian and African music, having graduated from playing Western and Cuban-based music to an authentic blend of Senegambian music. They were managed and promoted by the likes of the late Alieu Kah and Ousu "Lion" Njie.

Oko Drammeh, the current doyen of Gambian promoters, vigorously promoted them as well as the work of promising young Gambian musicians and artists. Youssou N'Dour, Senegal's *mbalax* superstar, who has performed globally and won every conceivable award in his relatively long profession, including a Grammy and an Oscar for his acting, performed with numerous Western performers, including Peter Gabriel, and follows in the tradition of Ifang Bondi and Laba Sosseh. What is little known is that N'Dour received his early training as a backup singer for the famous Super Eagles. Ifang Bondi singer Pap Touray's late mother, Marie Samuel Njie, along with Sosseh Jagne were also famous griot singers in their own right. And long before Senegal had Koumba Gawlo Seck and Viviane N'Dour, The Gambia had Vickie Blain, who sang beautiful melodies in English and Krio/Aku. She also sang popular old Wolof songs. Though never making it big internationally, Vickie Blain laid the foundation for future female and male Senegambian stars.

Youssou N'Dour's enchanting voice, accompanied by his band, Super Et-tiolle de Dakar, has a global fan base. He continues to set the pace for Senegambian music with innovations deeply steeped in Senegambian culture and musical traditions. The outcome is a heartwarming rhythmic blend of drum percussion punctuated by his wailing, sometimes piercing, modulated voice. Many Senegalese musicians have followed in his path by singing songs critical of Senegal's current government under Abdoulaye Wade. In 2011 N'Dour won approval from Wade's government to operate his own television station, which provides critical analysis of national events and news that would otherwise not air over the government-controlled stations.

In sum, Gambian music is a branch of the greater Senegambian culture, drawing on Fula, Wolof, Jola, and Manding cultures but influenced by music from Cuba, R&B, rock, reggae, and several other musical traditions. It too has influenced other music traditions, especially those of Cuba, Latin America, the United States, and black music in the United States specifically. The banjo, many believe or theorize, may very well have come from The Gambia/ Senegal, brought to these shores by enslaved Africans. Jazz, as well as the blues, major black contributions to world and American music, may have also originated in Senegambia or The Gambia specifically. The Wolof word *jaxas*, which means to mix, may have given this black music genre its name. It is more likely, however, that both jazz and the blues derive from Gumbay, a rich musical tradition in The Gambia and Senegal. Alan Lomax's *The Land Where the Blues Began* provides fascinating evidence of this.[4]

Music Genres

Music in African culture generally and Gambian culture specifically is central to all sorts of social interaction—weddings, naming ceremonies, wrestling matches, war times, and working on farms. Each institutionalized social event has its genre of song and sometimes dances to accompany it. The instruments used for these purposes can range from simple instruments that include a calabash over a pan of water struck with sticks, to the *kora, balafong, xalam,* as well as contemporary Western instruments accompanied by singing and dancing. Kings and generals in the past were said to be inspired during warfare by their griots through song, poetry, and praise. Similarly, music that accompanies a king, queen, or chief is distinct from drum music that announces his or her death. At beach and house parties and open concerts, music takes on a more contemporary dimension and genre, even though its initial inspiration is rooted in the more traditional, using local instruments for local entertainment.

Both contemporary and traditional music, especially in Senegal, Gambia, Mali, and Guinea, is infused with religion and verses from the Qur'an, making the distinction between secular and religious music all the more blurry. The contemporary music of Jaliba Kuyateh, Youssou N'Dour, and Kinneh Lam, especially, is replete with praise to religious leaders and Qur'anic verses. In his earlier career, Thione Seck, another Senegalese contemporary superstar, sang songs of praise for both secular and religious leadership and for listening purposes mainly, using the *xalam* primarily. Today, his band, *Ramdan,* boasts both traditional and modern instruments along with huge speakers—all calibrated to produce a tantalizing boom effect. Like Baba Maal, who sings mostly in Fula/Tukulor, Thione performs internationally and is a big draw in the West and among diaspora African communities who dance to his music, which he intersperses with quotes from the Qur'an. Thus, the type of music played in The Gambia and Senegal, specifically, as elsewhere is a function of the context or situation and purpose for which the music is played.

Court Music

The genre of court music is reserved for royalty. The *jungung* drum, in particular, was once reserved only for the listening pleasures of a king and his guests. A king on his way to a meeting with a colonial administrator, typically the district commissioner, or other kings or chiefs of similar status would be accompanied by an elaborate retinue of drummers. In the colonial days, Gambian chiefs played relatively important roles in the colonial administration, which were punctuated with *mansa bengo* (kings/chiefs conference). These *mansa bengo* were an occasion for Gambian kings/chiefs to be paraded past their subjects, dressed to the hilt in rich traditional garb accompanied by musicians and praise singers. Such music was played with deliberate and sometimes slower tempos to go along with the king's walk, or the slow gallop of the horses ridden by the chief and his entourage. In general, the *kora* and *xalam* music were reserved more for the chief and his guests at his palace, where much praise singing and accounts of valor and generosity of the king and his ancestors were recounted.

Music for Entertainment

Ultimately, music in The Gambia, as elsewhere, whether performed in the courts of kings in precolonial and colonial times or thereafter, has high entertainment value. Singing and drumming at wrestling matches or even male circumcision festivals are different in style and purpose, yet still carry with them immense entertainment value and provide continuity to these cherished institutions. Wrestlers receive inspiration from songs of praise just as much as listeners or audiences derive pleasure from hearing them. Songs of the *n'gansingo* (Mandinka) or *n'juli* (Wolof) initiates are mostly devoid of references to Islam—betraying their origin in pre-Islamic cultures. However, the *juju*, Qur'anic verses encased in leather and also known as amulets, are won by wrestlers and ordinary folk and serve as a protective against evil and *mangkaneh*, the spells of opponents. The *safara* is the solution obtained from washing slates inscribed with Qur'anic verses and is also used for protection. Even at soccer matches, these are used to increase a team's chances of winning, accompanied by rattlers, whistles, and drums. The use of *safara, mangkaneh,* and *juju* are routinely described as witchcraft practices by Western scholars without adequate understanding of their function; they do not constitute witchcraft but instead are part of a wrestler's intimidation kit. Today, training rather than these kits is given priority.

Music that accompanies rituals is performed within and by secret societies and is also intended to entertain as much as to safeguard the mystique and secrecy that surround them. The *egugu*, among the Igbo, for instance, has a place in the celebration of Gambians, especially during the Christmas season alongside the *kumpa* among the Jola, *kankurang* (Mandinka), *simba* (Wolof), and *mamaparra* (Sussu). In all, these masquerades and the identity of the individual performer is kept a secret and seldom revealed, leaving many spectators guessing. Identities can often be guessed, however, by the way, for instance, that a particular *kankurang* dances, or a certain limp gives away a performer's identity. Yet even in instances where a performer's identity is known, they are believed to assume another spiritual persona, one possessed by the spirit of ancestors who transform them into nonhumans capable of incredible feats. Performers may also assume the spirit of an ancestor to serve at trials as the *egugu* or perform at burials of secret society members, especially elders. Again, despite Christianity and Islam's stronghold, these forms of entertainment represent pre-Islamic and pre-Christian rituals that in turn are used to celebrate important religious holidays—this is known as syncretism. Christmas in urban centers during the 1960s, and perhaps as late as the 1980s, would be incomplete without these masquerades. Today, these performances are smaller in scale and conducted by younger and inexperienced performers, if they are conducted at all.

During Christmas, especially, *kankurang*, *simba*, and *egugu* roam the streets from one compound to another, soliciting money. They routinely stop individuals they come across in the street to solicit gifts of money, and a failure to deliver could result in a quick flash of a whip. The *simba* is more often taunted and subjected to blows on the body by the young for thrills. In response, a *simba* runs in hot pursuit and retaliates in kind. A *mamapara* is saddled on at least two 10-foot stilts and walks awkwardly, sometimes scaling fences of compounds with its long legs. Being so tall, a skilled *mamapara* can elicit much laughter among onlookers as he stands next to a tall tree or tries to run after members of the audience. All these performers and performances are shrouded in secrecy. The *kumpa*, among the Jola, specifically, is covered completely in shredded raffia palm leaves with at least a four-foot pole attached to its head. While dancing, the *kumpa* plants the pole superficially on the ground and twirls around it to produce a continuous movement of its body, to the sheer wonder of onlookers.

Religious Festival Music

Recitations of the Qur'an during religious festivals, including the two Eids that mark the end of Ramadan, the feast of the sacrifice, and Mawlood'Nabi, Prophet Muhammad's birthday, are occasions for Muslims to engage in worship, praise, and singing. *Gammo* is an all-night affair that celebrates the life of the Prophet and is accompanied by sermons to highlight his character, piety, and the virtuous life. These accounts of the Prophet's life by an imam or scholar are very often interrupted by singers who sing hymns dedicated to the Prince of Peace, as Muhammad is often called. Sung acappella, these hymns are sung in all the national languages, depending on the ethnic community, and Arabic. They attest to the musicality and beauty of the human voice and the poetic nature of the Qur'an, which is written in classical Arabic. The Qur'an in the hands of an able reciter is transformed and brought to life as a deeply moving poetic expression. Even the call to the five daily prayers by the *mauwazzin*, prayers during Ramadan, or Friday prayers are in themselves deeply musical. Thus, recitation of the holy book is a music tradition by itself in Islam with several genres that have led many an audience to tears because of its beauty. While *gammo* is seldom accompanied by drums, among some Banjul Wolof Muslims it once was a common practice called *gammo-sabarr—gammo* with the *tabala*. It is also common among the *Muride* Brotherhood to use drums to accompany hymns during *gammo* or as they roam the streets seeking alms from believers.

Christians also use drums in their various celebrations, even though this is more common among Catholics in Senegal. Hymns at church gatherings, celebrations that honor the Virgin Mary, Christmas, Easter, and other Christian holidays and Sunday Mass are celebrated with hymns in local languages, but mostly Wolof. These hymns also have special significance and beauty, especially when sung in Serer. It is routine on Thursday nights, the eve of the Muslim Sabbath, which is Friday, for television and radio stations in both Senegal and The Gambia to air Muslim religious hymns. Sunday morning is reserved for Christian hymns and church service broadcasts. This balance in terms of religious media coverage has engendered a strong sense of tolerance and respect among and between religious communities.

WORK AND RECREATIONAL MUSIC

The majority of Gambians are intimately tied to agriculture, as they cultivate groundnuts, corn, sorghum, coos, and other cereal crops for export and subsistence. Farming or tilling the land was once recognized as a noble profession, and many held onto it until the industry began to fail due to lack of government support. Yet it was the case several decades ago, and still now to a lesser degree, that a head of a household would organize his family or labor to produce a bumper crop for their collective survival, along with petty trading in used clothes, for instance, during the dry season. Praise songs would implore young men to attack the *warr* (large tract of land in Wolof), often under the intense gaze of the sun. Groundnut farms almost overtaken by weeds were cleared by the young who were inspired by songs. Women also use songs as a source of inspiration while working in rice fields or to critique social and gender arrangements regarding work on farms and at home. Thus, Gambian women have resisted through song, but many men take it for entertainment, without grasping the true meaning.

In Saloum, some 40 or more years ago, there was a song performed by two iconic drummers and singers: Damm Ceesay of Kaur and Kebba Haddy of Njau. The song went thus: *du ma sai legi yea, du ma sai legi yai mbarro tuti na aah; du mai sai legi yea, munu ma khei bodje, sokhe, ngone jot ma tali rerr aah* (I cannot get married now, mother, I cannot get married now, because I am too young. I cannot get married now, mother, because I am unable to awake at dawn to pound and prepare the grain and in the evening, prepare dinner). Conversely, a woman yearning to be married laments for her prospective husband. Now a classic, this song was performed by Senegal's premier traditional female singer, Aja Harr Mbaye Majagga: *dungah, dungah, dungah kaeign lai sai, kaeign la madie sai, sokhe njael be talib rerr, anna dungahaaa, kaeign lai sai dungah?* (When will I ever get married, when will I ever get up at dawn to pound and prepare the grain and later light the dinner fire; when will I ever get married?) Songs in Senegambian culture are therefore important vehicles for social protest, criticism, or commentary. Male songs will often counter criticisms against men with songs that seek to maintain the status quo.

Games such as *sosalla' so*, a popular Mandinka boys' game, is one in which the objective is to retrieve a ball and avoid being hit by it and in the process eliminate all players by hitting them with the ball to become the lone player at the end. It was played with songs and included call-and-answer invitations to join in the fun. Wrestling songs and chin, lower lip, and gum tattooing for women produced songs just as beautiful as the wedding songs of old. In The Gambia and Senegal there is a song and possibly a dance for every occasion. Among the Serer and Jola, elders who journey to the other world are often given a big send-off befitting their status. These too are celebrated with song and dance, just as plays, drama performances, and storytelling are punctuated with song.

MUSICAL INSTRUMENTS AND SINGING STYLE

Musical instruments include drums of numerous sizes and shapes made from animal skins and locally produced wood. String instruments include the *kora, xalam, ngoni, riti* (a concave one-string instrument), and hand pianos. There are animal horns, calabashes and gourds, and various iron instruments—the last played by women to accompany a *kora* player and singer(s). In general, these instruments are not vested with mystical properties even though the *tamma* (talking drum) is believed to be an instrument inspired by spirits because of its resemblance to the human voice under the hands of a master player. As mentioned earlier, some drums, like the *tabala*, have an important social function besides their entertainment value—announcing the death of a chief or elder, or announcing to the village an upcoming event. Some, however, are invested with ethnic identities. Animal horns, for instance, were once used by approaching village wrestling teams to announce their arrival at the host village. The *lambe*, a large drum that produces a hollow sound, serves as the base to the drums played during wrestling matches. Its deep and hollow sound could be heard deep into the night for miles by adjoining villages as it signaled an ongoing wrestling match.

DANCE

Dance, song, and music are deeply interconnected in Gambian and African cultures generally. Not all music is meant to be danced to, however. *Kora, ngoni,* and *xalam* are meant for listening, for the most part, and so is religious music, which one could sway to. Each ethnic group typically has distinctive dance styles or moves. Fula dances, especially women's, are generally graceful and given to less movement and bursts. Dances by women tend to be more of a swaying movement from left to right accompanied sometimes by clapping and singing. Fula men's dances tend to be more energetic. With oversized *chayas* and a calabash, which they stroke with oversized rings on their fingers, they too sway to the music as they sing along. As the pace of the music from the calabashes quickens, so do the dance moves, sometimes resulting in dizzying turns and acrobatic moves like summersaults, similar to break dancing. In fact, the break dance, a dance genre that was very popular in the United States during the 1980s, could very well be an offshoot of Fula male dance styles.

The dance of Mandinka women, especially with the dance style called *lenjeng; dimba' jullo,* a fertility dance; and *barra' wullo,* a work song dance, involve vigorous stamping of the ground as arms flap up and down to the side. With the head cocked to the side, sometimes straight, the dance resembles a graceful bird in flight. Gambian men generally and Mandinka men in particular are not likely to dance to traditional *seiruba* or *sabarr* drumming in public, unlike their Senegalese cousins, who generally are better dancers. Gambian Wolof men also shy away from dancing in public but participate more in public dancing than their Mandinka brothers. Yet when a specific dance style called *sara, gajo,* or *samtamuna* is played, it is an invitation for the young men to dance. *Sara,* like many Gambian dances, starts out slowly, and a male dancer circles the *gew* (dance circle) before he gives or receives the signal to speed up the pace. Other males might join in to support the first dancer, and so would his female kin and friends, who throw in their head ties in support of the male dancers. The outcome is a fast-paced yet intricate dance that results in rapturous laughter. Wolof males also perform a dance called *k'hokmbel*, which involves flapping the legs and thighs while hands are thrust outward toward the sky. Other male dancers hold onto their heads or assume a saluting pose as they dance to the scintillating music, while flapping their legs. In Saloum, specifically, women also dance *gajo* with deliberate ease and elegance. The highlight of a drumming event in Kaur was when Ndey Kani Touray took to the *gew*. Like the men, she too would dance around the *gew* and speed up her pace as she performed the intricate dance instructions from the drummer (Damm Ceesay). Everyone looked forward to her performance, often accompanied by the phrase *Kani ku daega gallan la* (Kani hears and understands the drumbeat beyond normal proportions).

Jola dance and music, *buka'rabu*, resemble that of the Mandinka, and vice versa. Years of intermarriage and cohabitation between the two groups has resulted in the near fusion of dance styles and moves. Both are characterized by a flying bird dance style amid loud hand clapping, sometimes amplified by hand-size wooden boards in each palm. Whistles are commonly used by both Mandinka and Jola drummers, unlike their Wolof counterparts, which add to the rhythmic richness and flow of the music and dance. As mentioned earlier, the Narr women's dance is similar to that of the Fula. That too may be due to years of cohabitation in the northern part of Senegal and Mauritania.

However, when Gambians and Senegalese dance to the modern music of Youssou N'Dour, Omar Penn, Madda Bah, Jaliba Kuyateh, and the younger generation of artists, ethnic dance styles and distinctions almost disappear. To the astute listener or the observant onlooker, it is relatively easy to detect traces of various ethnic music elements. For example, Baaba Maal's music is explicitly Tukulor. Not only does he sing in *pularr*, but his beat, depending on the genre of music he chooses to play, is in general less *m'balax* in style. This is also the case for Jaliba Kuyateh's music, which relies heavily on Mandinka traditional songs and dance, just as the Senegalese band *Toure Kunda* had done before him, in the southern Casamance region of Senegal.

POPULAR MUSIC AND FOREIGN INFLUENCES

Modern Gambian music has for many years been influenced by music from foreign lands. Young and middle-aged Gambians alike are drawn to reggae music because of the late Bob Marley, Peter Tosh, Jimmy Cliff, Third World, and other musicians and bands from the Caribbean, which have been adopted by African stars such as Ivory Coast's Alpha Blondie and the late South African performer Lucky Dube, who died a senseless death during a robbery. As mentioned earlier, music from Cuba and Congo deeply influenced Gambian music. Some of Super Eagle's best music repertoires in Wolof or Mandinka, Fula and Jola, like Badda Touray, have deep rumba influence and beat. R&B, rock, and music from the Middle East likewise influenced the Senegalese music scene and by extension Gambia's as well. Ghana's Osibisa, Cameroon's Manu Dibango and Fela Ransome Kuti, and Sunny Ade of Nigeria have also influenced Gambian music in significant ways, not to mention Bembeya Jazz Band and Horroya Band of Guinea. The *highlife* when played at parties is a sure invitation to dance.[5] Bembeya Jazz of Guinea had an interpretation of a *highlife* tune called *Mamie Wata* (mermaid), originally a Ghanian tune, that was a big hit in the early 1970s and to this day will elicit excitement among middle-aged folks.

World-beat music, a music genre that became popular in the 1980s and beyond and is a fusion of several music traditions, African and Western, specifically, continues to increase its fan base in The Gambia. Wolof rap music from neighboring Senegal is also leaving a mark on young Gambian rap artists, just as rap music from the United States has done. Rap music is not new in Senegambia, however. It is part and parcel of a rich poetic tradition that spans centuries. Gambian hip-hop artists like their counterparts in Senegal blend their hip-hop with styles from the United States to give their music international appeal. Groups like Pencha B, Masla B and Dancehall Masters, as well as young artists like Freaky Joe, also known as Singhateh, and Amie Dibba, based in the United States, have all performed internationally with a growing fan base, especially among diaspora Gambians. Other young Gambian artists with considerable talent include not only Singhateh but also Novagambia, whose style of play also includes raga-tone, hip-hop with an Afro-Manding backdrop and who sings in Mandinka and Wolof. Gambiaboy, as well as the Pepper House Crew, and many more are likely to break sooner than later into the international music scene. This crop of new artists has tapped more directly into the world-beat genre and is likely not to be limited to the more traditional *m'balax* or *ndaga* in The Gambia. Though the industry is young, it stands to grow internationally, partly because of the talent and the global appeal of hip-hop.

Raga-ton and Bangra music also have growing appeal in The Gambia, as elsewhere. These Spanish and Indian musical styles resonate well with Gambians given that Raga-ton has a distinctly African beat to it, with a heavy drumbeat similar to that of Bangra. The latter combines elements of hip-hop, African music with an Indian overlay. Bangra's appeal may also lie in the fact that many middle-aged Gambians, especially those over 50 years of age, grew up watching Indian films, captivated by the songs, the courtships and the fistfights that broke out occasionally.

Thus, Gambian music has been remarkably successful in absorbing elements from several music styles globally, and has also, in turn, influenced music in other parts of the world. Dance styles from the subregion such as *highlife*, and *juju* music from Ghana and Nigeria, respectively, *sokous* from the Caribbean and Congo, *meringue*, *charanga*, *son*, and *salsa* from Cuba and South America have had their mark, especially before the music renaissance of the 1960s spearheaded in The Gambia by the Super Eagles and Ifang Bondi. The jerk, foxtrot, and the bump and grind were also popular at one point or another. Black artists of the 1960s, including Otis Redding, James Brown, Etta James, and Jimmy Hendrix, as well as the Beatles, Deep Purple, and Carlos Santana kept many young people up as they danced the night away. Gambians therefore have a rich and eclectic taste in music that also includes European and American classical music traditions among the elite. In an era of globalization, contemporary Gambian music and its traditional variants have been exported to the rest of the world where they are included in musical performances by Gambian cultural groups in Oslo, Norway, and Birmingham and London, England, or as part of jazzercise programs in these countries.

YouTube has a diverse repository of all music genres from The Gambia and Senegal, as well as dance videos. Dance and music styles are likely to evolve and change while keeping some traditional forms intact. Dance styles like *ventilator*, which was popular less than a decade ago and involves hip gyrations to mimic a fan or ventilator, is a modern adaptation. However, *mbabass* as well as other dance styles from various ethnic groups, especially those related to work and fertility for young women, are likely to be around for some time to come.

NOTES

1. Sedia Jatta, "Born Musicians: Traditional Music from The Gambia," in *Repercussions: A Celebration of African American Music,* ed. Geoffrey Haydon and Dennis Marks, 19–23 (London: Century Publishing, 1985), 23.

2. Conversation with Professor Hayib Sosseh, September 2011.

3. Conversation with Mr. Tom Cocker, September 2011.

4. In this fascinating book, Lomax traces the blues to Senegambia and the griot (*gewel* or *jeli*). Alan Lomax, *The Land Where the Blues Began* (New York: Pantheon Books, 1993).

5. The *highlife* is a happy and gracious dance with slow movements enjoyed by all age groups, especially the middle aged.

9

Changing Landscape

IT SHOULD BE clear by now that The Gambia, in spite of its small size and limited mineral resources, is home to a dynamic culture and traditions that are part of the great Manding, Fula, Wolof, and other ethnic-based cultures of the subregion. Rather than being static, Gambian culture is dynamic, having helped shape major cultural traditions and music genres of the old and new worlds. This influence is felt more readily in the southern United States, South America, and the Caribbean, including Cuba and Jamaica. Gambians, too, have been the recipients of various influences from the outside, making Gambian culture and music, in particular, truly global and developing among Gambians an eclectic and rich appreciation and taste for music.

What also comes out distinctly from our discussion is that centuries of cultural exchange and mixing produced a cultural mosaic while maintaining the distinct ethnic qualities that constitute and differentiate them. This mosaic also illustrates to some degree the fluidity of ethnic identities, leading many to assume or construct various social identities. Thus, what is constant in Gambian society, as in many other societies around the world, is the permanence of change. Gambian society and Gambians themselves have been particularly adaptive to Arab and Western influences for centuries. Yet rather than these influences being forces of destruction, they have for the most part integrated into Gambian cultures and have never been subordinated, per se.

The Soninke-Marabout Wars of the mid-1800s were a pivotal event in the evolution of Gambian society insofar as it violently overthrew an already decaying political and economic order that was based and sustained by the trade in enslaved Africans. These wars were very much a part of the jihadist wave that began in northern Nigeria and culminated in The Gambia under Maba, Foday Sillah, and Foday Kaba. Therefore, the end of these wars of purification effectively ushered in a new religio-politico-social order, aided in large measure by combined British and French pacification wars. When unarmed Foday Kaba was shot and killed by the French in 1901, Gambian/ Muslim resistance to British colonialism effectively ended, and with it the trade in human beings. The protagonist in this bloody saga is none other than Foday Kaba, who although a slave trader himself, resisted to the very end. His 40 wives were not so lucky, as they died tragically in a bunker adjoined to the armory that exploded, killing all of them.

A century and a half later, following many years of resistance by Fula, Jola, and Serer traditional worshipers, The Gambia is today a Muslim-majority state with less than 1 percent of its population practicing traditional religions. Yet it was Maba Jahou Bah, the Tukulor cleric jihadist, who effectively overran the Soninke kings or aristocracy on both banks of the river and in the north to ransack the Wolof-Serer states of Cayor and Sine before his death at the battle of Somp. Under the British colonial policy of indirect rule, the Mandinka river states and their leaders became important instruments in the British colonial apparatus, with considerably reduced powers. One of the lasting effects of the jihadist wars was the movement of large numbers of inhabitants in the colony into the river states, making many of these states truly multiethnic and multicultural. These population movements were in subsequent years the fabric from which the cultures and customs described and analyzed in this book were fashioned.

Another legacy of these wars is the piety and generally laid-back Gambian personality, following decades of religious revolutionary wars and bloodshed only to culminate in French and British wars of pacification. Out of these ashes emerged a conservative religious social order bent on preserving peace at all cost. Thus, these jihads deeply shaped Gambians and their dogmatic pursuit of peace. To this must be added the *Mansa* syndrome—the tendency among modern chiefs, even the president of the republic, and to some degree pockets in the population, to emulate the former grandeur of former kings in today's modern political system. Patron-client relationships permeate The Gambia's social and political landscapes, which can be used for good purposes but when used in excess breed corruption and abuse of power. Yet interethnic and religious tolerance, as well as stability, remains The Gambia's strongest card and bodes well for the country and its current and future development goals. Not surprisingly, many investors, teachers, builders, tailors, and others from the subregion flock to its shores.

Today, there are visible signs of infrastructure development in the form of new gas stations, private banks, insurance companies, and road construction in Banjul and elsewhere. These roads have eased travel and enhanced commerce, growth, and development in coastal and rural areas alike. There is a boom in urban residential construction in newly designated areas developed by the government for Gambian nationals at home and abroad. Yet this new and growing relative affluence is not limited to urban areas, as signs of the construction boom can also be seen in the most remote parts of the country.[1] Similarly, the availability of, and access to, education, clean water, telephone services, and medical care grew since independence and more so since 1996 under Jammeh. Following the completion of the Farafenni and Bwiam hospitals, and the graduation of doctors from the University of The Gambia's Medical and Nursing schools, the health status of Gambians has improved, even though many die from easily preventable diseases. Still, the University of The Gambia is a necessary institution for national development, and its creation by the regime in 1999 fills an important gap in The Gambia's education and development needs. Accordingly, Gambians today are worldlier, are widely traveled, and are keenly aware of global and regional forces at play, thanks to globalization and the opportunities it provides to many people.[2]

Employment for women, especially in senior civil service jobs, seems to have increased but still lags behind that of men. As a result, many enterprising urban women engage in international commerce, making trips to the United Kingdom, United States, India, Dubai, and neighboring African states to sell and buy merchandise. Women also continue to dominate the street-vendor category, selling everything from roasted peanuts and cashew nuts to fruits and vegetables. These positive aspects of The Gambia's current development are in large measure attributable to the efforts and will to succeed of the average Gambian, and together they have important economic effects. The regime has also contributed modestly to these by way of infrastructure and a liberal import-export policy.[3]

Clearly, one positive and stabilizing tendency in The Gambia's political system is the apparent popularity of Jammeh. If the November 24, 2011, presidential election in which he won over 70 percent of the popular vote is any indication, then his popularity is increasing. There appears to be tremendous civil service support, but many contend this support is coerced and self-serving. Consequently, opposition to President Jammeh or his policies is generally perceived as opposition to The Gambia's national interest.[4] Thus, many Gambians in opposition strongholds, and perhaps even among regime supporters, harbor deep-seated fears for The Gambia and its people. Deepening poverty, now estimated at 60–65 percent, has heightened resentment

Africell Headquarters on Kairaba Avenue at Latrikunda, German, is one of several cell phone service providers in the country. It is located on the busy commercial strip Kairaba Avenue, named after the The Gambia's founding president. (Courtesy of Buharry Gassama)

and frustration toward the regime. The rift between the haves and have-nots is widening and perhaps unbridgeable. Deep-seated resentment is also widespread among those whose families were financially hurt by the coup, and certainly among those who lost jobs and loved ones since 1994. There is also mounting resentment against President Jammeh himself, those closely associated with him, and his regime.[5]

The greatest threat to Jammeh and his regime, however, does not lie here or in the ballot box, but within the military. The growing perception that the country in general and the army in particular are run by Jolas, and the perceived exclusion of other more populous ethnic groups like the Mandinkas, is a trend that is likely to have bloody consequences within the army, and within society at large. Accordingly, there is a mounting fever for revenge or settling of scores within the army.[6]

And as opportunities for promotion and improved rank and social status for non-Jolas are impeded, the expectation for civil strife and political violence heighten. The desire for revenge has also led to declining morale within the army and civil service. To this must be added the growing pool of unemployed, educated youth, the product in part of Jammeh's successful efforts to expand educational opportunities for the less advantaged. Like their counterparts in the army, they are growing restless because of their exclusion from income and wealth-making opportunities in society. Many unemployed youth contend that those in power today owe their wealth not to any special skills or gift(s) but to brute force.[7]

In sum, The Gambia has both integrative and disintegrative tendencies and is full of possibilities and opportunities for investment, growth, and development. While size and location clearly pose severe constraints, they likewise offer boundless opportunities for investors and enterprising individuals. Thus, given an enabling political and economic environment, the goals of sustainable development, gender equity, and an improved standard of living for the population are attainable in the long run. The Gambia has the right mix of a resilient people and culture, a warm Florida-like climate without the hurricanes, and an abundant and relatively inexpensive labor force and is less than six or seven hours from London and New York, respectively. Being an agricultural country, The Gambia has surprisingly abundant land to grow many products in addition to the diverse food crops that already exist. Yet The Gambia's greatest assets are the river and the ocean not to mention its people. These provide numerous opportunities for agriculture, energy production, recreation, fishing, and tourism. Certainly, with these opportunities will come many changes, opportunities, and challenges. Yet as in centuries past, Gambians will harness them to strengthen themselves, their country, and their culture while, it is hoped, addressing traditional practices that disempower women, girls, the poor, and marginalized groups.

NOTES

1. For a detailed discussion of these trends and tendencies, see Abdoulaye Saine, "The Gambia's Changing Political, Economic and Social Landscape," *Africa Insight* 33, no. 3 (2003): 57–64. Portions of this chapter have been adapted from that article. Also, see Abdoulie Sallah and Colin C. Williams, "The Illusion of Capitalism in Contemporary Sub-Saharan Africa: A Case-study of The Gambia," *Foresight* 13, no. 3 (2011): 50–63.

2. Saine, "The Gambia's Changing," 58.

3. Ibid., 59.

4. Ibid., 60.

5. Ibid., 62.

6. Ibid., 58.

7. Ibid., 63.

Glossary

Aa'bedi   How is it? (Mandinka)

Aa' da saeli   How are you? (Fula)

Affra   Smoked/grilled and well-seasoned beef or chicken (Narr)

Ajaratou   Religious title for a woman who has performed the hajj (pilgrimage) to Mecca (Arabic)

Alhaji (Al Hajj)   Religious title for a male who has performed the hajj (pilgrimage) to Mecca (Arabic)

Alkali   Village headman (Arabic)

Almamy   Religious and political leader (Arabic)

Asobi   Clothing of the same or similar color and pattern worn by both men and women for a special occasion (Yoruba)

Attaya   Brewed sweet green tea (Narr)

Baku   Self-praise poetic expression by wrestlers to intimidate opponents (Wolof)

Bantaba   A tree-shaded platform where men meet for conversation or gossip (Mandinka)

Benachin (Jollof Rice, Thiep)   Rice cooked in a spicy tomato-based sauce with vegetables and eaten with beef, fish, lamb, or chicken (Wolof)

Bissap   Hibiscus-sweetened juice from the sorrel plant (Wolof/Senegal)

Bororoje   A Fulani subgroup devoted to cattle herding

Bundi' neke   Serahule dish

Butut   Unit of Gambia's currency; 100 butut equals one dalasi (Mandinka)

Cadi   Religious judge (Arabic)

Challit   Forgetting a personal belonging—clothing, shoes, and so on—at the site of a meal (Wolof)

Cheerh' basseh   Couscous-like cereal made from coos, millet, or corn and eaten with a light and spicy peanut butter sauce (Wolof)

Dairra   Religious organization (Arabic)

Darra   Traditional Islamic school (Arabic)

Datte   A tree-shaded platform where men meet for conversation or gossip (Wolof)

Dempeteng   Roasted rice snack made from a new crop/harvest (Mandinka)

Dimo   Freeborn (Fula)

Ding-follo   First child (Mandinka)

Fai   When a married woman temporarily leaves her husband and stays with relatives to protest physical and other forms of abuse

Fiqh   Islamic law based on the Qur'an and jurist interpretations (Arabic)

Fitna   Stress (Arabic)

Gammo   Night of worship and praise celebrating Prophet Muhammad's birthday (Wolof)

Gewel   Third tier in Wolof stratification system of historians, entertainers, and diplomats (Wolof)

Griot   Entertainer belonging to the third strata of Wolof society (French)

Hajj   Pilgrimage to Islam's holy sites in Saudi Arabia (Arabic)

Hallpullar   Speakers of Fula and other sublanguages within it (Fula)

Jeliyaa   Tradition associated with being a jeli, griot, gewel (Mandinka)

Kafo   A social organization built around age and sex (Mandinka)

Kambaniya   An almost carefree existence for teenage boys or young men, a time to experiment (Mandinka)

Kanno   Love (Mandinka)

Kinkiliba   A leaf used for tea believed to have medicinal properties (Mandinka)

K'nohorr   Wizard (Wolof)

Kora   Twenty-one string harp-like instrument (Mandinka)

Kulembeng   Long skirt worn by girls with openings along both legs (Serahule)

Mansa' bengo   King/chief's conference (Mandinka)

Mawlood'nabi   Celebration marking Prophet Muhammad's birthday (Arabic)

Mbageul   Love (Senegalese Wolof)

Mbaring'ndingo   Niece (Mandinka)

Murr   Last rite before a wife joins her husband (Wolof)

Naa'da Slippery green vegetable stew with okra, eaten with rice (Mandinka)

Nan'mburu A pap-like meal eaten with a sweet mixture of peanut butter and sour milk with a touch of liquefied baobab fruit; could also mean Easter (Wolof)

Ndagga Dance style (Wolof)

Ndongo Student or street-smart kid or teenager (Wolof)

Neit' ack' taransu The traditional monetary bride price of less than $US10

N'gansingo Newly circumcised/initiated boy or girl

Rang' be Market or lineup for unmarried women (Wolof)

Saafara Water solution derived from washing a slate inscribed with a verse(s) from the Qur'an and believed to cure illness and protect from evil

Sarre Village (Fula)

Shari'a Islamic law (Arabic)

Sunni An Islamic sect (Arabic)

Talibe Student (Arabic)

Tariqa Religious Order (Arabic)

Taw Firstborn child (Wolof)

Teranga Senegambian hospitality (Wolof)

Tiko Head scarf (Mandinka)

Tomma Namesake (Mandinka; used by most Gambian ethnic groups)

Tura'ndor Namesake (Wolof)

Vous A social group that meets to play card and other games and drink green tea (French)

Xalam Three-string lute (Wolof)

Zakat Charity/alms given to the poor (Arabic)

Selected Bibliography

Austin, Allan. *African Muslims in the Antebellum America: A Source Book*. New York: Garland, 1984.

Austin, Allan, *African Muslims in Antebellum America: Transatlanic Stories and Spiritual Struggles*. New York: Routledge, 1997.

Barry, Boubacar. *Senegambia and the Atlantic Slave Trade*. Cambridge: Cambridge University Press, 1989.

Barry, Cherno Omar. "Gambian Fiction: An Analytical Study." In *The Gambia: Essays on Contemporary Issues and Future Direction: 1965–2011*, edited by Abdoulaye Saine, Ebrima Ceesay, and Ebrima Sall. Tenton, NJ: Africa World Press, 2012.

Beck, Linda. *Brokering Democracy in Africa: The Rise of Clientelist Democracy in Senegal*. New York: Palgrave, 2008.

Broughton, Simon,. *World Music: The Rough Guide*. London: Rough Guide, 1994.

Brown, Stewart, "Gambian Fictions," Wasafiri, Vol. 7, Issue 15, (1992): 2–7.

Carney, Judith. "Agro-environments and Slave Strategies in the Diffusion of Rice Culture to the Americas." In *Political Ecology: An Integrative Approach in Geography and Environmental-Development Studies,* edited by Karl S. Zimmer and Thomas J. Bassett, 256–73. New York: Guilford.

Ceesay, Ebrima. *The Military and Democratization in The Gambia*: *1994–2003*. Toronto, Canada: Trafford, 2006.

Chant, Sylvia, and Alice Evans. "Looking for the One(s): Young Love and Urban Poverty in The Gambia." *Environment and Urbanisation* 22, no.2 (2010): 353–69.

Chant, Sylvia, and Gareth A. Jones. "Youth, Gender and Livelihoods in West Africa: Perspectives From Ghana and The Gambia." *Children's Geographies* 3, no. 2 (2005): 185–99.

Chaplin, Karen. "Domestic Violence in International Law: The Criminalization of Domestic Violence in The Republic of The Gambia." Unpublished M.A. thesis, Lancaster University, United Kingtom.

Chongan, Ebrima. *The Price of Duty: 994 Days in The Gambian Military Junta's Dungeon.* London: Lulu Center, 2010.

Curtin, Philip. *Economic Change in Pre-Colonial Africa: Senegambia in the Era of the Slave Trade.* Madison: University of Wisconsin Press, 1975.

Darboe, Momodou. "Islam in West Africa: Gambia." *African Studies Review* 47, no. 2 (2004): 73–81.

Davidson, B. *The Black Man's Burden: Africa and the Curse of the Nation-State.* New York: Random House, 1992.

Davidson, Basil, with F. K. Buah. *A History of West Africa to the Nineteenth Century.* New York: Doubleday & Company, 1966.

Diouf, Sylviane. *Servants of Allah: Africans Enslaved in the America's.* New York: New York University Press, 1998.

Faal, Dawda. *A History of The Gambia; AD 1000–1965,* 2nd ed. Serrekunda: Edward Francis Small Printing Press, 1999.

Falola, Toyin. *Key Events in African History: A Reference Guide.* Westport, CT: Greenwood Press, 2002.

Falola, Toyin. *Culture and Customs of Nigeria.* Westport, Connecticut: Greenwood Press, 2001.

Gailey, Harry. *Historical Dictionary of The Gambia.* Metuchen, NJ: The Scarecrow Press, 1975.

Gamble, David. *Contributions to a Socio-economic Survey.* London: Colonial Office, 1949.

Garren, Samuel Garren, *"Exile and Return: The Poetry and Fiction of Tijan Sallah,"* Wasafiri, Vol. 7, Issue 15 (1992): 9–14.

Godwin-Sonko, Patience. *Ethnic Groups of Senegambia Region: Social Political Structures, Pre-colonial Period.* Banjul: Book Production Unit, 1986.

Gomez, Cornelius. *Gambian Folktales and Fables.* Banjul: Ndab Li Productions, 2009.

Gomez, Michael. "Muslims in Early America." *Journal of Southern History* 60, no. 4 (1994): 671–710.

Gray, John. *History of The Gambia,* 2nd ed. London: Frank Cass, 1966.

Herlund, Ylva, and Betina Shell-Duncan. "Contingency, Context, and Change: Negotiating Female Genital Cutting in The Gambia and Senegal." *Africa Today* 53, no. 4 (2007): 43–57.

Hiskett, Meryvn. *The Development of Islam in West Africa.* London: Longman, 1984.

Hughes, Arnold, and David Perfect. *Historical Dictionary of The Gambia,* 4th ed. Lanham, MD: The Scarecrow Press, 2008.

Hughes, Arnold, and David Perfect. *A Political History of The Gambia: 1816–1994*. Rochester, NY: University of Rochester Press, 2006.

Hunt, Paul. "Children's Rights in West Africa: The Case of the Gambia's Almudos." *Human Rights Quarterly* 15, no. 3 (1993): 499–532.

Jallow, Baba Galleh. Review of *The Comforts of Home: Prostitution in Colonial Nairobi*, by White, Luise (1990).Chicago: The University of Chicago Press, 2011 (Unpublished).

Jatta, Sedia. "Born Musicians: Traditional Music from The Gambia." In *Repercussions: A Celebration of African American Music,* edited by Geoffrey Haydon and Dennis Marks, 19–29. London: Century Publishing, 1985.

Jawara, Dawda K. *Kairaba*. Burgess Hills, West Sussex, UK: Domtom Publishing, 2009.

Jeng, Abou. "From Hope to Despair: Travails of Constitutional Law Making in Gambia's Second Republic." In *The Gambia: Essays on Current Development and Future Direction(s),* edited by A. Saine, E. Ceesay, and E. Sall. (Trenton, NJ: Africa World Press, 2012).

Jeng, Abou. *Peacebuilding in the African Union: Law, Philosophy and Practice* Cambridge: Cambridge University Press, 2012.

Juffermans, Kasper, and Caroline McGlynn. "A Sociolinguistic Profile of The Gambia." *Sociolinguistics* 3, no. 3 (2009): 329–35.

Khapoya, Vincent. *The African Experience*. Upper Saddle River, NJ: Prentice Hall, 1998.

Langley, Jabez.A. *Pan-Africanism and Nationalism in West Africa 1900–1945.* Oxford: Clarendon Press, 1973.

Levtzion, Nehemia, and Randall L. Pouwells, eds. *The History of Islam in Africa.* Athens: Ohio University Press, 2000.

Littlefield, Daniel. *Rice and Slaves: Ethnicity and the Slave Trade in Colonial South Carolina*. Urbana: University of Illinois Press, 1991.

Lomax, Alan. *The Land Where the Blues Began*. New York: Bantam/ Doubleday, 1993.

Lovejoy, Paul. "Background to Rebellion: The Origins of Muslim Slaves in Bahia." *Slavery and Abolition* 15, no. 2 (1994): 151–81.

Lovejoy, Paul. *Identity in the Shadow of Slavery*. London: Continuum, 2000.

Mahoney, Florence. "Government and Opinion in Gambia." Unpublished Ph.D. thesis, SOAS, University of London, 1963.

Mahoney, Florence. *A Signare: Mulatto Lady*. Gambian Studies. Banjul, 2008.

McPherson, M. F., and S. Radelet, eds. *Economic Recovery in The Gambia: Insights for Adjustment in sub-Saharan Africa*. Cambridge, MA: Harvard Institute of International Development, 1996.

Ndiaye, Boubacar, Abdoulaye Saine, and Mathurin Houngnikpo. *Not Yet Democracy: West Africa's Slow Farewell to Authoritarianism*. Durham, NC: Carolina Academic Press, 2005.

Nugent, Paul. "Putting the History Back into Ethnicity: Enslavement, Religion and Cultural Brokerage in the Construction of Mandinka/ Jola and Ewe/Agotime

Identities in West Africa, c 1650–1930." *Comparative Studies in Society and History* 50, no. 4 (2008): 920–48.

Nyang, Sulayman. "Ethnic Relations in the Gambia: An Historical Perspective." In *State and Society in Africa: Perspectives on Continuity and Change,* edited by Feraidoon Shams, 88–115. Lanham, MD: University Press of America, 1995.

Nyang, Sulayman. "Islam in the Gambia." In *Oxford Encyclopaedia of Modern Islamic World,* edited by John Esposito, 41–42. New York: University Press, 1995.

Nyang, Sulayman, and Jacob Olupona. *Religious Plurality in Africa: Essays in Honor of John S. Mbiti.* Berlin: Walter de Gruyter & Co., 1993.

Owomoyela, Oyekan, ed. *A History of Twentieth Century African Literatures.* Lincoln: University of Nebraska Press, 1993.

Philips, John, ed. *Writing African History.* Rochester, NY: University of Rochester Press, 2005.

Quinn, Charolotte. *Mandingo Kingdoms of the Senegambia: Traditionalism, Islam, and European Expansion.* Evanston, IL: Northwestern Universitity Press, 1972.

Rice, Berkley. *Enter Gambia: The Birth of an Improbable Nation.* London: Angus & Robertson, 1967.

Robinson, David. *The Holy War of Umat Tal: The Western Sudan in the mid-Nineteenth Century.* Oxford: Clarendon Press, 1985.

Robinson, David. *Paths of Accommodation: Muslim Societies and French Colonial Authorities in Senegal and Mauritania, 1880–1920.* Athens: Ohio University Press, 2000.

Saho, Bala. "Appropriations of Islam in a Gambian Village: Life and Times of Shaykh Mass Kah, 1827-1936." *African Studies Quarterly* 12, no. 4 (2011): 1–21.

Saine, Abdoulaye. "The Gambia's Changing Political and Economic Landscape: A Regime Performance Evaluation, 1994–2002." *Africa Insight* 33, no. 3 (2003): 57–64.

Saine, Abdoulaye. "The Gambia's Elected Autocrat: Poverty, Peripherality and Political Instability, 1994–2006: A Political Economy Assessment." *Armed Forces and Society* 34, no. 3 (2008): 450–73.

Saine, Abdoulaye. "The Gambia's 2006 Elections: Change or Continuity." *African Studies Review* 51, no. 1 (2008): 59–83.

Saine, Abdoulaye. *The Paradox of Third-Wave Democratization in Africa: The Gambia Under AFPRC-APRC Rule.* Lanham, MD: Lexington Books, 2009.

Saine, Abdoulaye. "Post-coup Politics in The Gambia." *Journal of Democracy* 13, no. 4 (2002): 167–72.

Saine, Abdoulaye, N'Diaye Boubacar, and Mathurin Houngnikpo. *Elections and Democratization in West Africa, 1990–2009.* Trenton, NJ: Africa World Press, 2011.

Sallah, Abdoulie, and Colin C. Williams. "The Illusion of Capitalism in Contemporary Sub-Saharan Africa: A Case-study of The Gambia." *Foresight* 13, no. 3 (2011): 50–63.

Sallah, M. Tijan. *Wollof Ethnography*. New York: Rosen Publishing, 1996.

Sanneh, Lamin. *The Crown and the Turban: Muslims and West African Pluralism*. Boulder, CO: Westview Press, 1997.

Sanneh, Lamin. *The Jakhanke Muslim Clerics: A Religious and Historical Study of Islam in Senegambia*. Lanham, MD: University Press of America, 1990.

Sanneh, Lamin. *Piety and Power: Muslims and Christians in West Africa*. New York: Orbis Books, 1996.

Sarr, Samsudeen. *Coup d'état by The Gambian National Army*. Philadelphia, PA: Xlibris, 2007.

Schroeder, Richard. *Shady Practices: Agroforestry and Gender Practices in The Gambia*: Berkley, CA: University of Berkley Press, 1999.

Senghor, Jeggan. *The Politics of Senegambian Integration: 1958–1994*.Oxford: Peter Lang Publishers, 2008.

Shell-Duncan, Betina, and Ylva Hernlund. *Female "Circumcision," in Africa: Culture, Controversy and Change*. Boulder, CO: Lynne Rienner Publishers, 2000.

Southorn, Lady. *The Gambia: The Story of the Groundnut Colony*. London: George Allen & Unwin, 1952.

Soyinka, Wole. *Myth, Literature, and the African World*. Cambridge: Cambridge University Press, 1976.

Stevens, Peter J. R. "Bachama Joking Categories: Toward New Perspectives in the Study of Joking Relationships." *Journal of Anthropological Research* 34 (1978): 47–71.

Swindell, Kenneth, and Alieu Jeng. *Migrants, Credit and Climate: The Gambia Groundnut Trade, 1834–1934*. Leiden: Brill, 2006.

Touray, Isatou. "Sexuality and Women's Sexual Rights in the Gambia." *International Development Studies Bulletin* 37, no. 5 (2006): 1–7.

Touray, Omar. *The Gambia and the World: A History of The Foreign Policy of Africa's Smallest State, 1965–1995*. Hamburg: Institute of African Studies, 2000.

Trimmingham, Spencer J. *Islam in West Africa*: Oxford: Clarendon, 1961.

Wallerstein, Emmanuel. *The Modern World System: Capitalist Agriculture and the Origin of the European World System in the Seventeenth Century*. New York: Academic Press, 1976.

White, Luise. *The Comforts of Home: Prostitution in Colonial Nairobi*, Chicago: The University of Chicago Press, 1990.

Wiseman, John A. "Letting Yahya Jammeh off Lightly?" *Review of African Political Economy* 72 (1997): 265–76.

Wright, Donald. *Oral Traditions from The Gambia, The Mandinka*, vol. I. Athens: Ohio, Center for International Studies, 1979.

Wright, Donald. *The World and a Very Small Place in Africa*. New York: ME Sharp, 1997.

INTERNET SOURCES

Barry, Cherno Omar. "Discovery of Gambian Literature Writing," 2004. http://gambianliterature.blogpost.com/2004/11/history-of-gambian literary-writing.html.

Barry, Cherno Omar. GAMWRITERS: Gambian Literature and Publications. 2011. http://gamwriters.com/user/gambianwriters.

Barry, Cherno Omar. "History of Gambian Literature Writing," 2008. http://gambi anliterature.blogpost.com/2004/11/history-of-gambian literary-writing.html.

Barry, Cherno Omar. "Mariam Khan." *Gambian Literature and Writings*, July 2003, April 2008. http://www.gamwriters.com/29.html.

Barry, Cherno Omar. "Ndaanan: First Gambian Literary Magazine," December 2004. http://gambianliteratureblogpost.com/2004/12/ndaanan-firstliterary-literary_01.html.

"Emerging Art in The Gambia." *African Colours,* 2008. http//www.gambia.african colors.net/content/11952.

Evans, B. "AVery Short History of The Gambia." About.com Guide. http://www.google.com/search?sclient=psy-ab&hl=en&source=hp&q=+Gambia+Guide.+Access+Gambia+%282008%29.&oq=+Gambia+Guide.

"Fashion and Design: Gambia's Elegant Designs," 2008. http://babyface.wow.gm/contacts.

Gambia Guide, The Gambia Information Site, 2011. http://www.accessgambia.com/information/.

"Gambia's Ritual Wooden Masks." *Gambia Guide*. Access Gambia, 2008. http://www.gambia.co.uk/Docs/About-Us/Customers/Gambia-Guide.aspx.

Jawara, Sanna. "Gambia: Art Community Describes Lack of Schools." *The Daily Observer,* June 2007. http//allafrica.com/stories/200706111272.html.

Rilly, Claude. WOW.gm: Gambian News Community, 2011.

Saine, Abdoulaye. "The Gambia Women's Bill 2010: A Promise yet to be Realized." *The Gambia Echo* (Raleigh, NC), May 2010. www.TheGambiaecho.com.

Saine, Abdoulaye. "Violence against Women (Wife-beating): A Bastion of Male Domination that Must End." *The Gambia Echo* (Raleigh, NC), March 2010. www.TheGambiaecho.com.

Sallah, M. Tijan. "To My Late Friend Dr. Lenrie Peters: The Gambian Vessel Emptied of Its Poetry." *Binda Gambia,* 2009. http://bindagambia.blogspot.com/2009/06/to-my-late-friend-dr-lenrie-peters.html.

Whiteman, Kate. "Ebou Dibba." *The Guardian,* Tuesday, April 3, 2001. http://www.guardian.co.uk/news/2001/apr/03/guardianobituaries1.

THE GAMBIA STUDIES SERIES BY PROFESSOR DAVID GAMBLE

Gambian Studies No. 1: A Conversation with Kaba So, an Elder of the Roroobe, From Jalakoto, Niani District, The Gambia

Gambian Studies No. 2: Mandinka Narratives from Kibaro—with a literal translation

Gambian Studies No. 3: Mandinka Dilemma Stories, Puzzles, Riddles & Proverbs

Gambian Studies No. 4: Accounts of Supernatural Beings, Spirits, Witches, Were-wolves, Ninkinanko, etc., from the Mandinka Newspaper, Kibaro

Gambian Studies No. 5: Medical Mandinka (Useful phrases and vocabulary)

Gambian Studies No. 6: Mandinka Stories from Books Published Prior to 1960

Gambian Studies No. 7: Mandinka Tales from the Newspaper 'Kobaro': 1951–1955

Gambian Studies No. 8: Mandinka Stories—Dictated, Written or Recorded

Gambian Studies No. 9: A Mandinka Narrative—"Manding Kuno" by A.K. Rahman

Gambian Studies No. 10A: Wolof Stories from Senegambia Mainly from Old Published Sources

Gambian Studies No. 10B: Wolof Legends from Published Sources

Gambian Studies No. 12: Gambian Fula—English Dictionary (Firdu Dialect)

Gambian Studies No. 13: Gambian Fula Stories Told by Mary Umah Baldeh

Gambian Studies No. 14: Firdu-Fula Grammar (Gambia Dialect)

Gambian Studies No. 15: Gambia Government Serial Publications of the Colonial Period: A Provisional List

Gambian Studies No. 17: Peoples of the Gambia—The Wolof

Gambian Studies No. 18 A General Bibliography of The Gambia up to 31st December 1977 Supplement 1

Gambian Studies No. 19: A General Bibliography of the Gambia Supplement II 1978–1982

Gambian Studies No. 20: Elementary Mandinka

Gambian Studies No. 21: Intermediate Gambian Mandinka-English Dictionary

Gambian Studies No. 22: Verbal and Visual Expressions of Wolof Culture

Gambian Studies No. 24: A General Bibliography of the Gambia, Supplement III 1983–1987

Gambian Studies No. 25: Elementary Gambian Wolof Grammar

Gambian Studies No. 26: Early Published Vocabularies of the Wolof Language

Gambian Studies No. 27: John Hill's Vocabularies of Wolof, Compiled in 1808 on the Island of Goree (Senegal)

Gambian Studies No. 28: Terms Found in Old Writings About Senegambia

Gambian Studies No. 29: A General Bibliography of the Gambia Supplement IV 1988–1992

Gambian Studies No. 30: The South Bank of the Gambia: Places, People, and Population (A) Kantora and Fulladu

Gambian Studies No. 31: The South Bank of the Gambia: Places, People and Population Nyaamina, Jaara, and Kiyang Districts

Gambian Studies No. 32: The South Bank of the Gambia: Places, People and Population The Fonyui Districts

Gambian Studies No. 33 A: General Bibliography of the Gambia Supplement V: 1993–1995

Gambian Studies No. 34: Mandinka Ceremonies

Gambian Studies No. 35A: The Gambia: Place Names on Maps and in Travellers' Accounts up to 1825 (A) Descriptive Text

Gambian Studies No. 35B: The Gambia: Place Names on Maps and in Travellers' Accounts (B) A selection of maps

Gambian Studies No. 35C: The Gambia: Place Names Given by Travellers & Residents in the 19th and 20th centuries

Gambian Studies No. 36: The North Bank of the Gambia: Places, People and Population (A) Nianija, Niani, Sami, Sandu, & Wuli Districts

Gambian Studies No. 37: The North Bank of the Gambia: Places, People, and Population (B) The Wolof Area: Sabah & Sanjal, Lower Saalum, Upper Saalum

Gambian Studies No. 38: The North Bank of the Gambia: Places, People, and Population: (C) The Nyoomi, Jookadu, and Baddibu Districts

Gambian Studies No. 39: Postmortem: A Study of the Gambian Section of Alex Haley's 'Roots'

Gambian Studies No. 40: Abbreviations and Acronyms Used in the Gambia: (Past and Present)

Gambian Studies No. 41: Maps of the Gambia in the Map Collection and Senegambian Book Collection of David P. Gamble

Gambian Studies No. 43 A: General Bibliography of the Gambia, Supplement VI 1996–1999

Gambian Studies No. 44 A: General Bibliography of the Gambia, Supplement VII 2000–2002 (with some earlier items)

Gambian Studies No. 45: Errors, Confusions, and Misinterpretations in Writings about the Gambia

Gambian Studies No. 48: Thoughts on Gambian Folktales

Gambian Studies No. 49: Traditional Mandinka Agriculture

Gambian Studies No. 50: John Hill's Account of Life on Goree Island 1807–1808

Gambian Studies No. 51: The South Bank of The Gambia: People, Places and Population (D) The Kombo Districts

Gambian Studies No. 52: Gambian Linguistic Material in the David P. Gamble Collection

With many thanks to William (Bill) Roberts and St. Mary's College, Maryland, USA, for housing the works of Professor Gamble and making them available to students and researchers.

GAMBIAN NEWSPAPERS

The Daily Observer: www.thedailyobserver.gm
The Point: www.Thepoint.gm
Foroyaa: www.foroyaa.gm

ONLINE NEWSPAPERS

Freedom newspaper: www.freedomnewspaper.com
Gainako: www.gainako.com
The Gambia Journal: www.thegambiajournal.com
Jollof News: www.jollofnews.com
all.Gambianet: www.allgambian.net
Maafanta: www.maafanta.com
Senegambia news: www.senegambianews.com
The Gambia Echo: www.thegambiaecho.com

Index

About the Author

ABDOULAYE SAINE is Professor of African Studies and International Political Economy in the Department of Political Science at Miami University, Oxford, Ohio. He has written widely on the military in politics, democracy, and democratization in West Africa and The Gambia. He is the author of *The Paradox of Third-Wave Democratization in Africa: The Gambia under AFPRC-APRC Rule, 1994–2008* (Lexington Books, 2009), and co-editor of, The Gambia: Essays on Contemporary Issues and Future Directions, 1965–2011 (Africa World Press, 2012).